NORMAN LEBRECHT

Why Mahler?

Norman Lebrecht has written several best selling works of nonfiction, including *The Maestro Myth* and *Who Killed Classical Music?* He is also the award-winning author of the novels *The Song of Names* and *The Game of Opposites.* He writes regularly for Bloomberg.com and *The Wall Street Journal,* and he presents *The Lebrecht Interview* series on BBC Radio 3 and *The Record Doctor* on WNYC. He lives in London.

www.normanlebrecht.com

Why Mahler?

HOW ONE MAN
AND TEN SYMPHONIES
CHANGED OUR WORLD

Norman Lebrecht

ANCHOR BOOKS
A Division of Random House, Inc.
New York

CONTENTS

PREFACE TO THE ANCHOR EDITION
AFTER MAHLER, ANOTHER DELUGE?

More than any other composer, Gustav Mahler owes his posterity to anniversaries. It was the centenary of his birth in 1960 that caused BBC producers in London and Leonard Bernstein in New York to put on groundbreaking cycles of his symphonies, restoring his music to concert circulation. Sixty years after his death, in 1971, Luchino Visconti's film *Death in Venice* introduced Mahler's music to a mass audience. The seventy-fifth anniversary, 1986, prompted Claudio Abbado to form a pan-European orchestra, the Gustav Mahler Youth Orchestra, which in turn yielded the Mahler Chamber Orchestra, applying the composer's name as a hallmark of excellence. Anniversary by anniversary, stage by stage, Mahler's fame extended to a point where, in December 2010, the Philharmonie in Berlin opened an exhibition under the evangelical title His Time Is Come. In half a century, Mahler had gone from near-zero to folk hero.

The one hundred and fiftieth anniversary of his birth in 2010, running into the centenary of his death in 2011, enabled slow-moving orchestras to plan a surge of symphonic cycles for this second coming—in Sydney, Seoul, Beijing, Rome, Leipzig, Stockholm, Krakow, Paris, Manchester, Birmingham, Amsterdam, Prague, Düsseldorf and Munich, not to mention triennial cycles in Pittsburgh, Boston, and more. On London's South Bank, there were twenty-seven Mahler concerts over the two years, and as many again across the city at the Barbican, Royal Albert Hall, and elsewhere. Listeners were spoilt for choice—two *Resurrections* in the UK on the same Saturday night; Rattle in the Third or Oramo in the Tenth on a gray Wednesday in February. Musicians complained of overkill. Some foretold a post-centennial backlash.

Over the two anniversary years, I covered the Mahler trail once again, checking in on past omissions and discovering fresh derelictions. I found the birthplace at Kaliste lovingly restored into a guesthouse of unusual tranquillity.[1] At Jihlava, where he grew up, the burned-out synagogue was converted into a Gustav Mahler Park, but the family home, flushed with Euro funds, was turned into a museum of ineffable blandness. The Budapest Opera, which he led at age twenty-seven, unveiled a Mahler statue. The New York Philharmonic, which he reinvented, did nothing (having got its Mahler cycle out of the way a year early). Upstate, a man in Syracuse erected a stone bench memorial on the site where Mahler conducted, but the town orchestra cancelled a Mahler concert for want of funds.

Vienna, where he lived and died, equivocated in classic style. A Mahler route for tourists was established, but not publicized. A Theatre Museum exhibition displayed, with squirming intimacy, the linen shirt that he wore as he died. Its label said "made in New York." In death, Vienna still stamped him an outsider.

At the graveside in Grinzing, I was discussing the social significance of tomb statuary with the cultural commentator Dr. Wolfgang Herles when he broke into a pleasant ditty his grandmother used to sing. It was a jolly little polka that went something like this: "when I die, die, die, let the hearse horses go clip-clop, and the zither play, play, play, all the way to my grave."[2] The song rumbled through my mind all year long, underlining the perpetual conundrum of how much in Mahler is original and how much cultural and environmental.

Morbidity, for instance, is taken to be a Mahlerian characteristic. That's understandable given that his earliest infant work was a polka with introductory funeral march, and that death runs through every symphony from the third movement of the First to the agonized finale of the Tenth. The same funereal preoccupation is found, however, extensively in Viennese culture, along with a parallel interleaving of mourning and merriment. Wolfgang Herles's granny song and the Frère Jacques episode of the First Symphony share common roots. So how much of Mahler's was typical to him, and how much to his life and times?

The question would not have troubled Mahler, who set little store by new tunes and shrugged when condemned as derivative. For Mahler, message was all. It was not so much which melodies went into a symphony—"the music is not to be found in the notes," he avowed—as how a symphony might embrace and reflect the world. The meaning beneath the music was the most important thing: *das wichtigste*. Beyond this, he gave few clues. He set conductors free to interpret the works in their own way and refused point-blank, after early misadventures, to explain what his music was about. A future age would understand, he proclaimed: *my time will come!*

His ironies and ambiguities remain matters of contention. Maestros struggle to convey double meanings to orchestral players without losing their authority and music critics are required by impatient editors to deliver decisive, star-rated reviews. Mahler defies box-ticking conventions. He also resists a classifiable niche in musical evolution. Pierre Boulez once defined the history of music as a continuum that runs Bach-Haydn-Beethoven-Wagner and then on through Mahler to the modern age, an argument that is simultaneously defensible and indefensible. Mahler might be seen in retrospect as the missing link between classical and modern. Yet much of Mahler's work is tangential to tradition, or in direct contravention of it. A worthy attempt by Simon Rattle to preface a performance of Mahler's Third Symphony with two songs of Brahms and Wolf revealed only the hole in the road left by Mahler. It seems to be running straight ahead from Brahms and then Mahler rips up the surface to explore the unseen and unmentioned. This is not the straight line that Boulez described.

The route is further complicated by Mahler's personal evasiveness. As this edition went to print I received a sorrowful email from Knud Martner in Copenhagen, listing a dozen errors and omissions in his catalogue of *Mahler's Concerts*, published in 2010 by the Kaplan Foundation. No researcher is more dogged, more meticulous than Knud. He has spent his life chronicling every day of Mahler's and, at the end, was misled by Mahler's smokescreens, his deliberate vagaries, his covering of tracks.

Some find these evasions infuriating. For me, they are Mahler's secret weapon. His refusal to be pinned down allows him to respond to changing circumstances. To experience Brahms in 2011 is no different from hearing him in 1891, a great composer at full blast. Mahler, by contrast, varies from one day and one listener to the next. Mikhail Gorbachev in the dying months of perestroika and America in the aftermath of 9/11 (see pp 232) did not hear the same Mahler, attentively as they may have listened to the music. Mahler moves with the times, past, present, future. It is encouraging that the end of the Mahler centennial will mark the start of a Mahler Project in Los Angeles and Caracas by the most exciting interpreter of a new generation, Gustavo Dudamel.

Beyond the statutory fifteen minutes of fame no-one can predict an artist's posterity, but even if Western civilization were to be submersed by an alien culture and all that remained were the summits, among the protruding relics I suspect there will always be an enduring Mahlerian moment of universal appeal. Picture a small boy, terrified of domestic violence, who runs away to hide in the heart of the forest where, sitting alone all day on a log, he finds a new way to listen to the world. Out of that listening, he imagines a music that *must be like the world, all-embracing.* As a young man, age twenty-seven, he inscribes the sound he heard through the pine-tops: a harmonic A on open strings, at the start of his First Symphony. That's the beginning of the Mahler story. Like all good stories, it has no end.

NL, March 2011

INTRODUCTION
DESPERATELY SEEKING MAHLER

My search for Gustav Mahler began in 1974 in a London edifice where a Beatle once got married and paparazzi hung out each morning in hope of another payday. Marylebone Town Hall and its adjoining public library embodied Victorian values of public order and enlightenment. The library stocked books in all disciplines, from trivial romances to nuclear science, and readers were encouraged to recommend new titles. I lived nearby in a dank basement flat, working unsocial hours in television news. Whatever leisure I had was spent reading and practicing the piano. My musical tastes were turning away from the confrontational sounds of my own generation to the challenging complexities of classical music. Sitting on backless choir benches at concerts in the Royal Festival Hall, I trained my eyes on conductors of many kinds in an effort to discover how gesture shaped sound. Subtler than rock, whose rhythm and dynamics contained little variation, orchestral music opened a door to a world of feeling and ideas—if only I could fathom how it worked.

The concert notes I read were not much use to a struggling autodidact, rattling on as they did about subtonics and dominants, and newspaper reviews worshipped each morning at a shrine of Great Composers whose sanctity was taken for granted. As a child of my time I rejected established hierarchies. To find music that mattered to me, I attacked the music section at Marylebone library from top shelf to bottom, Alkan to Zelter, in pursuit of human affinities, relishing Charles Burney's bird's-eye view of the 1784 Handel Commemoration, Stendhal's life of Rossini, and the wonderfully acrid diaries of Hector Berlioz. William Reed's *Elgar As I Knew Him*, Marguerite Long on Ravel, and Agatha Fassett's observations of Bartók in exile added a flesh-and-blood dimension to the poignancy of their subjects' music.

My reading was advancing at a rate of six loans a week when two books stopped me in my tracks. Alma Mahler's memoir of her marriage to a composer was so vivid, so incisive, so intrusively possessive, that I was consumed by a need to understand a man who could inspire such passionate ambivalence. It was published in 1940, when Mahler was widely banned, and there was a desperation to Alma's tone, as if she feared that his life and hers had been wasted. Mahler's voice, crisp and assured, rang out in his letters. I ran back to the shelves, but there was nothing more to read until, weeks later, there arrived from the publisher Victor Gollancz the 980-page first installment of a projected biography by a French baron, Henry-Louis de La Grange, who seemed to know what Mahler was doing practically every waking minute. The mountain of intimate detail in this first volume (of four) drew yelps of astonishment from me, reading on shift at the BBC's *Newsnight* show, and prompting the newscaster to ask if war had broken out.

What struck me in these accounts of Mahler's life was my familiarity with his experience. There was not much I could relate to in the lives of Bach, Mozart, and Beethoven: Their loves were unfathomable, their routines dull, their diseases medieval, and their fortunes dependent on patronage. Mahler was a self-made man, driven by ambition. He dealt with issues I could recognize: with racism, workplace chaos, social conflict, relationship breakdown, alienation, depression, and the limitations of medical knowledge. "My time will come!" he vowed, confident that his works would someday find a sympathetic audience. I also took this to mean that he was living outside his time frame, fast-forwarding to a future date. It struck me that the best way to approach Mahler was to treat him in the present continuous, as a man of my own time.

My search for Mahler would, I realized, need to cover every footstep of his odyssey from a land without a name to world fame in Vienna and New York, as well as every aspect of his personal conduct, from the way he made love to how he knotted his tie. (Arnold Schoenberg once said you could learn more about music from watching Mahler get dressed than from any conservatory lecture.) I first went to Vienna in 1983 to write a feature for the *Sunday Times* and, after a rehearsal of Mahler's Second Symphony in the Musik-vereinsaal, walked twice around the Ring on a subzero winter night. I talked my way into Mahler's apartment (where his bathtub was still in use), stroked Rodin's cast of his head in the Opera foyer, and placed a pebble on his grave in Grinzing. Broad-minded travel edi-tors helped me to visit Mahler's birthplace, the small towns where he made his career, and the summerhouses where he composed. Reel-ing with vertigo, I scaled a mountain peak that inspired the Third Symphony. In Helsinki I relived the crossroads encounter between Mahler and Sibelius. In the Czech Philharmonic archive in Prague, I studied symphonic scores with Mahler's red-and-blue pencil marks. In the pin-quiet reading room of the Pierpont Morgan Library in New York, I looked at side-by-side manuscripts of his Second, Fifth, and Ninth Symphonies, charting the changes in his handwriting.

Along the route I found relics. A grungy bookshop in Amsterdam yielded a copy of stage designer Alfred Roller's scarce iconography. A riffle through a Munich railway terminus store produced an uncat-alogued photograph of Mahler on the podium. A chat at a cocktail party disclosed unpublished letters. By 1987 I had acquired so much Mahleriana that, needing to clear the desk, I wrote *Mahler Remembered*, a portrait of Mahler through the eyes of those around him. The month that book came out I moved into a flat in St. John's Wood, London, where, it turned out, the old lady on the top floor had attended Mahler's wedding and had the invitation to prove it. Mahler, it seemed, was following me to my lair as much as I was pur-suing him.

Down the years the book I wanted to write changed from musical biography—there were several in existence by now—to one that would try to address the riddle of why Mahler had risen from near-oblivion, to displace Beethoven as the most popular and influential symphonist of our age:

Why Mahler? Why does his music affect us in the way it does? Are we hearing what he meant us to hear, or a figment of interpretation? Why does Mahler make us cry?

Who is Mahler? Using his own life as a template for his music, Mahler exposed dark, private traumas to public gaze in a bid to analyze and alleviate human misery. His was not a simple or a nuclear persona. Calling himself "three times homeless," he claimed three identities: his Jewish roots, his German language, and his ineluctable sense of not belonging anywhere in the world. That alienation, so prevalent in a culturally diverse twenty-first century, gives a vital clue to Mahler's contemporary relevance. In an age when a half-African man from Hawaii could rise to become president of the United States, Gustav Mahler is finally able to find a home in our lives.

But *Whose Mahler* is it we are hearing? Mahler told conductors to perform his music as they saw fit, matching it to the acoustics of the hall and the mood of the moment. No composer had granted such license before, nor does other music accommodate much flexibility. Richard Strauss's *Symphonia Domestica,* or Jean Sibelius's Third, will sound much the same from one night to the next; but two concerts of a Mahler symphony can vary in length by up to ten minutes and in mood from black to white. Mahler's instructions often point in more than one direction; it is up to the conductor to decide how the work is to be resolved. This fluidity, a strikingly postmodern concept, makes each performance of a Mahler symphony an occasion without precedent, a potential world premiere. It also encourages the interpreter of Mahler's life and work to look beyond explicit statements and literal texts, seeking the meaning of Mahler in the context of his ancestry, his contemporaries, and of our own preconceptions as to how symphonic music might affect us. Mahler, for the modern reader, is not always what he seems.

Where does that place Mahler in the pantheon of great composers? Not among the monoliths, that's for sure. He is, rather, a composer for today, a maker of music that interacts with what musicians and listeners are feeling (see pp. 9–10, 244–46) in a fast-changing, often threatening world. In a quest that has taken up half my life, Mahler has been a warm and sympathetic companion. He never preaches or prescribes, neither gloats nor grumbles, but through a long life span he talks to us as a cognate, sensate, laughing, suffering fellow member of the human species, always trying to work out the meaning of it all. Mahler lives. Here and now. This book is my attempt to understand how and why.

PART I

Why Mahler?

1. Some Frequently Asked Questions

CAN MAHLER CHANGE YOUR LIFE?

In August 1991 Mikhail Gorbachev was meeting military officials at his holiday home in the Crimea when, resisting a demand for a return to totalitarian rule, he was placed under house arrest. The phones went dead, and he was held incommunicado for three days. His wife, Raisa, collapsed with a hypertension attack. In Moscow protesters massed in the streets, and the president of the Russian republic, Boris Yeltsin, led an armed vigil outside Parliament, televised live around the world. The coup crumbled, and Gorbachev was restored to office, only to be deposed at the year's end by the drunken and rapacious Yeltsin.

On one of his last nights in office that December, Gorbachev and his wife went to see Claudio Abbado conduct Gustav Mahler's Fifth Symphony, music they had not heard before. It affected them deeply. "I had the feeling," wrote Gorbachev, "that Mahler's music somehow touched our situation, about the period of perestroika [reconstruction] with all its passions and struggles." Raisa said: "I've been shaken by this music. It left me with a feeling of despondency, a feeling that there is no way out." Abbado assured her that this was not Mahler's intention, nor his own, but she was not reassured. The second most powerful couple in the world had been unsettled by something in the music that felt personal to them. "In life," reflected Gorbachev in his memoirs, "there is always conflict and contradiction, but without those—there is no life. Mahler was able to capture that aspect of the human condition."[1]

"Conflict and contradiction"—not a bad piece of music analysis from a world leader—are the essence of Mahler's art, but they do not account for its instantaneous impact on a politician hardened by quotidian confrontation. Something in the music had pierced his public carapace and attacked the individual unconscious. Something else was going on, and I think I know what it was: What the Gorbachevs failed to recognize was that they had been listening to Mahler unawares all their lives. Through decades of mass murder, hot and cold wars, state larceny, and comic inefficiency, Communism had imposed a mold of conformity on Soviet arts, sending poets and writers to exile and death if ever they deviated from the fixed party line. Music in the Soviet Union amounted to an official, upbeat sound track to everyday life.

Musicians, however, had a way of bending the line. Dmitry Shostakovich, in fifteen symphonies and fifteen string quartets, charted life under Stalin in ways his audience could understand and commissars could not prosecute. Alfred Schnittke described the start of Soviet disintegration without getting sent to the salt mines. Both employed a device they borrowed from Gustav Mahler—the application of irony in a musical score.

Irony, in Samuel Johnson's definition, is "a mode of speech in which the meaning is contrary to the words," a way of saying one thing and meaning another. Music, before Mahler, had a lexicon of simple emotions: joy, sorrow, love, hate, uplift, downcast, beauty, ugliness, and so on. Mahler in his First Symphony (see pp. 49–54) introduced the possibility of parallel meanings, a child's funeral broken by a delirious orgy, an apparent lament that turns absurd without losing its tragedy. Using the same duality, composers were able to buck and mock the Soviet system, liberating a part of themselves from its manacles. Shostakovich, outwardly a timid man, applied Mahlerian irony (among other hidden codes) in many of his works, most daringly in the Eleventh Symphony, where a Communist revolutionary ode is tauntingly laced with snippets from Mahler's *Resurrection*. Alfred Schnittke developed "Polystylism" out of the flurry of mixed messages in Mahler's First Symphony.[2] Mahler, through the ingenuity of Soviet musicians, became a subversive undercurrent, scarcely performed by state orchestras but as pervasive as vodka in the national bloodstream. It sounded to the Gorbachevs like everyday music, but with an ominous twist.

Even as he was infusing Russia with dissident freedoms, Mahler, on the far side of the cold war, was feeding two tracks of the American mind as the official sound of public mourning—and the commercial backdrop to popular amusement. A week after John F. Kennedy's assassination Leonard Bernstein conducted Mahler's Second Symphony in memoriam; at the funeral of Kennedy's brother Robert, he performed the Adagietto from the Fifth Symphony. After the terror attacks of September 11, 2001, many U.S. orchestras and radio stations switched to Mahler. "The songs and symphonies of Gustav Mahler prophetically mourn the victims of twentieth century catastrophes," noted one American composer.[3] Along with Samuel Barber's *Adagio*, itself a Mahlerian imitation, Mahler's Second, Fifth, and Ninth Symphonies were America's music of lamentation.

The same music, at the same time, was also its engine of mass entertainment. In Hollywood, composers Erich Wolfgang Korngold, Max Steiner, Franz Waxman, and Alfred Newman found in Mahler a sonic underpinning for epic movies, a dialect that extends from Korngold's Errol Flynn swashbucklers to John Williams's score for *Star Wars*. When Harry Potter mounts his broomstick, the liftoff takes its thrust from Mahler's *Resurrection*. Of the twenty-five "greatest" film scores listed by the American Film Institute, more than half are by Mahler-influenced composers.[4] Mahler can be heard in the rock music of the Grateful Dead, Pink Floyd, King Crimson, Blue Nile, and John Zorn. His music crosses all cultural and ideological barriers.

This universality is not easily explained. Mahler is accused of emotional indulgence, yet his music affects dark-suited audiences in Japan as much as open-shirted Mediterranean crowds. He can sound derivative, yet he is extensively imitated. Schoenberg and Stravinsky may have been bolder, Strauss and Puccini more melodic, but Mahler is the most widely performed. None of his symphonies is short or simple. He took the form to extremes of gloom (Sixth), size (Eighth), and quietude (Ninth), and his meaning is often willfully perverse. "Whatever quality is perceptible and definable in Mahler's music," said Bernstein, "the diametrically opposite is equally so."[5] The Adagietto of the Fifth Symphony, played at funerals, was written as a love letter—another instance of Mahler's writing music that points in opposite ways.

The paradoxes pile up. He expressed intimate, furtive, even shameful feelings in pages that were written for a hundred players and an audience of thousands. This contrast of message and medium is innate: It may also lead us toward the secret of Mahler's intense appeal. Mass society overwhelms the individual in us with the encroachments of ephemeral fashion. Mahler turns that formula on its head, using orchestral mass to liberate the individual unconscious. Among three thousand people in a concert hall you are always alone when Mahler is played.

DID MAHLER INVENT THE MODERN WORLD?

The last five years of the nineteenth century and the first ten of the twentieth changed the world as *we* know it. Few of our ancestors alive at the time realized that Picasso, turning blue in 1901, was taking art away from recognizable portraiture into abstract forms that hinted, rather than specified, a meaning. James Joyce, in *A Portrait of the Artist as a Young Man* (1904), led linear narrative toward the meandering interior monologue of *Ulysses*. Albert Einstein apologized each morning to Isaac Newton's picture on his wall for altering his order of the universe by adding a fifth dimension of time. Sigmund Freud in 1899 explored the unconscious mind in *The Interpretation of Dreams*, moving on to discover the sexual origins of neurosis and the talking cure that he called psychoanalysis.

Among these breakthroughs Mahler's contribution might seem conservative and of comparative insignificance. Mahler wrote in a mold that dated back to Haydn, and for an audience made up in the main of the complacent middle classes. He was not, by concurrent estimations, a pathbreaker. Nevertheless each of Mahler's innovations echoed or anticipated the epoch's advances. Mahler departed from the pastoral canvas of Beethoven, Brahms, and Bruckner (a depiction continued by Richard Strauss in *An Alpine Symphony*) for a work that hinted at multiple meanings, mostly subconscious. The fragmented, angular faces of Picasso's breakaway work (*Portrait of*

Kahnweiler, 1910) are the mirror image of Mahler's multiple layers of optional connotation.

Like Franz Kafka he conjoined autobiography, autoanalysis, and social criticism with daring, dreary mundanity. Like Joyce he described the world in its untidiness. His language is not astringent, novel, or surreal like Schoenberg's or Apollinaire's. It is, rather, an everyday vernacular made new by flashbacks and fast-forwards, stray colloquialisms, misplaced consonants, and forbidden thoughts: "For this, o dearly beloved, is the genuine Christine, body and soul and blood and ours. Slow music, please. Shut your eyes, gents. One moment. A little trouble about those white corpuscles. Silence all." Joyce or Mahler? Your call.

Einstein, in 1905, wrote five transformational papers, culminating in a theory of special relativity and an equation, $e=mc^2$, which discovered energies in the atom that could destroy the world. Mahler knew of Einstein's theories from a mutual friend, the Hamburg physicist Arnold Berliner. He discussed "atomic energy"[6] with Bruno Walter and grew very excited in 1907 about an unsigned newspaper article titled "Matter, Ether and Electricity." Mahler understood that "laws of nature may change; for instance, the law of gravity may no longer hold; doesn't Helmholtz, even now, assume that gravity may not apply to infinitely small distances?"[7] He was not just aware of Einstein but closely attuned to his reconfiguration of the universe.

Einstein, a dedicated violinist, defined science as "what was seen and experienced, portrayed in the language of logic" and art as "forms whose connections are not perceptible to the conscious mind."[8] Mahler, grasping the importance of that distinction, shied away from revealing such "connections." In his Third and Seventh Symphonies he hinted at a future ecological disaster; in the Sixth he warned of imminent world war. Like Einstein he reordered perceptions of musical time by avoiding the metronome in all but the earliest of his works. Einstein found that time slows down in higher gravitational fields and is perceived differently by moving and static objects. Mahler understood time as a dimension varied by the mood of a given moment.

Mahler's closest affinity with a maker of the modern world was with Sigmund Freud, four years his senior and from a similar Czech-

Jewish provincial background. Both built works out of incidents in their early lives. Freud predicated the oedipal theory on memories of urinating in his parents' bedroom, being his mother's favorite, and seeing his father racially humiliated. Mahler, a boy who saw five of his brothers carried in coffins from the family tavern where the singing never stopped, composed a child's funeral with a drunken jig in his First Symphony.

Both men observed their world from the outside. Personal experience, for Freud, was a sourcebook of psychoanalysis; for Mahler it yielded a parallel track of music and commentary, involved and detached, a Bible text equipped with exegesis. Both men, intellectually Jewish, could sustain discrete lines of thought within a single argument. Freud's free association is modeled on Talmudic discourse, in which rabbinic opinions from various places and centuries preclude a straight logical line. Mahler's interpolation of stray horns and folksongs reveals the same methodology.

Both used their Jewishness as a shield and a sword. "Because I was a Jew I found myself free from many prejudices which limited others in the employment of their intellects," said Freud, "and as a Jew I was prepared to go into opposition and to do without the agreement of the 'compact majority.' "[9] Being Jewish, said Mahler, was like being born with a short arm, having to swim twice as hard. Being "three times homeless," he could ignore fixed rules. Both men felt a sense of mission to repair the world, undertaking a *tikkun olam* to assist and complete God's work of Creation.

When Mahler told Jean Sibelius in 1907 that "the symphony is like the world, it must encompass everything,"[10] he was stating that music had a duty to reflect the whole universe, and to repair it. Sibelius countered with a blinkered argument for textural purity. It is perhaps no coincidence that the Finn spent the last third of his life in silence while Mahler composed, in anguish, to the end of his last summer.

Music, in Mahler's view, did not exist for pleasure. It had the potential for a "world-shaking effect" in politics and public ethics.[11] His First Symphony tackled child mortality. His Second denied church dogma on the afterlife; the Third addressed ecological damage; and the Fourth proclaimed racial equality. No symphony had done such things before. Mahler, said a disciple, was "a Redeemer in his profession."[12] ("I don't know what I'm supposed to be redeemed from," snorted Richard Strauss.[13]) Mahler never made his meanings explicit. "What is best in music," he hinted, "is not to be found in the notes." It was up to musicians and listeners to interpret the meaning behind them. Some of the Einsteinian "connections" I have just drawn are open to debate. The opposite, as so often in Mahler, may also be true.

What cannot be disputed is that Mahler is received by many in modern times as a source of spiritual revelation. On the Mahler-List, an Internet chat site, one fan describes "an identifiable moment of conversion,"[14] another his "road to Damascus."[15] In the aftershock of September 11, 2001, a schoolteacher posts: "Only music, and Mahler's music particularly, can bring me such a deep sense of the human connection that makes it possible to bear the unbearable."[16] An orchestral musician, after playing Mahler, feels "proud to be a human being."[17] In a TV documentary, *A Wayfarer's Journey*, a pediatric oncologist, Dr. Richard J. O'Reilly, speaks of Mahler's "healing power." At a Mahler festival in Boulder, Colorado, a Jesuit priest, John Pennington, reports playing Mahler to the dying: "The music's ultimate optimism makes it valuable to those caring for people as well as the patients."[18]

Vast and irresponsible claims are made for a supposed "Mozart effect" that improves the intelligence of newborns by playing them *Eine Kleine Nachtmusik* in the womb. The Mahler effect, far from being a panacea for all human woes, is more of a dormant presence in our collective unconscious, available when needed and touching even those who actively reject his music. The neurologist Oliver Sacks, musically aware but indifferent to Mahler, was disturbed by a "hateful, hallucinatory music" during an unhappy dream. "Have you abandoned young patients, or destroyed some of your literary children?" asked a colleague.

"Both," admitted Sacks. "Yesterday I resigned from the children's unit at the hospital and I burned a book of essays I had just written."

"Your mind is playing *Kindertotenlieder*, Mahler's songs for the death of children," was the diagnosis.[19]

Mahler's music has a peculiar capacity for catching us unawares, unsettling heads of state and harassed professionals, unlocking repression, coloring dreams, and inducing a state of awareness that leads to self-content. "He does not exactly propose a therapeutic solution," writes the Chicago-based philosopher Martha Craven Nussbaum. "He just expresses the thought that one may simply overcome primitive shame and stand forth in one's own being, without disgust, without envy."[20] Mahler, like Freud, tells us that it is all right to be who we are; it might even be admirable. His music stands for the resilience of our individuality in a pressure-cooker society. The most we can expect from art is that it helps us live in peace with ourselves. This, at best, is Mahler's contribution to the modern world.

DID GUSTAV MAHLER SKI?

Living his life as a resource for art, Mahler held that nothing he did was insignificant. "You want to know what I have been doing?" he demanded at eighteen. "I have eaten and drunk, I have been awake and I have slept, I have wept and laughed, I have stood [on] mountains, where the breath of God bloweth and where it listeth, I have been on the heath, and the tinkling of cow-bells has lulled me into dreams. Yet I have not escaped my destiny."[21]

He made his sisters keep his letters and encouraged friends to write down his sayings. An infatuated viola player, Natalie Bauer-Lechner, recorded "the great power naturally radiated by a being of genius in his daily life."[22] Mahler's wife, Alma, wrote fervent diaries and false memoirs. His stage designer Alfred Roller wrote a precise description of the stark naked man:

> The most beautifully developed part of him, quite an outstanding sight because it was so well delineated was the musculature of his back. I could never set eyes on this superbly modelled sun-tanned back without being reminded of a racehorse in peak condition. His hands were real workman's hands, short and broad and with unmanicured fingers ending as if they had been chopped off.[23]

A Swiss fan and his Slovak lover kept diaries. Two would-be biographers hovered, pens in hand.[24] Nothing Mahler did passed unnoticed. In Vienna he magnetized café attention:

> Someone shouted: "There he is!" Everyone got up and rushed to the window. They stood there, pressed up against each other, peering out. On the other side of the Wallfischgasse, Mahler was walking along with his wife. He was swinging his hat back and forth in his right hand and stamping with his left foot as if he were trying to pacify the ground. He laughed, partly devil-may-care and partly with the ease and innocence of a child. . . . Everyone stared at this bareheaded little man and then, of an instant, all awoke from their staring and looked at each other. They smiled, perhaps trying to diminish the fact that this "bungler," this "so-and-so" . . . was able to make such an impression.[25]

More eyewitness accounts exist of Mahler than of any composer except Richard Wagner. There are descriptions of his funny walk, his vocal register (baritone when relaxed, tenor when agitated), and his unaccented High German speech, with rolled rs. We know that he stood one meter sixty in socks and that he liked a glass of beer on a summer's night. Hardly any aspect of his being is undocumented. Mahler, working like Freud from small observations to grand human theories, welcomed the scrutiny. He would have agreed with James Boswell who, in his *Life of Johnson,* quotes a twelfth-century rabbi, David Kimhi (on the verse "his leaf also shall not wither," Ps. 1:3), to demonstrate that "even the idle talk of a good man ought to be regarded."[26] Every aspect of Mahler's life matters intensely to someone and, in a life that was turned into art, none can be overlooked. Even if it has no apparent bearing on the music, the fact may be of urgent personal concern: *"Was Mahler circumcised?"*

I am standing in the aisle of the Golders Green Beth Hamedrash, an ultra-Orthodox London synagogue, on Simchas Torah, the day of Rejoicing the Law, and a thickset man in a woolen prayer shawl is demanding an answer. His great-grandfather, born a day's ride away from Mahler's birthplace, went uncircumcised because his village had embraced Reform Judaism. He cannot accept circumstantial assumptions in respect to Mahler. So I go away and find proof (see p. 23). My friend is happy and so am I. We have emulated Mahler's minute concern for trivial detail.

"What's that Ninth Symphony all about?" It's a bleak night in Liverpool and, after a dreary sponsors' dinner, the conductor Libor Pešek and I are stumbling about in search of a nightcap. Entering a cellar club, we are barred by a king-size bouncer who looks as if he can lift whole ships from the harbor with one hand. "Great concert, maestro!" booms the giant, crushing Libor's fingers to matchsticks, "but what was that Mahler's Ninth Symphony all about?" So we tell him. Mahler has brought us another seeker, forcing us to look with different eyes at a hard man.

"Am I related to Mahler?" The most frequent of FAQs, always to be expected at the end of a Mahler lecture. The family names Mahler, Hermann, and Bondy (or Bondi) are prevalent among Czech Jews, and not alien to Gentiles. Among those who claim kinship to the composer are the Vienna-born Connecticut conductor Fritz Mahler (1901–73), the inventor Joseph Mahler (1900–81), the Ukraine-born Israeli composer Menachem Avidom (Mahler-Kalkstein, 1925–95), and the American pop singer Beyoncé Knowles (who is said to be an eighth cousin, four times removed). You never know who, when, or where—and most perplexingly why—it should matter to have Mahler in your bloodline. In Tel Aviv my nephew Moshe introduces his parents-in-law, Gad and Vivi. Gad is from the Czech town of Aussig (now Ústí nad Labem). His maternal grandmother, Sofie (1850–1923), was the daughter of Joseph Mahler (1830–80) of Lipnice, an uncle of the composer. *"Does this make my great-nephew a Mahler?"* Let's stop this right here.

Here are some other regular FAQs. Did Mahler smoke? Was he gay? Did he like jazz? What strength glasses did he wear, and what was his favorite dessert? Did he speak English? Was he good in bed? *Did Gustav Mahler Ski?*[27] is, it so happens, the title of a 1991 short story that opens in Toblach, where Mahler wrote his last symphonies. To

Mahler seekers the question seems perfectly reasonable. *"So did Mahler ski?"*

Evidently not: He went to the mountains in June, too late to slalom. In Toblach the first thing he did was to buy an umbrella so he could walk out in all weathers to collect mail and order coffee at the grand hotel. At night he "slept a lot better when he felt slightly chilly."[28] Many of his best ideas came, Alma noted, while he sat in the earthen closet after breakfast, gazing out onto the slopes. The composer Alban Berg, a fervent admirer, kept a sheet of Toblach toilet paper, otherwise unused, on which Mahler sketched a theme from the Ninth Symphony. Do we really *need* to know this?

"Was Mahler a good man?" When that question was put to Mahler he replied, "There are no great men without some goodness."[29] Arnold Schoenberg proclaimed him "a martyr, a saint";[30] orchestral musicians saw menace and venom. He was, said a biographer, "at once just as portrayed, and yet quite different."[31] Both genius and demon, was Bruno Walter's first impression.[32] Finding the real Mahler is an expeditional battle through a blizzard of contradictions. His life is a jigsaw with far too many pieces.

WAS MAHLER MAD?

I am sitting in the London house where Alan Turing was born, meeting an authority on manic depression, or bipolarity in the current anodyne euphemism. Turing, the computer genius whose Enigma machine cracked Hitler's army codes, killed himself in June 1954 by eating an apple laced with cyanide, a ceremonial act. Was Turing mad? Demonstrably not. He was being hounded by the secret services for homosexuality and, seeing no hope of relief, he made a calculated exit in a cryptic manner that was designed to protect his elderly mother from the taint of suicide. The London maternity home where he was born in June 1912 is now a quiet hotel in Little Venice.

In the lobby Kay Redfield Jamison is eager to discuss Mahler's madness. A hyperarticulate, handsome woman with shoulder-length blond hair and a glow of Californian well-being, Kay, herself bipolar, has made a specialist study of links between creativity and manic depression. She finds a high incidence in composers. Robert Schumann and Hugo Wolf both died in asylums. Hector Berlioz and Anton von Webern were wildly unstable; Bellini and Donizetti had their ups and downs; and George Frideric Handel could turn in a trice from amiable to apoplectic. "If Handel entered your consulting room," Kay asks students, "would you prescribe lithium?" If they say yes, she counters: "And risk losing *Messiah?*" Through two conversations, in London and Washington, D.C., she makes a strong case for Handel, whose look, wrote Charles Burney, "was somewhat heavy and sour, but when he did smile, it was his sire the Sun, bursting out of a black cloud."[33] Similar mood swings are found in Mahler: "If he is engaged in lively conversation with anyone, he grabs him by the hand or the lapels and forces him to stand where he is. Meanwhile, he himself, growing more and more excited, stamps the ground with his feet like a wild boar."[34] He has panic attacks, "scarcely able to breathe,"[35] and is abnormally self-absorbed. Drinking coffee, he stirs the cup with his cigarette and, imagining he has inhaled a mouthful of smoke, blows a jet of black coffee into his hostess's face.[36] His wife fears for his sanity: "Gustav is crazy—still—and I am afraid he will remain so."[37] *So was Mahler mad?*

The document Kay brings as proof is from the beginning of his adult life, a letter he wrote when he was eighteen, to a school friend, Joseph Steiner, with whom he had been writing an opera. No longer: Mahler is now "a different person . . . the most intense and joyful vitality and the most consuming yearning for death rule my heart in turn, very often alternate hour by hour. One thing I know: I can't go on like this much longer!" The threat of suicide is explicit.

When the abominable tyranny of our modern hypocrisy and mendacity has driven me to the point of dishonouring myself, when the inextricable web of conditions in art and life has filled my heart with disgust for all that is sacred to me—art, love, religion—*what way out is there but self-annihilation?* Wildly, I wrench at the bonds that chain me to the loathsome, insipid swamp of this life, and with all the strength of despair I cling to sorrow, my only consolation. Then all at once the sun shines upon me and gone is the ice that encased my heart; again

I see the blue sky and the flowers swaying in the wind, and my mocking laughter dissolves in tears of love. Then I *needs must* love this world with all its deceit and frivolity and its eternal laughter.[38]

The transition is so sudden you have to read the letter twice for comprehension. In one sentence Mahler is ready to give up life, in the next the sun is shining and all is bright and beautiful. What is going on? In the third week of June 1879, Mahler has a summer job on a farm at Puszta Batta, outside Budapest, teaching music to three sons of Moritz Baumgartner. He is bored, lonely, and upset that Baumgartner won't give him a pay advance that could get him into town. He tells another friend that he is "filled with the most terrible yearning, I simply can't stand it any longer,"[39] but this means only that he wants out. The dishonoring he mentions may have been a sexual escapade with a farm girl, and the hypocrisy a clash of values with his employer. He does not know what to do with himself in the long days and hot nights. So he pours out a stream of guilty consciousness to a friend from whom he is drifting apart.[40]

The next day he writes to Steiner "in a gentler mood," and the day after "in merry mood." He is out at six in the morning with Farkas the shepherd, who is playing his shawm, a reed instrument. "The flowers growing at his feet trembled in the dreamy glow of his dark eyes, and his brown hair fluttered around his suntanned cheeks. Ah, Steiner! You are still asleep in bed and I have seen the dew on the grasses!"[41] cries the former would-be suicide. The Baumgartners are off to the seaside that day, leaving him "free as a finch." He might even spend the next summer with them.

This is not a lunatic on the loose but a young artist in search of a style. Mahler's "joy in life and the desire for death" is borrowed from the popular storyteller E.T.A. Hoffmann, whose *Fantasies in the Manner of Callot* have left a lasting impression. The *Fantasies* carry a preface by a fellow romantic writer, Jean Paul (Richter). Mahler's First Symphony is named *Titan*, after a Jean Paul novel; its third movement is titled "a funeral march in the manner of Callot." "What the flowers in the meadow tell me" appears in the Third Symphony and "shawm-playing shepherds" appear in the margins of the Eighth.[42] The suicide letter, far from expressing a death wish, contains the birth pains of a new composer, the point at which young Gustav becomes mature Mahler. Seldom in the history of art is the transition from pupa to chrysalis so graphically revealed.

And there is more to the letter than raw materials for future works. "With all the strength of despair," writes Mahler, "I cling to sorrow, my only consolation." This is an extraordinary revelation. Most people shun sorrow; Mahler embraces it. Sorrow is his retreat, the place he calls home when he is Lost to the World. Rather than avoid pain, he seeks it as a creative incubus. Time and again in his life, exhausted and infertile, he drives himself to a state of lonely despair, as he does in this letter, and all of a sudden a dam breaks and he is in the full flood of a new symphony. The moment he mentions sorrow in this letter, "all at once the sun shines upon me and gone is the ice that encased my heart." The threat of self-harm is his route to self-repair: He has discovered that the way to mend his life is by making art.

Mahler never again considers killing himself, neither in bereavement nor in the most hurtful betrayal. From now on he takes strength from adversity. When faced with mortal illness, his response is not to acquiesce to fate but to resist to his last breath. If grief can heal, death can be defeated. Mahler's attitude to life is clinically sane. He addresses the most harrowing of personal tragedies, the death of a child, with heartrending grief and creative resilience, extracting from his darkness a *Song of the Earth (Das Lied von der Erde)* that affirms the essence of human connection. He loves life, no matter how badly it treats him. He affirms. As he says in the "madness" letter, *"needs must."*

SO WHY MAHLER?

"And why now?" The two FAQs are joined at the hip. Why does a discarded composer displace Beethoven in twenty-first-century playlists, and what took him so long? Two popular misapprehensions, of suppression and overnight resurrection, require correction.

Except under Nazi rule, Mahler's music was never fully silenced. From his death in 1911 until the Second World War, his works were performed 2,200 times worldwide (Germany 900, Holland 400,

Austria 300),[43] more than any twentieth-century composers except Sibelius and Strauss. He did, however, provoke intense antagonism. In the United States, Arturo Toscanini and Walter Damrosch damned his symphonies as tedious. *Time* magazine, under the headline "Wormy Mahler," warned that "the brooding melancholy of his music gets many a listener down."[44] In Britain his works were said to be "laboriously put together and lacking that vital spark of inspiration."[45]

As a boy the philosopher Ludwig Wittgenstein met Mahler. He later wrote: "If it is true that Mahler's music is worthless, as I believe to be the case, then the question is what I think he ought to have done with his talent. For quite obviously it took a *set of very rare talents* to produce this bad music."[46] A less doctrinaire thinker might have asked himself why, if the music was so bad, it elicited a violent response. Bad art does not require intelligent deprecation. Mahler kept getting under people's skin even during the years when he was least performed.

His revival came in three waves. Centennial cycles by the BBC (1959–60) and the New York Philharmonic (1961–65) were "a test of fashion,"[47] sustained by Bernstein's recordings and Luchino Visconti's use of the Fifth Symphony Adagietto as the sound track for *Death in Venice* in 1971. In the 1980s the vastly improved sound of compact discs rekindled demand for Mahler as a hi-fi experience. By 1995 there were 1,168 Mahler CDs; fifteen years later there were twice as many.

A third wave was powered by the Internet, where every known thing became infinitely reusable. Mahler featured on more than twenty film tracks between 1990 and 2010—mostly the Adagietto, but also the Ninth Symphony in Woody Allen's *Husbands and Wives* (1992), "I Am Lost to the World" in Jim Jarmusch's *Coffee and Cigarettes* (2004), and *Kindertotenlieder* in Alfonso Cuarón's disturbing *Children of Men* (2006).[48] The "Drinking Song" from *The Song of the Earth* played in an episode of the U.S. TV funeral-parlor comedy *Six Feet Under.* T-shirts with the slogan "I've Been Mahlered" were sold on street corners. Newspaper editors no longer prefaced Mahler's name with an explanatory noun. His time had come, and proof abounded.

One morning in October 2007, commuters in Toronto, Canada,

awoke to foot-high "Gustav Mahler" graffiti on the Queen Street Bridge and along Lake Shore Boulevard East. "Who is the mystery Mahler among us?" demanded a Web reporter,[49] but answer came there none. Mahler was just there, written on the walls.

"Why Mahler, why now?" Is it the music, or the man? Or is it, perhaps, the melting pot of turn-of-the-century Vienna, a time and place like our own, where confidence and fragility were tantalizingly interwoven? The Vienna of Freud, Mahler, Mach, Wittgenstein, Schnitzler, Herzl, Trotsky, and the young Hitler forged the world we know today. It was a meeting point of individualism and collectivism, egotism and idealism, the erotic and the ascetic, the elevated and the debased. At its center whirled Gustav Mahler. A hero to some, to others a sick neurotic, the man and his music are central to our understanding of the course of civilization and the nature of human relationships.

Art that is both high and low, original and derived, breathtaking and banal, Mahler's music resists textbook analysis. It is an open-ended mind game of intellectual and ironic discourse, a voyage of discovery that combines self-revelation, consolation, and renewal. Mahler's remedy is there whenever we need it. Each symphony is a search engine for inner truths. To know Mahler is ultimately to know ourselves.

PART II

Who Is Mahler?

The Life and Times

2. Living in a Nowhere Land (1860–1875)

A PLACE, A NAME, A FAITH, PERHAPS

The landscape in high summer is a wash of gold and green. The harvest is ready for reaping, and the hillsides are in leaf, the forests thick and dark as a warrior's beard. There are blue lakes in the glades and ruined castles, magical haunts for a solitary boy. Birdcalls in the pines above are punctuated with inblown wafts of cowbells, coach horns, and tavern bands. This is the land that gave birth to Mahler, the landscape that infuses his music, the view he will call to mind each summer as he sits down to compose. It is preserved unaltered when I first visit; and the next time it is gone.

Mahler needs a remembrance of boyhood sights and sounds before he can write a note. His first composing studio is beside a lake, the second deep in woods, the third on a mountain meadow. "Don't look up there," he tells a visitor who admires the view. "I have already used it up and set it to music."[1] He mines topography and memory for musical stimulus. Once, walking in woods, he hears a distant fairground, the crackle of shooting galleries, puppet shows, a military band, a choir. "You hear that?" he cries. "That's polyphony, and this is where I get it from! Even as a small child in the Iglau woods, it used to affect and impress me strangely. It's all the same—a racket like this, a thousand birds singing, the howling of a storm, the slap of waves or the crackle of a fire. Just like this—from different sides—the themes appear, different from each other in rhythm and melody . . . and the artist orders and unites them into a harmonious whole."[2] Mahler wants us to know where he comes from and how he is formed.

His landscape has no name. It is neither Bohemia nor Moravia but an undrawn borderland where the river Iglawa (Jihlava) divides one province from the other in an empire that covers half of Europe from Split on the Adriatic Sea to Czernowitz in the Ukraine. A garrison town, Iglau (now Jihlava) guards the road from Prague to Brünn (now Brno) and beyond to the capital, Vienna. Iglau (population 13,000[3]) is historically a German-speaking island (*deutsche Sprachinsel*) in a Slavonic sea of Czechs. It remains so until May 1945, when the Czechs expel the Germans after six years of Nazi occupation.

Czechs and Germans aside, the region has a third ethnic group, oppressed by the other two. Jews, who have lived here for centuries, are treated as aliens. They must report to the police on entering Iglau, pay a fifteen-kreuzer fine, and be gone by nightfall.[4] Their freedom to trade, move home, and travel is restricted. They have no sense of permanence. "I am three times without a *Heimat*," says Mahler, "as a Bohemian in Austria, an Austrian among Germans and as a Jew throughout the world—always an intruder, never welcomed."[5] *Heimat* is German for "homeland," for roots and birthright. As a Jew, Mahler has no place to call home.

Mahlers have lived in this province since before they were called Mahler. The first to bear the name does so in 1787 when Emperor Joseph II forces Jews to take German surnames for administrative convenience. Some, for a bribe to the clerk, become beautiful mountain (Schoenberg), peace (Fried) or joy (Freud). Others, less fortunate, are given pejorative labels: short (Klein), crinkled (Kraus), or blue head (Blaukopf). Many are defined by occupation: Schneider (tailor), Schnitzler (chopper), Lehrer (teacher). Abraham, son of Jacob, registers at Chmelna, near Humpolec, as Abraham Jacob Mahler; he is a seller of spices, a synagogue singer, and a *shochet*, a kosher slaughterer. Mahler, a variant of Maler (artist) or Müller (miller), has no bearing on Abraham's livelihood. It appears to be a clerk's misspelling of *mohler*, which is a local Yiddish variant of the Hebrew *mohel*, a man who carries out the rite of circumcision on male infants. The *shochet*, trained in the precise use of lethal knives, often serves the community as a *mohler*.

Abraham, son of Jacob, the first Mahler, has seven sons; his eldest, Bernard (Bernhard), has six. Under an oppressive law only one child in any Jewish family is allowed to register a civil marriage. Bernard's son Simon (born 1793) lives out of wedlock with Maria, daughter of Abraham Bondy, kosher butcher of Lipnitz (Lipnice); his eight children are listed as bastards. Maria's father and Simon own a distillery in Kalischt (Kaliště, "muddy pond" in Czech). They leave it in 1855 to Simon's eldest son, Bernhard (born 1827).

Bernhard is a driven man. Riding from village to village selling his brandy, this fourth-generation Mahler has a book on his knees—a French grammar, a work of science or history. Fellow peddlers call him "the cart-seat scholar." He gives private lessons to children of rich families and, in 1857, he marries Marie Hermann from Ledeč, a lame girl with an augmented dowry. Marie is twenty years old to Bernhard's thirty, shy and devout where he is bluff and skeptical. "She did not love him, hardly knew him," says their son. "They belonged together like fire and water. He was all stubbornness, she gentleness itself."[6] The couple occupy the Kalischt alehouse. A son, Isidor, born March 1858, dies in a domestic accident. The next, born Saturday, July 7, 1860, is Gustav Mahler.

The Hebrew date is the seventeenth day of the month of Tammuz, the Fast of the Fourth Month, when Jews begin three weeks of mourning for the destruction of Jerusalem in the years 586 BC and AD 70. The fast is a warning from history, an omen of homelessness. Gustav Mahler enters the world on a day of dispossession.

A week later, on July 14, 1860, in [Dolní] Kralovice, near Ledeč, he is brought "into the Covenant [bris] of our Father Abraham" by the act of circumcision. The mohel is David Kraus from Ledeč, and the godfathers (sandekim) who hold the child during the ceremony are Ignatz Weiner and Anton Kern;[7] Weiner is Marie's favorite uncle.[8]

Male circumcision is a religious and social imperative for committed Jews, a bonding with tradition and community. It is a quick procedure. The mohel takes a scalpel and severs the prepuce from the head of the penis, after which a blessing is recited over a cup of wine and the baby is given his Hebrew name. Gustav is medieval German, from the Swedish, meaning "God's staff."

Sigmund Freud, at his bris, becomes Shlomo. Franz Kafka is Anshel, Theodor Herzl is Benjamin Ze'ev. For Gustav Mahler, no Jewish name has been traced, though he must have received one.

Let's try to work it out. Bible names beginning with G are scarce—Gad, Gershom, Gedalia, Gideon, Gavriel. In Yiddish there is the diminutive Getzel, for Gottfried or Gustav. Was he Getzel? Unlikely, when other Mahlers had proper Hebrew names. A Hebrew match for Gustav, with two phonetic affinities, might be Yaakov (Jacob). The end syllable is the same, and in regional dialects the initial G softens to Y (*Yustov*). Jacob was the patronymic of the first Mahler, Abraham. It is a family name. So is Gustav also Yaakov? Gustav means "God's staff," awesome and unbending. This name, throughout life, is Mahler's shield against intimacy. No one (apart from his wife) calls him anything but Gustav, never slurred or truncated.

Yaakov is Isaac's sneaky son who deceives his father with a mess of pottage, a very different character. Yet Jacob is Mahler's hero, a "tremendous symbol of creativity,"[9] quoted in rehearsal when musicians cannot fathom his intentions. Facing a bemused Viennese chorus in the *Resurrection* Symphony, he calls for silence and summons his alter ego: "This is Jacob wrestling with the Angel, and Jacob's cry: I will not let you go until you bless me!"[10] The biblical Jacob has nothing to do with any narrative of resurrection, and the singers cannot have been much enlightened. But to Mahler, Jacob is an indomitable fellow struggler, a man who has to fight the angels to earn his rightful due. "God won't give me a blessing," he grumbles. "I have to wrest it from him in my terrible struggles to realise my works."[11] Just like Jacob, he adds, the son who "struggles with God until he is blessed." Mahler's art, his whole life, is a fight for that blessing. Like Jacob, who dons goatskin to claim his birthright, Gustav "changes his coat"[12] upon becoming a Catholic to gain power in Vienna. Everything he does, even in deceit, is a bid for God's blessing. Dying, he scrawls on his last symphony: "Oh, God, God, why have You forsaken me?" Gustav, also Jacob, will not let go until he receives that blessing.

Three months after he is born, the Mahlers move into town. The emperor Franz-Joseph, easing some antiminority laws, allows Jews to live in Iglau. On October 22, 1860, Bernhard Mahler rents a house on Pirnitzergasse, at the lower end of the town square, and opens a tavern on the ground floor. His brother David joins him in the bar. Business is brisk. The garrison yields bored conscripts and the market thirsty traders. At night officers in uniform dance with girls in billowing skirts, vanishing with them into nearby fields. Bernhard rents the house next door and starts a vinegar factory and a bakery. He gets into trouble over unpaid licenses, prostitutes in the pub, late taxes, and insulting a police officer. He is a busy, blustery man who cuts corners and grabs serving girls. At home he is an educational paragon, with a set of classical and modern literature in a glass-fronted sideboard.[13] While Bernhard is on the make, Marie suffers headaches and "a weak heart."[14] Every year or two she has another child, fourteen in all. There are two bedrooms. Eight infants die before the age of two. As the coffins leave by the rear, the singing continues in the bar out front.

Business aside, the family's migration to Iglau is dictated by religious needs. Kalischt, "a scattering of huts," has three Jewish families, insufficient for a prayer quorum. Iglau is building a synagogue and a cemetery. By 1869 the town has 1,090 Jews, 5.4 percent of the population, and "anti-Jewish riots and disturbances"[15] are reported.

Bernhard, friendly with the synagogue cantor, is elected chairman of the Jewish education board. Marie lights candles on Friday nights and keeps a kosher home. Judaism, however, is in a state of flux. From the east Hasidism blows happy-clappy ecstasies into a scholastic faith. In the north Moses Mendelssohn brings Jews into ethical dialogue with Christians. Reform rabbis relax the old rules, allowing mixed-sex seating in synagogues and one-day festivals; some even permit the eating of pork. A counterreformation is driven from Moravia by a university-educated German rabbi, Samson Raphael Hirsch, who preaches a coexistence of Torah and science. Iglau is in the thick of these controversies. Its rabbi, Jacob Joachim Unger, has a doctorate in philology from the University of Berlin.

The Judaism in which Gustav Mahler is raised is lukewarm mainstream Orthodox with infusions of other trends. He encounters Hasidic melody from itinerant klezmer bands, their music shifting, at a nod of the head, from morbid to manic and back. Klezmer is a music that obeys no code of conduct, unlike the military bands that parade daily in Iglau's town square. A collision of army discipline and smiley, Jewish individualism is imprinted on the boy's mind.

The first language he hears at home is Yiddish, made up of German, Hebrew, Aramaic, and Slavonic terms with a syntax all its own. Known as *mameloshn,* "mother's tongue," Yiddish allows Jews to communicate in code. Double negatives are designed to confuse alien ears, along with a courtesy so elaborate that only by listening to tone and observing hand motions can anyone be sure whether a word is flattery or insult. Yiddish rings loud in Mahler's adult response. "Am I a wild animal?"[16] he shouts at celebrity gawkers, using a Yiddish term, *vilde khaye,* that conveys both feral danger and boyish mischief, terror and endearment, in one useful obfuscation. "So many fingers and none to be stirred,"[17] he yells at his sisters, when they keep him waiting. He teaches his gentile wife the word *schlemiel* (which she understands as "fool" when he means "clumsy"), and he employs *Unserer,* a Yiddishism denoting fellow Jews but to Mahler signifying any sympathetic soul.[18] Crucially, Yiddish gives his music the possibility of sustaining two contrary meanings. Everything that Mahler innovates derives from his tribal origins.

The synagogue is the scene for one of the earliest reported incidents in his life. The congregation is singing in unison one Sabbath morning when, "from his mother's arms," the three-year-old boy shouts, "Be quiet! that's horrible!" and starts singing "Eits a binkel Kasi (Hrasi)," "one of his favorite songs."[19] "Eits" is a Czech peddler's ditty about a swaying knapsack. Sung in polka rhythm, it is a bawdy ballad, unsuited for a place of worship. Mahler relates the story as a token of his refusal to tolerate bad music. There is an element of mythmaking involved in his narration. He is leaving false trails for future biographers like me, playing us along a line of no return.

INTRODUCED BY A FUNERAL MARCH

At his grandparents' house in Ledeč, the little boy disappears. He is found in the attic, on tiptoe, his fingers tapping a disused piano. Grandfather Hermann asks if he would like to have it for his own and delivers the instrument to Iglau by oxcart. Gustav is four years old when he learns to play. At six he writes a Polka with an Introductory Funeral March. His mother promises him a reward if he makes no blots on the page.

If he catches her listening at the door he stops playing, then castigates himself for depriving her of pleasure. When she suffers a headache, he stands behind her chair and begs God to make her better. There is a clinical term for small children who care for needy parents: "Pathological nurturance," it is called, and it aptly describes Mahler as he protects his lame, child-ridden mother from his robust, frightening, and uncontrollable father. Bernhard abuses his wife and has sex with servant girls. During a marital row Gustav runs out of the house in a panic, into the path of an organ-grinder who is playing the old plague song, "Ach, du lieber Augustin." Dr. Freud will find this most interesting, telling Mahler that it explains why his music mixes intense emotion with cliché and banality. What Freud does not mention is that Mahler is being conditioned by a clash of parental temperaments to fuse opposites in a single phrase.

Bernhard demands a composition to match the one he wrote for Marie. Gustav sets a poem by Gotthold Ephraim Lessing about Turks who chase girls but drink no wine. His first attempt at irony? He is surely too young and too scared to satirize his lustful, teetotaler father. Bernhard, delighted, rewards the boy with the key to his bookcase. Gustav becomes a constant reader. Hurting his finger, he howls "for hours" until he is given *Don Quixote*. Moments later he is roaring with laughter, all pain forgotten.[20]

To escape misery at home he hides in the forest one summer's day until he is "overcome by a shudder of Panic dread."[21] He bursts into tears for no reason. He loses himself in music. Catching sight of a band on the way home from school, he is so absorbed by the sound that he forgets he needs the toilet and soils his pants.[22] His brother Ernst, a year younger, is his happy acolyte, shining his brother's shoes and doing his share of household chores in exchange for Gustav's playing him tunes on the piano. Between one crib death and the next, a healthy sister, Leopoldine, "Poldi," is born in 1863, followed by Louis, "Alois," in 1867 and Justine, "Justi," in 1868. Justi places candles around her bed, pretending to be dead. Ernst never fully recovers from an attack of rheumatic fever. A specter of death hangs over the house.

The town choirmaster, Heinrich Fischer, who lives next door, recruits Gustav to sing in his church. At school Rabbi Unger marks him "Excellent" in religion (Jewish). In other subjects he is barely "Adequate." He goes swimming with Fischer's son, Theodore, and hears folk tales from his nursemaid. One is called "Das Klagende Lied," the song of sorrow. Mahler remembers that.

On December 20, 1869, the town crier announces in the square that a purse has been found with three gold coins and sixty-four and a half kreuzers. It has been handed in at the police station by "the schoolboy Mahler," who found it "under the snow on the corner of Pirnitzergasse, near the sewer drain-cover." It is a large sum, two weeks' wages for a bricklayer.[23] Picture "the schoolboy Mahler," solitary and contemplative, scuffing snow in the gutter outside his house. He sees a purse and, with no thought of reward, relinquishes it to the authorities, an act of selfless renunciation.

The following year, on October 13, 1870, the boy commands public attention once again. A piano recital takes place at the Iglau theater:

A nine year-old boy [sic], the son of a Jewish businessman here by name of Maler [sic], gave his first public performance on the piano before a large audience. The success that the future virtuoso achieved with his audience was great. It would have been greater still on an instrument of the same quality as his fine playing.[24]

Bernhard, delighted by his son's success, takes Gustav to Prague and enrolls him at a gymnasium, an advanced secondary school. He boards with a Jewish family in the leather trade, Grünfeld by name, two of whose sons are making musical careers. Alfred is a pianist and Heinrich a cellist. They are eight and five years older than Gustav, who later complains that they stole his shoes and clothes. It seems unlikely, given the disparity in age, but he is in all sorts of torment. One day he enters a room and sees a servant girl writhing on the floor beneath Alfred or Heinrich. In "shock and disgust," he rushes to help her only to get "soundly abused by both of them."²⁵ It is a brutal introduction to the act of love, inculcating a lifelong prudishness, but is it true? No such incident is mentioned in Heinrich Grünfeld's memoirs,²⁶ nor is there lasting rancor between him and the family. Mahler employs a third brother, Siegmund, as a coach at the Vienna Opera; Alfred attends Mahler's funeral.²⁷ Mahler is sowing false clues again, casting himself as Candide, an innocent among the depraved.

Bernhard, visiting Prague in February 1872, finds the boy at the bottom of his class, his pallor severe. He feeds him in a restaurant and whisks him home for three more years of mothering. In his months away, however, Gustav has acquired emotional distance. In letters home he reports nothing of his inner life, only how he is sleeping, what he eats and excretes: "I upset my stomach in the train compartment and in the dining car on a steak and salad and, upon my arrival, I had to lie down after an extremely severe rash and a terrible headache."²⁸ He suffers from "damned haemorrhoids,"²⁹ as well as migraines, "angina"³⁰ and "stomach catarrh." Even when feeling "excellent," he adds: "as is seldom the case."³¹ Marcel Proust, in letters to his *maman*, indulges in a similar hypochondria, a substitute for meaningful communication.

His bar mitzvah approaches. He is due to recite from the Torah on Saturday, July 12, 1873, chanting verses from the portion of Balak (Num. 22:2–25:9). Three months beforehand "the young virtuoso Mahler" takes part in synagogue events to honor the wedding of Archduchess Gisela; three weeks before his bar mitzvah Marie gives birth to a boy, Otto. Although there is no record of his chanting his bar mitzvah portion, it is inconceivable that a son of the education chairman could have failed to pass this rite of passage. Mahler, after leaving Iglau, retains his respect for Jewish tradition and his affection for its synagogue. Years later, as head of the Vienna Opera, he meets a singer, Max Davidsohn, who once served as a synagogue cantor. Mahler takes Davidsohn to the music room of his hotel and demands to hear a Hebrew prayer. The singer intones, "Do not forsake us in old age, when strength gives out," from the Yom Kippur liturgy. "Yes," sighs Mahler, "that is religious. That is how I heard it as a child, sung by the old cantor at our synagogue."³² He sits at the keyboard, improvising on the tune, gripped by *Sehnsucht*, a longing for lost roots and heritage. If his bar mitzvah has been obliterated, that may be due to a parallel event, a tragedy unfolding in the family.

Ernst is dying, wasting away from congestive heart failure brought on by rheumatic fever. Gustav sits by his bed for months,[33] spinning stories. "I invented all sorts of gruesome fairy-tales for him: about giants and monsters in the most terrifying forms, with two heads and four arms, doing the most frightful things. When these monsters no longer made an impression, they were given more arms and ten, twenty, a hundred heads—until even that did not satisfy the fevered, wandering imagination of my charge and they had to have thousands and millions. Finally, instead of monsters, what appears on the scene but a normal person."[34] Ernst is Gustav's adoring fan, his security blanket. His death on April 13, 1875, is a devastating loss. Gustav mourns as never before (or again), and then, abruptly, he stops.

That summer he takes a job on a farm, copying music for its manager, Gustav Schwarz. At night he writes an opera with Joseph Steiner, son of another employee. The opera, *Ernst, Duke of Swabia*, is based on an 1818 Ludwig Uhland play about Ernst's love for his friend Werner. Mahler is writing about his brother. Schwarz, hearing the boys sing arias from their opera, secures Gustav an audition with Julius Epstein, professor at the Vienna Conservatory of Music. Bernhard refuses point-blank, fearing he will "be corrupted by bad company in Vienna."[35] Schwarz persuades him to let the boy go. In Vienna, Epstein declares, "Herr Mahler, your son is a born musician." Bernhard says he wants Gustav to study commerce and run the distillery. "The young man has spirit," quips Epstein, "but not for the spirits trade." On September 10, 1875, Gustav Mahler registers as a full-time student in the empire's foremost music college.

Leaving home at fifteen is a defining act. I left at sixteen to study in another country, a foreign language. A lone, bright youngster is a magnet for all types of adult ambitions, the object of more attention than he seeks or can always handle. But to be young and far from home is no bad thing. Others invent roles and opportunities for you to fulfill, or not. Like Mahler, I felt no homesickness, no regret at leaving tragedy and faith behind. Leaving home liberates the creative faculty to convert sorrow into art. Mahler is not yet a composer, but he is on the way to finding a destiny.

Iglau froze in time for the next century, fossilized like a pterodactyl at the onset of the ice age. On my first visit in the mid-1980s, little had changed since Mahler left. The town square, dating back to Good King Wenceslas, was unaltered apart from a gray concrete store at the far side and a flutter of red-banner slogans around the town hall. The vaulted stairwell of Mahler's boyhood home on the Pirnitzergasse, now Malinovského, felt suitably spooky, the interior decayed. Balconies crumbled over the courtyard, their rails at crazy angles. Boiled cabbage and fresh sewage were the prevalent smells. A bronze plaque was affixed to an outer wall, but no mention of Mahler could be found in the town's guidebook, printed in Czech, German, French, English, and Russian. As a foreign journalist, I was shadowed by government guides. A cloud of dogma and disinformation hung over the wretched town.

A visit had been arranged to the municipal archives. In the cellars of the town hall, by some state order that had never been revoked, all school registers and examination papers of the past century and a half had been kept on file. With a minimum of fuss I could read the name of every boy who had sat in Mahler's class and every essay he wrote. Rabbi Unger's signature leaped off the foot of a Religious Studies paper. I asked if I could make photocopies. A curator confided in German that photocopiers were banned in the "workers' paradise." I transcribed a few quick lines of what seemed the most remarkable essay, "On the Influence of the Orient on German Literature," which had been marked "less than Adequate."[36] It was easy to see how an adolescent in this numb place might reach out to a distant East, a point of flight. Mahler felt very close to me at that moment.

I rode on to Kaliště, formerly Kalischt. Mahler's birthplace, struck by lightning, had burned to the ground and been rebuilt to scale. "Such a miserable little house," he called it. "None of the windows even had glass. In front of the house was a little pond. The village, a few scattered huts, was nearby."[37] The house was still a tavern.

A quarter of a century later, it no longer was. After Communism, the nowhere land glimpsed opportunity. In September 1998 a Mahler birthplace museum opened in the Kaliště inn, an official-looking edifice with safety notices and fire extinguishers. Invited to embed a message in a foundation capsule, I wrote a few words about Mahler's being a man of modern times and, as I wrote, regretted the onset of sterile modernity in this static, silent place.

Jihlava, too, was refurbishing the Mahler home to European Union specifications and in a kind of institutional Kitsch at what was now Znojemské ulice 265/4. The archives were gone, and a Hotel Gustav Mahler, thirty-seven rooms with private bathrooms nestled at the top of the square. At the southern end grinned Ronald McDonald, serving identimeals to 47 million customers daily, in 119 countries.[38] Mahler's town was being progressively homogenized.

In search of Mahler, I walked out of town and into a forest where the composer David Matthews told me he could hear the opening of the First Symphony in "the wind whistling through the trees . . . a sound uncannily like that six-octave A on string harmonics."[39] It was a windless day. I sat on a fallen log like that dark-eyed boy called Gustav, all alone. Suddenly a story came into my head.

THE BOY ON A BICYCLE

One morning in July 1937 a boy heard bells ringing at the Humpolec firehouse and followed the trucks on his bicycle to Kaliště, where the inn was ablaze. "Remember," said his mother that evening, "a famous musician was born there." Twenty months later, on March 16, 1939, the boy saw flames licking the sky at Jihlava. The Germans had torched the synagogue under orders from Gauleiter Artur Seyss-Inquart, a local lout from Stannern (now Stonařov). On April 28 Seyss-Inquart organized a pogrom, evicting the town's twelve hundred Jews. "Remember," said Jiří's mother, "the famous musician sang in that synagogue."

And remember, he did. Through half a century of Nazism and Communism, Jiří Rychetský never forgot Gustav Mahler. He became a teacher in Humpolec, then headmaster, living under state terror and unable to speak his mind. "Even here," he told me at the dining table of his spartan apartment, "my wife and I could not talk to each other for fear the children might repeat something at school and we would all get into trouble. So we talked about Gustav Mahler, and the exhibition I was making."

Mahler had ups and downs under Czech Communism. The first culture minister, Zdeněk Nejedlý, had been a music critic, author of a Mahler biography, but his successors backed Czech-speaking composers. In July 1960 Jiří Rychetský affixed a centennial plaque to the Kaliště inn, "my first activity for Gustav Mahler,"[40] and began to plan a permanent exhibition in Humpolec. When I visited he took me to every ruined synagogue in the region. At Ledeč I saw the loft where Mahler touched his first piano. At the defunct Jewish cemetery of Humpolec I found his grandparents lying close to Kafka's uncle. Jiří kept the graves tidy.

Mahler mattered greatly to the headmaster of Humpolec, keeping him sane and humane in a moral vacuum. Pupils told me how Jiří had talked of Mahler as a light in darkness, *lux in tenebrae*, their escape from the deadly conformity of state socialism. "Mahler" was their secret word for freedom, for imagining a life elsewhere. Mahler meant more, in this nowhere land, than anywhere I have been or seen.

3. City of Dreams (1875–1887)

The Vienna that Mahler enters in September 1875 has been under scaffolding for fifteen years. By order of Emperor Franz-Joseph, the old town is being enclosed in a Ring of parkland and cultural buildings—the Opera (1869), the Musikverein concert hall (1870), the University (1873), the Arts and Crafts School (1877). In the interstices stand the palatial homes of courtly aristocrats and the Jewish nouveaux riches, the Ephrussis, Epsteins, Gomperzes, Todescos, Gutmanns, Rothschilds, and Wittgensteins, financiers of an economic boom. Rail termini open at the city's four compass points, and migrants surge in from every corner of the empire. The population of Vienna trebles, from 431,000 in 1851 to 1.36 million in 1890.[1] One in five is Czech-born. The Jewish component rises from 6,000 in 1867 to 147,000 by 1900, amounting to 9 percent of the population;[2] they congregate chiefly in the rundown second district of Leopoldstadt, known as Mazzeinsel, or Matzo Island.

Immigration transforms Vienna from a sleepy government town (think Ottawa, Canberra) to a hub of invention (Paris, Milan). Yet Vienna remains a byword for sybaritic indulgence, sunning itself in *Schlamperei*, a constitutional sloppiness. Ruled by a God-given emperor and his cousins, Vienna is stifled by history, fattened on the easy flow of coffee, cake, veal schnitzel, and sexual relief. Gustav Mahler is at once repulsed and intrigued. Like many an adolescent away from home, he craves experience and cannot afford much. He shares a room with fellow indigents and gives piano lessons to pay the rent. At the conservatory he goes to Julius Epstein for piano,

Robert Fuchs for harmony, Franz Krenn for composition. Epstein is a Schubert expert, Fuchs an imitator of Brahms, and Krenn a composer of masses. All three are reactionaries, stuck in the past. Then the revolution dawns.

On November 1, 1875, Richard Wagner arrives in Vienna to mount *Tannhäuser* and *Lohengrin* at the Opera. Although these are early and innocuous works, the mere mention of Wagner's name arouses apoplexy in the conservatory staff room and something akin to Beatlemania in the students. Wagner makes the loudest noise on earth, with the biggest orchestra and the most sustained fortissimi, striking the ear (in one celebrated caricature) as a miner strikes coal from the ground. His sensuality is provocative. In *Tristan und Isolde* he stretches the resolution of a chord over five hours of preorgasmic tension. He is exhilarating, disturbing, and tendentious. He has fought on the barricades in the 1848 Revolutions and had children with his assistant's wife. He writes about sex between brother and sister and attacks the Jew as "the born enemy of pure humanity and all that is noble in man. . . . We Germans especially will be destroyed by them."[3] Wagner splits any space he enters into old and young, prudent and curious, racist and liberal. Eduard Hanslick, Vienna's most influential music critic, condemns his music as downright dangerous.

In exchange for supervising two operas, Wagner gets to pick any singers he likes for his upcoming Bayreuth Festival. His presence drives Vienna wild. "You'll never guess who I've been with!!!" cries Mahler's classmate Hugo Wolf. "With the Master. With Richard Wagner. . . . He said: 'My dear friend, I wish you lots of luck in your career.' "[4] Mahler, too poor to attend the performances, reads up on Wagner's concept of opera as a *Gesamtkunstwerk*, a union of all arts, the apotheosis of creation. The Wagner redemption gives power to the conductor—no longer to be ruled by stout singers—as the linchpin of interpretation. Mahler, who has taken up conducting at college, sets his sights on fulfilling the Wagner mission by stamping his mark as a conductor on everything he performs. "Whenever I am feeling low, I have only to think of Wagner and my good mood returns," he declares. "Amazing, that a light like his could have entered the world!"[5]

He joins the Academic Wagner Society, founded by a fellow Iglauer, Guido Adler, and attends lectures by Anton Bruckner, whom Hanslick dubs "symphonic Wagner." A monkish bachelor, shambolic and maladroit, Bruckner writes hourlong unplayed symphonies. On Sundays, he plays the organ in the emperor's chapel. By the grace of good connections, Bruckner is given the chance to premiere his Third Symphony with the Vienna Philharmonic. The concert, on December 16, 1877, is calamitous. The musicians, irked by Bruckner's muzzy beat, play wrong notes and make rude faces. The audience slips away until, at the end, there are just twenty-five people left. Two of them, Mahler and his friend Rudolf Krzyzanowski, are so enthused they prepare a four-hand piano score. Aside from the Wagner sonorities, Mahler's ear has been caught by a funeral melody in the horns echoed by jollity in the strings, a hint that music has the potential to convey polar opposites.

The short score, written by the two students, finds a publisher, and Bruckner gives Mahler his original manuscript in gratitude; seeing him at lunchtime gnawing a roll with cheese rind, buys him a beer to wash it down. Mahler calls Bruckner his "father-in-learning,"[6] overlooking his repeated disparagements of Mahler's Jewishness. It is the price he has to pay for having a mentor.

Jews in Vienna are used to abuse, but the tone is turning nastier. An 1873 stock market crash is blamed on Jewish speculators. In 1879 a limit is imposed on Jews in university posts. Wagner, in the essay "The Work of Art of the Future," singles out "Jewish modernism" as "something quite miserable and very dangerous."[7] By doing so he makes the demonization of Jews culturally acceptable. A student fraternity club specifies: "Every son of a Jewish mother, every human being in whose veins flows Jewish blood, is from the day of his birth without honour and void of all the refined emotions. He cannot differentiate between what is dirty and what is clean. He is ethically subhuman. Friendly intercourse with a Jew is therefore dishonourable; any association with him has to be avoided. It is impossible to insult a Jew."[8]

"Anti-Semitism," as a dictionary term, does not yet exist. The term—credited to Wilhelm Marr, an agitator who marries three Jewish wives before discovering his abhorrence—first appears in print in January 1881, supplanting *Judenhass,* Jew hatred. Karl Lueger, a local politician, clambers on the bandwagon. "Without the Jewish newspapers, there would be no anti-Semitism," he proclaims, accusing the Jews of controlling the mass media. Lueger coins a classic equivocation: "Wer Jude ist bestimme Ich [I decide who's a Jew]." Adolf Hitler will be one of his admirers. The appalling prospect of genocide germinates around the Ring of Mahler's Vienna.

Mahler, feeling threatened, does what Jews have done down the ages: He huddles in a ghetto of close friends, almost all of them Jewish, and keeps his head down. He does not need to do much to get noticed. Older students, sensing talent, seek his company. Krzyzanowski and his brother Heinrich make sure he has something to eat each day. Anton Krisper shares his essays. Friedrich Löhr, an archaeology scholar, takes him to exotic lectures. Guido Adler, the Wagnerian, helps him find work. Emil Freund, a law student, gives financial advice. Natalie Bauer-Lechner, a plain-faced bookseller's daughter, flutters her eyelashes. In midwinter she sees him coatless in the street, correcting a sonata as he runs along, unaware that the sheets are scattering behind him. Someone should look after the lad, she thinks.

At the end of his first year Mahler wins the conservatory composition prize for a salon-pretty piano quartet movement in A minor. It is his earliest extant score, a work (he insists) of no originality; the manuscript, at New York's Pierpont Morgan Library, bears a stamp of Bruckner's new publisher Theodor Rättig, who must have turned it down. At eighteen Mahler fails his school-leaving exams in Iglau and is obliged to retake them before he can enter the University of Vienna to study ancient German literature, philology, art history, philosophy, and Greek art. Bored, he "spends time in the Vienna Woods,"[9] devouring Goethe, Nietzsche, Jean Paul, Schopenhauer, Hebbel, Hoffmann, Hölderlin, Dehmel, Dickens, Dostoyevsky. "Bücher fresse ich immer mehr und mehr [I gobble up more and more books],"[10] he says. Poetry becomes an obsession, to the point where he thinks of giving up music.[11] He reads the Persian mystic Jalāl ad-Dīn ar-Rūmī in an edition by Friedrich Rückert, translator of the Koran. Another Rückert book comes to hand, poems on the death of his two infants in the winter of 1883–84. It is called *Songs on the Death of Children.*

That summer, he falls in love with Marie Freund, a cousin of Emil's, and weeks later with Josefine Poisl, daughter of the Iglau telegraph master. "A new name is inscribed in my heart alongside yours," he tells Krisper, "only whisperingly and blushingly but no less powerfully."[12] In the winter he joins a Wagner club that meets in a vegetarian cellar restaurant. Its leaders are Dr. Victor Adler, founder of the Social Democratic Party; a fellow physician, Albert Spiegler; the archaeologist Löhr, and the writer Hermann Bahr. Mahler grows a full beard and gives up meat. "Over-exertion and under-nourishment made him highly strung," notes Emma Adler, the doctor's wife. "He talked loudly to himself in the streets and gesticulated with his arms."[13]

His new best friend in the club is Siegfried Lipiner, a Galician Jew whose 1876 drama, *Prometheus Unbound,* was praised by Wagner. Banned from Bayreuth for reciting Nietzsche, Lipiner and his writings win Mahler's undying adulation. "I am sometimes quite amused at how closely my 'music' is related to yours,"[14] Mahler tells him, mistakenly. Lipiner is a burnout who lands a job as librarian to Parliament. Why Mahler tolerates his "so very remarkable views"[15] is inexplicable, but the friendship is inextricably symbiotic. Lipiner goes on to marry two of Mahler's companions and to sleep with his mistress. He is not the only Mahler friend to chase his women. Are these clubmen more, perhaps, than just good chums? Might Mahler's circle be gay? Gender Studies experts who have outed Handel, Schubert, and Chopin on the skimpiest of evidence would love nothing better than to drag Mahler from a putative closet. There is, however, no hint of physical love between Mahler and other men, nothing more than a platonic affection, extravagantly expressed. At twenty Mahler has learned how to make friends and influence people. He is now ready to break out of Vienna's tight Ring and make his way in the great wide world.

THE YOUNG TRAVELER'S SONGS

Josefine Poisl's parents forbid her to answer his letters. Mahler writes three songs of rising despair. "I cry to you from the depths of my misery! . . . Farewell! My salvation! My light. . . ."[16] The songs are titled "In Springtime," "Winter Song," and "May Dance on the Green," innocuous enough, but the words are bleak beyond hope: "I am not blind and yet I do not see, I have no darkness and no light." He invites the girl to share an abyss of grief: "Our happiness is over, lost forever." The last word, *ewig*, is a Mahler archetype (see pp. 160–61). A Freudian psychoanalyst believes that this moment, this loss of Josefine, is the event that makes him a composer. "Typically the first great failed love affair of adolescence/young adulthood leaves an indelible imprint on the psyche: it is much more consciously accessible, and therefore painful, than the Oedipal catastrophe which remains buried deeply and is all but inaccessible. Suicide may also occur, so intense and desperate is the experience."[17]

Before the year is out Josefine marries the director of the Iglau College. Mahler responds with *Das Klagende Lied (The Song of Lament)*, "the first work in which I really found myself as Mahler."[18] It is a Grimm-like fable about a queen who pledges to marry the first man to bring her a red flower. Two brothers go searching in the forest. The good brother finds the flower, the bad one kills him. A minstrel makes a flute out of the victim's bone and plays it plaintively *(klagend)* at the wedding. Emotion, for Mahler, is a tale of two brothers, one of whom must die; himself or Ernst.

Not a formal cantata, *The Song of Lament* is more a *tableau vivant*, an after-dinner entertainment. Mahler is looking for a market. His classmate Hugo Wolf suggests an opera on the Rübezahl fairy tale about a Sudeten mountain sprite. Mahler decides not. Dropping out of university, he is sent by the publisher Rättig to an agent, Gustav Löwy (Levi), who offers a summer job in Hall, a spa near Bruckner's birthplace. Hall boasts a wooden theater, a medieval market square, and every requisite of kitsch: The urinals in its restaurant are labeled "beer," "wine," and "cider." Mahler conducts an orchestra of fifteen and, during intermissions, sometimes wheels the soprano's baby around the park. Putting the finishing touches on *The Song of Lament*, he suffers fierce diaphragm pains. It feels as if a second person is trying to burst out of his body.

In September 1881 Löwy sends him to Laibach (Ljubljana), capital of Slovenia, a province that is being repopulated with German speakers. Ljubljana has a Baroque theater, built in 1765, and an orchestra of eighteen. Over seven months Mahler conducts Weber, Verdi, Donizetti, Rossini, Gounod, and Mozart, as well as fifteen operettas. He lodges with Krisper's family in an apartment above a bookshop, opposite the town hall. At rehearsal he demands total attention. A soprano, irked by his austerity, jumps onto his piano lid and slaps her bare thighs in mockery.

All the while he is waiting to hear from the Beethoven Prize Committee. The contest is chaired by Johannes Brahms and judged by the composer Karl Goldmark, the conductor Hans Richter, Mahler's teacher Krenn, and the concertmaster, Josef Hellmesberger, Jr. With so regressive a panel, the result is a foregone conclusion. The winner is a B-flat-minor piano concerto by Professor Robert Fuchs, a sunny acolyte of Brahms. *The Song of Lament* does not even get a commendation. He sends it to Franz Liszt, hoping for a favorable citation, but the cassocked legend dislikes it, and Mahler resigns himself to "a hellish life in the theatre."[19] He spends Christmas 1882 in Iglau, where his mother complains of his slow progress, and Löwy comes to the rescue with a vacancy in Olmütz (Olomouc), a Moravian garrison town where the latest conductor has been fired for beating up the theater manager. Mahler goes there with four days to rehearse two Meyerbeer epics, *Les Huguenots* and *Robert le Diable*. His rehearsals leave singers hoarse and the orchestra in an uproar at his precisionism. "Accuracy," declares Mahler, "is the soul of artistic performance." "Curiously," notes a baritone, Jacques Manheit, "nobody dared to contradict."[20] This is the first sight of Mahler the musical purifier, fanatical in his fidelity to text.

"I suffer for my Masters," he complains, lonely, stressed, and desperately hungry. "In the restaurant, I starve because they only serve meat menus. In my apartment, I am plagued by noise from two pianos. I have nothing at all to read."[21] Manheit sees him one day at breakfast, looking glum. Mahler mentions that his father is sick.

[The] next morning on my way to the theatre [writes the baritone], I saw a man running demented, weeping loudly, through the streets. With some difficulty, I recognised Mahler. Remembering the previous day's events, I asked anxiously, "In heaven's name, has something happened to your father?"

"Worse, worse, much worse," howled Mahler. "The worst has happened. The Master has died."

It was 13 February 1883, Richard Wagner had been taken from us.[22]

After four months he moves on. Olmütz, between Dresden and Vienna, is on the theater route, and Mahler gets a job in Kassel, across the German border. Kassel has a hundred thousand inhabitants, an orchestra of fifty, and a theater run on military lines by Baron Adolph von und zu Gilsa, an Iron Cross hero of the Franco-Prussian War. Mahler is rebuked for tapping his feet in rehearsal and making the chorus laugh. A Royal Prussian Theater, he is informed, is no place for levity.

Patrons in the front row grumble that his nervous energy disturbs them, and the chief conductor, Wilhelm Trieber, gets jealous. Mahler is unhappy but he cannot leave, not yet. He is in love with a singer, Johanna Richter. She seems willing, but Mahler is beset by "a dread of the inevitable." On New Year's Eve it ends in tears.

When the bell tolled, tears spurted from her eyes. It felt terrible that I could not dry them. She went into the next room and stood for a while, silent at the window. She returned, still weeping. A nameless grief had risen between us, like an eternal [ewig] partition wall. All I could do was press her hand and go. As I came out of the door, the bells were ringing and the solemn chorale was heard from the tower. Ah, dear Fritz, it was as if the Great Director of the World had staged it to perfection. All night, I wept in my dreams.[23]

It reads as if he is observing them through a window, saving his pain for art. He writes six songs, "all dedicated to her," four of them a set: *Lieder eines Fahrenden Gesellen (Songs of a Traveling Apprentice)*. In the first, on the day his girl marries another man, a morning walk turns to misery; he considers self-harm with a knife; and two blue eyes beckon him wanly home. The verses are naive, even trite, but the music is utterly new, a voice that owes nothing to safe teaching. Mahler's melodies are reckless. He soars and swoops, shedding dignity for raw pain, attacking loneliness, poverty, and death. Like Freud, Mahler is drawing on personal experience to make sense of the world. He is starting to define a mission.

Unwilling to risk rejection, he shoves the songs into a drawer but does not forget them. The second *Gesellen* song, "Ging heut' Morgen," will be the opening of his first symphony. The fourth, "Die zwei blauen Augen," appears in its third movement. Mahler is storing up materials and experience for a big statement. Meantime he writes incidental music for a successful tableau, *The Trumpeter of Säkkingen*, and sends the reviews to Prague, Leipzig, and Hamburg in the hope of landing a better job. While he waits for replies Hans von Bülow arrives in Kassel with his Meiningen ensemble. Bülow is the assistant whose wife Wagner seduced during rehearsals for *Tristan und Isolde*. His conducting, intense and pellucid, leaves Gustav Mahler spellbound. "I beg you," he writes, "take me with you in whatever way possible and let me be your pupil even if I have to pay the tuition with my own blood."[24] Bülow is the wrong man to implore. Psychologically maimed by Wagner's betrayal, he hands Mahler's note to Trieber, who demands his dismissal.

Gilsa writes to Berlin for permission to fire Mahler (in Prussia they do things by the book). Mahler, showing no contrition, breaks his contract by agreeing to conduct Mendelssohn's oratorio *Saint Paul* at a prestigious summer festival. Gilsa appeals to Mahler's "sense of nobility" to hand over the festival date to Trieber. Mahler refuses. When Trieber pulls his orchestra from the festival, Mahler, with exceptional chutzpah, calls in the Eighty-third Infantry band. A professional soloist, Rosa Papier of Vienna, jots Mahler's name in her diary, and wealthy choristers shower him with gifts, including a gold watch to replace the one the bailiffs seized when he could not pay his rent. Mahler takes the first job in his mailbox, deputy to Arthur Nikisch at Leipzig, starting a year hence. Until then, he fills in at the German Theater in Prague, where, arriving from the station with a feverish throat infection, he hurls himself into a *Lohengrin* rehearsal. Mahler is twenty-five years old and has not a minute to waste.

THE FANATIC AT LARGE

Every job he takes, every performance he gives from now to the end of his life, is stamped by superhuman effort. "The new conductor, who put every ounce of energy into his task, seemed to us to move about too much on the podium,"[25] notes the canny Prague manager, Angelo Neumann. Mahler's first triumph is a *Don Giovanni* delivered with a smaller orchestra in a more authentic Mozart style.

Both in and away from the theater, he is a man possessed. At his lodgings he bawls out children for making noise. He romances a singer, Betty Frank, who sings three Mahler songs in April 1886, but breaks it off when gossip reaches Iglau. His intensity is terrifying. Acquaintances suspect a mental disorder, fearing he might be heading—like his classmates Hans Rott, Hugo Wolf, and Anton Krisper—for an asylum. Passersby make corkscrew motions with fingers to their brows as Mahler hurtles through the streets, colliding with pedestrians and vehicles. He cannot stop; he hears death at his door. His father's kidneys are failing, and his mother, in her forties, can hardly walk. His sore throats are recurrent, and he suffers crippling migraines—not just eye flashes and headaches but fullblown attacks that leave him feeling as if his head is about to explode. Often he drags himself half blind to work, only for his head to clear as the music begins. He varies his diet and takes furious exercise. Physically he is in top form. Inside he is in torment. He thinks of Ernst and wonders why he is alive while his brother is cold in the grave. He must make each day, each hour, every minute count in the most meaningful way.

After a year in Prague he transfers to Leipzig, a cultured city where Bach was organist, Mendelssohn led the orchestra, and Wagner was born. No respecter of pedigree, Mahler rips into the orchestra, whose members wail to the town council that "Herr Mahler has hardly been satisfied with a single [player] and . . . demands what is absolutely impossible."[26] Arthur Nikisch, the senior conductor, is a languid Hungarian, five years older than Mahler and already world famous for "hypnotizing" orchestras with his twinkling eyes. Musicians call him *Der Magier,* "the magician." He calls in sick before the season begins, and Mahler takes on his first *Ring* cycle, conducting seventeen nights in a month. He introduces Wagner tubas and has the pit lowered to achieve the same sound dispersion as Bayreuth. Audiences can tell the difference right away.

> Mahler is passion personified, nervous restlessness; Nikisch possesses cool, circumspect and level-headed sobriety. Mahler conducts in grand style, with broad strokes, with elemental power; Nikisch strives more for minute detail, for the refined nuance. Mahler is ingenious, unbridled, often whimsical; Nikisch always distinguished, smooth and graceful . . . his carefully arranged locks of hair undulate gracefully to the rhythm, his eyes shine with a melancholy, dreamy light.[27]

Max Staegemann, the theater director, keeps his two conductors well apart. He invites Mahler home and introduces him to Capt. Karl von Weber, grandson of Carl Maria von Weber, whose dead bones Wagner had repatriated from London. Weber is the father of German romantic opera, a martyr to the national art. Mahler knows *Freischütz,* and the captain shows him Weber's unfinished opera, *The Three Pintos.* Together with Captain Weber and his clever wife, Marion, Mahler sets to work adapting the clumsy comedy, about a Spanish don whose identity is stolen by two love rivals. "You'd be surprised how little of it is Weber's," says Mahler of the new version. "Not much more than a few wonderful themes, not a note of orchestration."[28] He plays excerpts of the score to Richard Strauss, who is in Leipzig conducting his F-minor symphony. Strauss calls *Pintos* "a masterpiece" and Mahler "a remarkably intelligent musician." An alliance of convenience is formed between the young composers, a tacit agreement that they will assist each other's progress.

Visiting the Webers every day while finishing the *Pintos* opera, Mahler falls in love with Marion, demure, Jewish, and a mother of three. "I have met a beautiful person here in Leipzig," he tells his friend Fritz Löhr, "the sort that tempts one to do foolish things."[29] What happens next is unclear. Mahler later says he is left standing on the platform, tickets in hand, waiting for Marion to show up for their elopement. The English composer Ethel Smyth, a student in Leipzig, hears that Weber boards the departing train, shooting in all directions. One way or another, Marion stays put.

Mahler is shaken and inspired by the loss of his latest love. Marion, he says, "gave my life new meaning."[30] He dreams he is in a coffin surrounded by wreaths when Marion arrives and removes the flowers. A storybook that he borrows from her children—*Des Knaben Wunderhorn (The Boy's Magic Horn)*—suggests an idea for a symphony, his first. "When I finished the first movement—it was almost midnight—I ran to the Webers and played it to them both. They had to help me at the piano, playing above and below to augment the opening harmonic A. We three were so enthusiastic and happy: I don't think I ever had a more wonderful time with my First."[31] He wears a "half-expectant, half-worried look." "I can't help it, I just have to compose," he tells friends.[32] "Everything in and around me is in a state of becoming."[33]

In January 1888 he conducts *The Three Pintos* to standing ovations, and the king of Saxony chats with him "in a most amiable way . . . for the entire intermission."[34] The opera is seen in Hamburg, Munich, Dresden, Kassel, Prague, and Vienna. Mahler pockets a ten-thousand-mark publisher's check and tells his parents he will find it easy to get his symphony performed "since I am now a 'famous' man."[35] But *Pintos*, which Tchaikovsky finds "idiotic," does not get revived, and Mahler, restless, picks a fight with a stage manager, forcing Staegemann to release him. He is out of work again but very much in play. Guido Adler sets up lunch with David Popper, head of strings at Franz Liszt's academy and a Budapest power broker. Popper sends Mahler to meet Baron Franz von Beniczky, commissioner in charge of theaters. Beniczky has lined up Felix Mottl as chief conductor but, finding that Mottl refuses to learn Hungarian, installs Gustav Mahler as artistic director of the Royal Hungarian Opera, the number two stage in the Hapsburg Empire.

4. A Symphony Like the World (1887–1891)

Budapest is a volatile place, isolated by linguistic particularity. Home to half a million people on either bank of the river Danube, it proclaims the superiority of all things Hungarian, starting with a language that, though eloquent, bears no relation to any other except, vestigially, to Finnish. Learning Hungarian is a challenge. With twenty-seven different cases, Hungarian is capable of exquisite refinement and an astonishing capacity for insult, interchangeable without warning. Budapest is alternately romantic and morose. Pest, it is said, smells of spring violets, while "autumn and Buda were born of the same mother." The city holds the world's suicide record, thirty-two a year per one hundred thousand inhabitants. There is even a suicide song, "Gloomy Sunday":

> Angels have no thought of returning you.
> Would they be angry if I joined you?

One in five of the populace is Jewish (Vienna's mayor calls the city "Judapest"); most of the rest are fervent nationalists. Yet, for all its separatism, Budapest is aggressively cosmopolitan, intent on equality with Vienna. If Vienna gets a new opera house in 1869, Budapest must have one by 1884. If the Vienna Opera is part of the imperial household, Budapest's must be a "gift of the [emperor]." The first task facing a director of the Budapest Opera is how to be a Magyar. Mahler sets out his program in October 1888.

I have been studying the situation in Budapest for three months now and have discovered many surprising facts. The most astonishing of these is that Hungary, richer in splendid voices than any other European nation, has made no serious attempt to create a national opera. . . . I am endlessly astonished that the question of the language of performance has not been the subject for serious concern.[1]

He promises to ban foreign singers from "a true Hungarian national institution" and, in tandem with Ödön von Mihalovics of the Liszt academy, to foster local talent. Two of Wagner's *Ring* operas will be sung in Hungarian before Christmas. By embracing nationalist rhetoric and equating it with artistic excellence, Mahler strikes the right note. Nationalists are reduced to sniping at his salary, his ten-year contract, and, at twenty-eight, his inexperience, never having run an opera house before. Mahler, however, has learned much in his apprentice years. At the first rehearsal he takes each singer by the hand and leads them to their spot on stage, establishing personal contact. With the orchestra he varies praise with fiery exhortation, working himself to a gray pallor.

Christmas comes and goes without a *Ring*, and the press starts muttering. It is January 26, 1889, before Mahler enters the pit, the lights dim, and the E-flats of the *Rhinegold* prelude growl upward from the pit. As the sound reaches the audience, a puff of smoke is seen billowing from the prompter's box, followed by a lick of flame. Mahler carries on conducting, his composure averting a stampede. When the firemen arrive, he calls a half hour break. Then the E-flats resume. This is Budapest's first experience of Wagner's saga of gods and greed. The next morning, critics write that Budapest's Wagner is better than Bayreuth's. "The way the mass of gold blazed up (from the Rhine bed) was sensational," gasps one review.[2] At *Valkyries* there are shouts of "Éljen Mahler [Long live Mahler]!" Beniczky, Mahler's boss, congratulates him in an open letter to the biggest newspaper, *Pester Lloyd:*

> Honoured Mr Director: . . . Producing these gigantic works in fairly short time and with musical and scenic perfection would have done credit to any opera house. . . . You, sir, have shown, that the greatest contemporary works of art can now be produced without external

assistance and completely in Hungarian. This situation fills every patriot with joy.[3]

But before the elation can build, the theater is shut down. On January 30, 1889, the crown prince, Archduke Rudolf, Franz-Joseph's son, shoots himself and his eighteen-year-old girlfriend at a hunting lodge in Mayerling, southwest of Vienna. Official mourning is declared amid fears of civil unrest. Rudolf is popular in Hungary, a champion of Magyar rights. The streets of Budapest are draped in black. Mahler, seething with frustration, receives more bad news. His father is in poor health. He sends two baskets of grapes and a crate of Seville oranges, assuring his sister Justi that "when the need is greatest, I will come immediately." On February 18 he is summoned by telegram: Bernhard is dead, aged fifty-two, and Gustav becomes head of an unruly family.

A TRIPLE BLOW

No account exists of Mahler's response to his father's death. Bernhard Mahler is buried in the Iglau Jewish cemetery. The widow and children rend their garments with a razor cut to the lapel. At the open grave the eldest son is expected to recite Kaddish, the sanctification of God's name. Does Gustav Mahler say Kaddish? He has given up Jewish observance, but he would not wish to hurt his mother or to offend Rabbi Unger. Bernhard would have expected Gustav to say Kaddish so that his soul might find rest. This may be the last religious rite that Mahler performs as a Jew.

Orthodox ritual requires the family to sit on low chairs for the week of mourning, receiving consolation visits. Mahler stays the full week in Iglau. There is much for him to do. Of his five surviving siblings, only Poldi is settled—married to a Vienna businessman, Ludwig Quittner, whom Mahler loathes so much he cannot pronounce his name correctly.[4] Alois, twenty-one, is going to the army; Justi, twenty, runs the house. Otto and Emma, fifteen and fourteen, are virtual strangers to him.

Gustav decides that Otto will study piano in Vienna, staying with Poldi. Justi will look after Emma and their mother. "I must avoid all unnecessary expenses," he warns her, adding that "naturally in the case of dear mother *nothing* must be spared and I will always be ready *gladly* if it is about *her* needs and wishes."[5] There is no regret for his father. Where Ernst's death was terrible and Wagner's sent him weeping in the streets of Olmütz, he treats his father's passing as a formality. The lack of sentiment in his letters is chilling. Death will not derail Mahler again from his vocation.

In Budapest a Roman Catholic priest, Ferenc Komlóssy, accuses him in Parliament of making the Opera a "Jewish national house." Driving himself all the harder, that summer he auditions singers in Prague, Salzburg, and Bayreuth. In Munich he undergoes surgery to treat bleeding hemorrhoids. He convalesces in Marienbad, then rushes back to Iglau on hearing that his mother is sick. He finds Justi emaciated with exhaustion and diarrhea. Without rest, he heads back to work, stopping in Vienna to check on Poldi, who is suffering severe headaches. A nervous complaint, he assures his mother, "completely innocuous."[6]

He opens the season with a short speech in unaccented Hungarian. A week later, while conducting Halévy's *La Juive*, he is brought a cable saying that Marie is poorly. He hastens to Iglau, makes his mother comfortable, and takes Justi to a doctor in Vienna. He is back at work next morning and in the podium that night. At the weekend Poldi dies. She is twenty-six years old, a mother of two children. Two weeks later, on October 11, Marie dies. "I can't get away,"[7] says Mahler. The boy who stood behind his mother's chair and begged God to ease her headaches, who presented her with his first composition and defended her from his father's rage, has no hesitation in missing her funeral. Mahler, like many successful men, has downgraded the personal in his scale of priorities. He cannot take time off to bury his mother because he is preparing to present his First Symphony.

A DIFFERENT KIND OF FUNERAL

He calls it a "symphonic poem" and tells *Pester Lloyd* it could be titled *Life* for the way it shows how life "throws marvels into the paths of youth" before, "with the first breath of autumn, [it] takes back piti-lessly everything."[8] He offers a further clue to its meaning, citing *The Huntsman's Funeral*, an 1850 drawing by Moritz von Schwind in which happy field animals gloat as they escort a dead predator to the grave, an odd analogy considering that he has just gotten out of attending his mother's burial.

The program booklet describes the work as a "Symphonic Poem in two parts (manuscript: first performance under the direction of the composer).

Part I: 1 Introduction and Allegro commodo, 2 Andante, 3 Scherzo, Part II: 4 Funeral march; attacca; 5 Molto appassionato.

At seven-thirty on November 20, 1889, Mahler warms up City Hall with a Cherubini overture. Once the applause fades he gives the strings a signal for a seven-octave sustained A. The world is about to hear an orchestra play a work by Gustav Mahler.

It goes down well, at first. After each of three movements, there is warm applause. Half an hour gone, Mahler is feeling good. Then, the reception changes. The second half of the symphony begins with a nursery rhyme, "Bruder Martin," or "Frère Jacques," played slowly and in a minor key with the "sepulchral whine of a muted double-bass"[9] and the sneer of a purse-lipped oboe. Suddenly it breaks into a dance, fast and grotesque. The audience grows uneasy. "We don't know whether to take this funeral march seriously or interpret it as parody," notes the critic Kornél Ábrányi. "The cym-bals clash, the clarinets and violins shriek, the drum thunders out, the trombone bellows; in a word, the instruments run riot in a mad witches' dance."[10]

Nothing upsets an audience so much as not knowing whether to laugh or cry. "The attacca leading into the last movement so alarmed an elegant lady sitting next to me," writes Mahler's friend Löhr, "that she dropped everything she was holding onto the floor." The end is greeted with tepid clapping and a spatter of boos. Mahler rushes backstage and out of the hall, not staying for the concert's second half. "My friends avoided me in terror," he recalls. "Not one of them dared to speak to me about the work or its performance, and I wandered about like a leper or an outlaw."[11]

"This . . . is the work of a young, unbridled and untameable talent, which must [learn to] stem the flood of melodic motifs," is one of the kinder reviews. "The second part is an enormous aberration on the part of a mind of genius," writes another, while a German-language paper tells Mahler to stick to what he does best:

> All our great conductors—Richter, Bülow, Mottl, Levi, &c.—have either recognised themselves or had it proven to them that they are not composers. Their reputations have not suffered. The same is true of Mahler. We shall be pleased to see him on the podium so long as he is not conducting his own music.

Wallowing in self-pity—"You were the only one who did not avoid me," he tells academy director Mihalovics—Mahler knows his symphony needs work. Over the next ten years he conducts five different versions, adding a title, *Titan*, and an explanatory note, which says the symphony is about "a powerful heroic figure, his life and sorrows, his struggles and defeat by fate; the true, higher redemption is brought in the second symphony"—in which "the hero of my D major [is] being borne to the grave."[12] The first was always intended as the introduction to a life history.

Two symphonies, two funerals—the point he is making is: "What did you live for? Why did you suffer? Is it all one vast, terrifying joke? We have to answer these questions somehow if we are to go on living; even if we are only to go on dying."[13] People in the audience are made uneasy by the intimations of their own mortality. This is not the entertainment they paid for.

Mahler, in the finished version of the work, drops the Andante (titled "Blumine") and withdraws his attempted explanations, crying "Death to all programmes!" and insisting that the music must be received as heard. This is disingenuous. Mahler always tries to convey a message in his music, and it is the complexity of that message that leaves his early audiences unhappy. What he does is without musical precedent. What makes the audience uneasy (as Löhr observes) is the nursery rhyme/funeral march and its sudden twist into ribaldry. Here, Mahler invests music with a means of saying two or more things at once. The lullaby/dirge is, by his own admission, a textbook irony, "in the sense of the Aristotelian *eironeia*."[14] He is saying one thing and meaning another because what he has to say is a message people do not want to hear.

Here is how it works: The nursery rhyme/death march is a disturbing aural image, indicative of the death of a child. The jig that disrupts it is a klezmer tune: Modern listeners may recognize its resemblance to the refrain of "If I Were a Rich Man" from the shtetl musical, *Fiddler on the Roof.* What Mahler is describing from boyhood memory is a child's coffin leaving the house to a blast of merriment from the tavern. The music is a protest against the world's indifference to infant mortality rates of 56 percent, a pestilence of diphtheria, smallpox, rubella, scarlet fever, and more that carries off one in two children before the age of five. Medical science at the time attaches greater priority to diagnosis than cure.[15] The death of a child is normal, every household has one. Mourning is perfunctory and burial nameless (we found my father's brother, who died at age five in 1906, in an unmarked plot in Plaistow, East London).

Mahler demands respect for the dead child and remedies for disease. His rage is not focused on any particular target, but he is writing as a Jew, and the irony he uses is not classical Greek but everyday Yiddish, which changes meaning by gesture and inflection. Any statement in Yiddish can be made to mean the opposite. "He is a wise man *[Er iz a talmid-khokhem]*," said with an emphasis on the pronoun *er*, suggests that the man is a fool. The syllable "Oh!", delivered with a raised forefinger, is not a gasp of surprise but an implied condemnation. Mahler invented his game of opposites as a boy, in his Polka with an Introductory Funeral March. Here he applies it to social policy without a specific target, covering his back by means of ironic euphemism.

His instructions in the score are, however, utterly specific. He tells the orchestra to play like "miserable village musicians,"[16] and wants "all the crudity, frivolity and banality in the world,"[17] to disrupt the funeral. He has a familiar image in mind. Marc Chagall, in *Fair at the Village* (1908), shows two parents carrying a small white coffin through the village under lowering skies. There are a harlequin, an acrobat, and a clown at the margins; in a horribly mundane detail a woman on her balcony tips her chamber pot onto the mourners' heads.[18] In the midst of death, there is messy life—and that's what Mahler is describing. Both symphony and painting contain a very Jewish recognition that no act is ever totally tragic or happy. At Hasidic funerals vodka is drunk to toast the soul's resurrection. The conjunction of gravity and gaiety is a facet of Jewish psychology and a driving motive of Mahler's First Symphony. Played without irony, the music sounds shallow. Played with too Jewish an accent, it attains self-parody. Mahler leaves it to interpreters to strike the correct balance.

This, in my understanding, is the most Jewish episode in the whole of Mahler's music, and my understanding is founded on a lifetime of studying undercurrents of Jewish ritual, the essential ambiguities of communal experience. Mahler, with a universal audience in mind, writes music that can be played with other accents and intuitions. Nevertheless it is impossible not to glimpse in it the boy Mahler following his brothers' coffins, deep in sorrow yet aware of all that is going on around him.

FIRST RAISE YOUR ARMS

In the spring of 1974 I went to lunch with the first of my friends to marry and have a child. After we had cleared the table, my friend R—— rose and walked over to the record cabinet to select some music. So vivid is my memory of this act that I can see the LP being tweaked from a crowded shelf, extracted from its glossy jacket and placed, in shiny blackness, to revolve at 33.33 revolutions a minute. My friend took the pickup arm and lowered it onto the record. Then, instead of joining me on the couch to listen, he stood in front of the player, his back to me, and raised his arms. As a seven-octave A sounded out, R—— began to conduct Mahler's First Symphony.

Neither he nor I knew how to conduct. We loved music, that's all there was to it, but some impulse in Mahler provoked my friend, a proud new father, to risk making an ass of himself by waving his arms at a robotic machine. The memory sticks in my mind not for any embarrassment or rancor—we are still friends all these years later—but for the realization that dawned on me, surreptitiously and with gathering force, that this music was written as a manifesto for a new breed of conductors.

Where Beethoven enlarged the orchestra to the point at which someone had to direct from a rostrum, and Wagner left time beating to assistants, no one before Mahler treated the conductor except as an extension of the composer's will. Mahler, in his First Symphony, freed the conductor from creator's writ. Where Beethoven and Brahms wrote metronome speeds in their scores, Mahler called the tick-tock device "inadequate and practically worthless"[19] and left the measurement of time to the maestro. He was delighted when friends with stopwatches pointed out that a passage could take five minutes longer from one night to the next. "It's all a matter of feeling," he would tell musicians. Watching my friend flex his biceps to the harmonic A's of Mahler's First Symphony, it dawned on me that this work was a portal to a new way of interpreting music, as radical in its potential as Einstein's theory of flexible time. Mahler, in his multiple meanings, makes conductors of us all.

OUT OF HUNGARY

No sooner does he recover from the premiere than he is caught up in national politics. After the tragedy at Mayerling, Budapest turns febrile and public discipline breaks down. Two singers challenge Mahler to a duel, and a music magazine claims that "in the last year and a half not a single Hungarian opera has been performed at the Royal Hungarian Opera House."[20] It is an outright lie, but he starts to feel unwelcome. In March theater commissioner Beniczky is replaced by Count Géza Zichy, a one-armed, ultranationalist pianist who changes programs "without consulting the artistic director," leaving Mahler to "learn about the repertoire from the newspaper."[21] Mahler looks around for a job and renews contact with Bernhard Pollini, a commercial impresario who runs the Opera in Hamburg. A Jewish boss called Bernhard sounds preferable to the Jew-baiting Zichy.

In his final months in Budapest, he makes formative connections. Johannes Brahms, dragged to see *Don Giovanni,* is enthralled by Mahler's conducting and declares himself his "fiercest partisan."[22] And the emperor Franz-Joseph comes out of mourning to see one of Mahler's new productions, Mascagni's *Cavalleria Rusticana.* He will remember the conductor's name when the moment is right. During his final winter in Budapest, a Vienna classmate, newly divorced, asks if she can come to stay. Mahler greets Natalie Bauer-Lechner like a long-lost cousin and gives her his apartment while he moves into a hotel. "I have practically forgotten how to talk,"[23] he tells her, enjoying her company so much that he begs her not to go to the opera "because then I would see too little of you."[24] Natalie, magnetized, falls in love. Waiting for a reciprocal spark, she becomes Mahler's recording angel, writing down his every word each night in her room.

Her notebooks over the next ten years capture Mahler in motion. Sometimes, through Natalie, he plays to the gallery of posterity, but most of the time he forgets she is there and speaks from the heart. Mahler is not, however, interested in Natalie's love. He sees her as a camera, a sheet of blotting paper, an instrument to record his ascent. When she tries to kiss him, he recoils. Natalie tells herself that he will come round, and settles down to play the waiting game, securing his sisters as her allies.

On March 14, 1891, Mahler is fired by Zichy and escorted off the Opera premises with a thirty-month payoff for eight contract years. He puts Budapest behind him with such alacrity that within a fortnight he is conducting *Tannhäuser* in Hamburg, to ecstatic reviews. Cranky Hans von Bülow (their past encounter forgotten) tells his daughter that "Hamburg has secured a really excellent opera conductor in Herr Gustav Mahler (a serious, energetic Jew from Budapest) who, in my opinion, equals the very best: Mottl, Richter and so on."[25] The German welcome is so effusive that it erases Mahler's feelings of failure in his first job as boss.

The morning after Budapest opened its National Concert Hall in March 2005, I passed by three men on a soapbox, haranguing a small crowd beside the Danube. A bystander told me that they were demanding the return of lands from Slovakia, Serbia, and Romania while spewing abuse at "the Jews." "Pay no attention," said my translator. "There are plenty more like that."

Calling the concert hall "national" had caused political strife, since the Hungarian adjective rekindles all the emotions of two world wars, civil wars, and revolutions. Budapest, in its rush to modernize, refuses to shake off the past. Walls are pocked with bullet holes, which locals can date at a glance—1956, 1945, 1919, even 1848. When I asked why no one dabbed plaster on those inglorious wounds, Hungarians stared with pity at my incomprehension. I found the Opera House much as Mahler left it, a bijou, beautiful stage with a boring program. I patrolled the warrens behind the Great Synagogue, streets that buzzed with Jews until 1944, when the Nazis sent them to Auschwitz. After the fall of Communism, the Hollywood actor Tony Curtis, of Hungarian descent, financed the synagogue refurbishment, and pale-faced outreach rabbis in black hats promoted a religious revival.

I had been told of a shop specializing in Mahler recordings, set up by a medical technician, Peter Fülop, when the state cut research grants. Fülop emigrated to Canada before I arrived, and most of the collectibles in his shop were already on my shelves. But his published discography was a subtle reminder of just how much the course of Mahler interpretation was Budapest-bred. There was Jenö Blau, better known as Eugene Ormandy, who made pioneer recordings of the Second Symphony in Minneapolis and the Tenth in Philadelphia. George Szell and Fritz Reiner introduced Mahler to Pittsburgh, Chicago, and Cleveland. Georg Solti and Antal Dorati played Mahler through long international careers. The brothers Iván and Adam Fischer founded a Hungarian Mahler Society. The Vienna professor Hans Swarowsky, teacher of such noted Mahlerians as Claudio Abbado, Zubin Mehta, Mariss Jansons, and Giuseppe Sinopoli, came from Budapest. "What's best in the music is not to be found in the notes" was a Mahler apothegm that Swarowsky drummed into his students.[26] Budapest, through its maestros and teachers, had left a large footprint on Mahler's performing legacy.

5. Rise Again (1891–1894)

The cafés of Hamburg have the world's newspapers on their racks. For the price of a small dark cup, one can read *Le Figaro* of Paris, *The Times* (of London), the Dutch *Handelsblaad*, Vienna's *Neue Freie Presse*, and more.[1] A city-state, Hamburg is rapacious for trade and famed for tolerance. "We in Hamburg perhaps allow the individual a greater deal of theological independence than is the case elsewhere,"[2] brags a senator. Faith thrives in many denominations, and God's blessings are denoted in an abundance of expansive villas and public amenities. Hamburg has high standards of health care and excellent schools. A few minutes' walk from the wealthiest residences, it also accommodates Europe's busiest red-light district, the notorious St. Pauli. This cohabitation of virtue and vice should not be mistaken for hypocrisy. It is as natural as the coexistence of rich and poor, a function of the free market.

Alone among German cities, Hamburg makes no public provision for art, leaving culture to private capital. The art gallery, the opera house, concert hall, even the public zoo—all are operated for profit. Hamburg's greatest son, Johannes Brahms, has moved to Vienna to earn a living. Hamburg is a business town, no place for dreamers.

For Gustav Mahler, escaped from Budapest, Hamburg's pragmatism is as bracing as the North Sea winds that screech across the estuaries. "The weather is dreadful," he informs his sister Justi, in Vienna. "On the other hand, one has a wonderful appetite. . . . It is splendid here, the city is really the most marvellous I know."[3] He is being paid 30 percent less, but the cost of living is low and he is "overwhelmed by invitations from the most prominent families."[4] At work he conducts a solid cast led by Katharina Klafsky, Max Alvary, and the statuesque Ernestine Schumann-Heink. After two months Pollini gives him a 20 percent pay raise and he goes off for a summer walk through Denmark, Sweden, and Norway, reading Friedrich Nietzsche's turgid and disturbing philosophies for light relief.

Although he is required to conduct every two or three nights, he has no management duties and expects to have time to compose. He rises daily at seven and, after a cold shower, sits down to resume his Second Symphony from where he left it four years before, after the Leipzig love affair. He has an opening movement called "Totenfeier [Funeral Rites]." But try as he might, he cannot take it further. Idle at his desk, he fills his head with family frets. Alois is in debt, Otto is neglecting his studies, Emma is a sulky teen, and Justi cannot manage on the money he sends her. The dress shirts she has made for him are short in the arms. He has "a vague feeling that everything is not in order,"[5] but he does not visit Vienna to see for himself. The composing block is driving him to depression.

He has a chat with Bülow, his colleague at the Hamburg Philharmonic, and wonders if he might spare a few minutes to listen to his music. After much hemming and hawing, Bülow consents. Mahler sits at the piano and plays "Totenfeier," his symphonic embryo:

> It occurred to me to look up and I saw Bülow holding both hands to his ears. I stopped playing. Standing at the window, he motioned me promptly to continue. I played. After some time I looked up again. Bülow was sitting at the table with stopped-up ears. . . . When I had finished, I waited quietly for the verdict. My lone listener remained at the table, silent and motionless. Suddenly, with a violent gesture of rejection, he said: "If that's music, I know nothing at all about music."[6]

His reaction leaves Mahler in such despair that he is ready to give up composing. He tells Richard Strauss: "You have not gone through anything like this and cannot understand that one begins to lose faith. Good heavens, world history will go on without my compositions."[7] To Löhr he writes: "I am getting tired of it."[8] But each morning at seven he continues to push himself until, in January 1892, the block lifts and five new songs flow, the nucleus of a second *Wunder-*

horn cycle, which, he tells Natalie, contains "five pieces of the Third and Fourth Symphonies."[9]

THE ENGLISH LESSON

Hamburg's *Ring* cycle is booked for London, so Mahler studies English with Arnold Berliner, a physicist at the lighting company Allgemeine Elektrizitäts-Gesellschaft (AEG). Soon he is ready to speak another language:

> Dear Mistress Ernestine [he writes to Löhr's sister]
>   I got your second lettre yesterday and your carte of corr. just now. I can wery well read and understand your english writing, and you must not be affread that I was angry—I must have laugh at your first lettre. . . . I become wery angry if I see that you all are unpractical sheeps and throw my money out the window. For instance: my brother Otto take teachers like a prince, so many and dear and all this for a little be examined. . . . There are certainly many mistaken in this lettre, but I hope you excuse me therefore.
>
> Gustav[10]

London is "stunningly magnificent."[11] He boards with a Jewish family in Torrington Square, near Covent Garden, and rehearses the orchestra in English. Herman Klein, the *Sunday Times* critic, recognizes Mahler's "remarkable magnetic power and technical mastery,"[12] and the playwright George Bernard Shaw reports that "the impression created by [*Siegfried*] was extraordinary, the gallery cheering wildly at the end of each act."[13] Mahler stays on to conduct *Tristan* and *Fidelio* at Drury Lane, leaving himself with less than four weeks for a summer break.

Justi and the family are waiting for him at Berchtesgaden, future home to Adolf Hitler (and *Sound of Music* tourists). Frustrated and unrefreshed, he is on a train back to work when news arrives of a cholera outbreak in Hamburg, the worst for a century. The authorities are in denial, telling the United States vice-consul on August 22,

1892, that there are no confirmed cases.[14] People continue to drink contaminated water. In a week seven thousand die. Mahler cables Berliner for advice. The scientist tells him to stay away, so he returns to the mountains, and it is mid-September before he shows up at work. Pollini, claiming breach of contract, threatens to fine him a year's wages. Mahler declares Pollini his enemy. Like many artists he sees work relations in black-and-white. For Pollini a row with Mahler is part of the job; for Mahler every fight is existential: Love me or kill me.

Bülow comes to the rescue, asking him to take over his concerts while he seeks winter sun. Mahler uses the opportunity to give the world premiere of Bruckner's Mass in D Minor, for which the composer is morosely grateful: "*Omnes amici me derelinquerunt* [All my friends have forsaken me]!"[15] he tells Mahler in church Latin. Still unable to make progress on his symphony, Mahler turns on his wastrel brothers—on Alois who is forever cadging money and on Otto, who is neglecting his music studies. Natalie finds Otto "unspeakably lazy."[16] "About Otto I am absolutely at my wits' end," Mahler rails. "Incompetent, ignorant and respectful of no-one. The lash in the army might perhaps do it. *I* give up."[17] Except he cannot—not with Otto, the kid brother who is following in his footsteps. Alois is the one he gives up on. "Do not, under any circumstances, count on getting so much as another kreuzer from me," he tells Alois. "It remains for me to express to you my best wishes for your well-being, and my hope above all to see you yet as a useful member of human society."[18] (Alois, rejected, changes his name to Hans Christian Mahler and finds work as a bookkeeper. He sails to America in 1905, 1910, and December 1912,[19] finally settling in Chicago, where the telephone directories show he changes address almost every year. His last home is at 3931 North Hoyne Avenue; in the 1930 U.S. Census, he is down as a real estate salesman; Alois dies, aged sixty-two, on April 14, 1931.[20])

WHAT THE LAKE TELLS ME

On a springtime jaunt in the Salzkammergut, a tract of lakes and mountains east of Salzburg, Justi and Natalie Bauer-Lechner find a summer home, a place where Mahler can compose during the long opera vacation. It is an inn on the outskirts of Steinbach village, beside the glacial Attersee, a lake that also catches the eye of Gustav Klimt in the next few years. Behind the inn there is a lakeside meadow and a jetty for swimming and boating. Justi books rooms for Mahler, herself, Emma, Otto, and Natalie—who is getting on Mahler's nerves. "I made it perfectly clear to her solely in what sense a friendly and comradely relationship between us could be imagined," he tells Justi. "Unfortunately, she did not take the right lesson."[21] Natalie fills her diaries all summer. From her we learn that Mahler rises at six-thirty and swims two or three kilometers across the lake and back. He works in his room all morning, and in the afternoons he takes long walks. He unwinds at night with a cigar and a beer, enjoying a gentle disputation with young Otto. They argue as to who is the greater composer, Bruckner or Brahms. Otto, trying to please big brother, says Bruckner. Mahler rebuts him. Music, he says, is more than just tunes. Bruckner can blow you away with magnificent themes but Brahms has richness and depth. "It's not enough to assess a work by content alone," he declares. "You have to grasp the whole picture. That's what determines its value, its survival and its immortality."[22]

He is speaking once more as a working composer. In Steinbach a flutter of four new songs takes him past the "Totenfeier" block into the body of the Second Symphony. "Totenfeier" takes its title from Lipiner's translation of *Dziady*, a Polish play by Adam Mickiewicz in which the hero, Gustav, kills himself when his beloved Maria (Marion, or his mother, Marie) marries another man. In Polish, Gustav is "the embodiment of his nation's martyrdom";[23] in Lipiner's German he is Everyman. The death of Gustav in his projected symphony has reduced Mahler to five years of creative silence.

The breakthrough comes in one of his new songs, "Urlicht," or "Primal Light." Its words, "I come from God and will return to God," point to a life after death for Gustav, "an eternal, blessed life." From the moment he sees primal light, the symphony unfolds with startling speed. On July 19, 1893, "Urlicht" is orchestrated; on July 30 he completes a twelve-minute Andante; on August 1 he inserts the song "Saint Anthony" from *Wunderhorn* as the theme of his third movement, "Urlicht" as fourth, "without knowing where it is leading."[24] He is writing "the content of my entire life, all that I have experienced and endured."[25]

Natalie, mystified by his creative revival, demands to know how the process works, how music is composed. "My God, Natalie, how can anyone ask such a thing?" he explodes. "Do you know how a trumpet is made? You take a hole and wrap tin around it; that's roughly how it is with composing."[26] Calmer, he admits that an idea can come from a poem or a melody. He likes to work from the middle of a tune outward. Before leaving Steinbach he pays a craftsman to build him a brick cabin on the lakeside meadow, so he can look out onto the water next summer while he composes. "The lake has its own language," he tells the builder's son. "The lake speaks to me."[27] His symphony is complete except for a finale.

In Hamburg, Pollini ups his workload to 125 performances[28] of twenty operas. He falls ill with stomach cramps. The doctor, suspecting cholera, wants him hospitalized. Justi objects, nursing him herself. He takes up Swedish gymnastics and swallows iron pills for his hemorrhoids. Between premieres of Verdi's *Falstaff* and Smetana's *Bartered Bride*, he tinkers with his symphonic score and despairs of finding a finale. "It began to look as if the symphony would remain a torso," observes Josef Bohuslav Foerster, the husband of a Czech soprano,[29] and himself an aspiring composer.

In February 1894 Bülow dies in Cairo. The Hamburg funeral, on March 29 at Saint Michael's Church, starts at nine in the morning with a Bach chorale, a reading from Scripture, and an extract from Brahms's *German Requiem*. Then from the organ loft, a boys' choir intones the "Aufersteh'n" hymn by the poet Friedrich Klopstock (1724–1803), in a setting by Karl Heinrich Graun (1704–59).[30] "Rise again," they sing. "Yes you will rise again, my dust, after a short rest. . . ."

"The hymn died away," reports Foerster, "and the old, huge bells of the church opened their eloquent mouths, those bells which had already lamented so many famous dead, and their mighty threnody brought mourning to the entire port."[31] In the afternoon Foerster calls on Mahler at home and finds him

> sitting at his writing-desk, his head lowered and his hand holding a pen over manuscript paper. I remained standing in the doorway. Mahler turned to me and said: "Dear friend, I have it!" I understood. As if illuminated by a mysterious power, I answered: "Rise again, yes you will rise again after a short sleep." Mahler looked at me with an expression of extreme surprise. I had guessed.[32]

His symphony is finished that summer in Steinbach, and his brother is the first to be told: "Dear Otto, I hereby announce the safe delivery of a healthy, strong last movement—father and child both doing as well as can be expected."[33] He is alone at the lake with his sisters, having dumped Natalie (who starts sleeping with Lipiner). Otto has a job in Leipzig as concertmaster and chorus conductor. Mahler arranges to meet him in Munich, on his way back from a visit to Bayreuth, but Otto refuses to join the family at Steinbach. They have a blazing row on a railway platform and go their separate ways. Mahler spends the rest of the summer tinkering with the order of movements in his new symphony. He calls it *Resurrection*.

WHOSE *RESURRECTION* IS IT, ANYWAY?

Anyone hearing the work for the first time must wonder (as I did) what it's all about. The title is weighted with eschatology, dusty as a crypt. Mahler's Second Symphony has been performed in the Vatican as a Christian affirmation, at Masada as a token of Jewish renewal, and in Communist China, where atheism is the state doctrine. It may be a mark of greatness that it can mean all things to all faiths, but what exactly does Mahler have in mind?

At first glance he appears to endorse the Christian narrative. He hears a hymn in a church service and finds himself "conceiving by the Holy Ghost."[34] In "Totenfeier," the dead come to life. "Saint

Anthony's Sermon" is based on a Gospel text. In the finale "What is created must perish, what perishes will rise again." What could be more Christian? Except that in Mahler, every perception can always mean the opposite.

In a non-Christian analysis Mickiewicz's "Totenfeier" is a pagan rite, "Urlicht" is a folk myth, while "Saint Anthony's Sermon to the Fishes" is pure irony: "The sermon pleases them, but they are just the same as before." Mahler's "conceiving by the Holy Ghost" is a meaningless colloquialism. And to prove his non-Christian affinity he cuts off Klopstock's text one stanza before the name of Jesus is invoked.[35]

Mahler's own explanations are not much use, the more so since he later retracts them. In 1901 he says: "We stand by the coffin of a well-loved person. . . . An awe-inspiring voice chills our heart: '. . . what is life? what is death? why did you live? why did you suffer? Is it all just a huge, frightful joke? Will we live on?' " He describes the Andante as a memory of life's happy moments and the Scherzo as "distorted, crazy," the world "seen in a concave mirror." Life "becomes meaningless," we are seized "by utter disgust for every form of existence." "Urlicht" sounds "the moving voice of naïve belief" before the finale brings the relief of a Last Judgment.[36]

So what kind of *Resurrection* is this? For Leonard Bernstein, the symphony is an avowal of Mahler's Jewishness, affirmed by opening strings that recall the shofar blasts of the Jewish Day of Judgment on Rosh Hashanah. Is that claim sustainable? Just about: The three short blasts of *shevarim* and the extended trembling sound of the shofar can be heard in the cello and double bass; the long *tekiah* blast is missing at either end. Is Mahler thinking Jewish? Unlikely. Edward Elgar, a Roman Catholic, simulates a shofar to describe daybreak on Temple Mount in his 1903 oratorio *The Apostles*; and Richard Strauss uses shofarlike blasts in *Salome*'s "Palestinian" music. You don't have to be Jewish to sound the shofar.

Max Brod, Franz Kafka's editor, maintains that, played at half speed, the finale reveals "Jewish foundations." He defines these as "a melodic line fluctuating between major and minor; a slow beginning in which the same note is repeated several times."[37] It's a nice try, but the obvious objection is that if Mahler had wanted the finale to sound Jewish, he would have halved the tempo.

The Marxist Theodor Wiesengrund Adorno, in a wonderfully convoluted dialectic, argues that the music of the Second Symphony directly contradicts the religious texts, acting as atheistic subversion: "The mute will of music penetrates speech. . . . Music addresses itself in words, as protest."[38] The Freudian Theodor Reik resorts to Oedipus theory, arguing that the symphony is driven by Mahler's guilt for wishing Bülow dead, a guilt revealed as the victim is laid to rest:

> It was no accident that brought the solution, that text, just at this moment! The . . . power of one's wish which had, so to speak, "killed" Bülow, was now transferred to the fact that the text of that chorale contained verses very appropriate for the finale. . . . It is as if Mahler had thought: *As my unconscious wish that you who rejected me as a composer should die was fulfilled, so my symphony will be finished and become a masterwork.*[39]

There are more theories about Mahler's *Resurrection* than there are symphonies by Mahler, yet none of them tells us why he is concerned with life after death and what he thinks music might add to the sum of human knowledge. Why is a man in his early thirties concerned with what happens after he is dead? Reik has a point: He is smitten with guilt, not over Bülow's death but over his refusal to find closure at his mother's funeral. Searching for catharsis, he finds it in his mother's faith. Resurrection is not a Christian invention. It is, says the Jesus historian Géza Vermes, "definitely a Jewish idea."[40] Early references are found in Moses' farewell ode (Deut. 32:39): "I shall cause to die and I shall bring to life"; in the prayer of Hannah (1 Sam. 2:6): "God causes to die and brings to life, he brings down to the grave and raises up"; and in the prophet Ezekiel (37:1–16): "I shall open your graves, and I shall raise you from your graves, my people." Two centuries before Jesus the book of Daniel spells it out (12:2): "And many of those that sleep in the dust of the earth will awake, some to everlasting life and some to shame and everlasting contempt."

The key difference between Jewish and Christian resurrections is that the Church holds that only the righteous will rise again, while

Judaism proclaims that all souls, good or bad, will return. Jews repeat this mantra thrice daily in the Amidah prayer, composed five centuries before Christ. It reads: "He sustains life with kindness, revives the dead with great mercy; supports the fallen and heals the sick; releases the imprisoned and keeps His faith with those who sleep in dust. . . . The King who causes to die and brings back to life, who brings forth salvation. Blessed are You, O God, who brings back the dead." Unlike other Amidah blessings, this section makes no self-limiting reference to "Your people, Israel." Mahler knows this text from boyhood; it is the second passage he would have learned from Rabbi Unger, after the Shema. "Excellent"[41] in his Jewish Studies grades, he reiterates the Jewish doctrine of resurrection in his original 1896 narrative of the symphony's finale:

> The end of every living thing has come, the last judgement is at hand and the horror of the day of days is upon us. The earth trembles; the last trump sounds; the graves burst open; all the creatures struggle out of the ground, moaning and trembling. Now they march in a mighty procession: rich and poor, peasants and kings, the entire church with bishops and popes. All have the same fear, all cry and tremble alike because, in the eyes of God, there are no just men.

Sinners and saints share the same fate. "What happens now is far from expected," Mahler continues. "Everything has ceased to exist. The gentle sound of a chorus of saints and heavenly hosts is heard. Soft and simple, the words gently swell: 'Rise again, yes rise again, you will.' "[42] And by that he means everyone. In 1901 he adds: "The glory of God appears. A wondrous light strikes us to the heart. All is quiet and blissful. Behold: there is no judgement, no sinner, no just man, no great and no small; there is no punishment, no reward. An overwhelming love . . ."

Mahler's *Resurrection* Symphony is deliberately Christless. It is denounced by one early critic as "cynical impudence," which translates as the cheek of a Jew to sneak heresies into the concert hall—and by another for "contempt for the limitations of art,"[43] meaning that these issues are church property. No such complaints are heard when Richard Strauss writes *Death and Transfiguration*, partly because

Strauss merely depicts the afterlife as a painter might, where Mahler seems to believe that music can heal the human condition, bringing peace to grieving souls: What was created, must pass away; what passes away must rise again. His presumption is, in contemporary perceptions, preposterous. A century will pass before Pope John Paul II, hearing the symphony in the Vatican in January 2004, speaks of its quest for "a sincere reconciliation among all believers in the one God,"[44] erasing—as Mahler has intended—the artificial divisions of doctrine.

A DEATH IGNORED

A pudgy youth of eighteen is in Pollini's office. "Schlesinger," says the lad, stretching out a hand.

"New voice coach and chorusmaster," grunts Pollini.

"Do you play the piano well?" demands Mahler.

"Excellently."

"Do you sight-read music?"

"Oh yes, anything. . . ."

"And do you know the main repertoire operas?"

"I know all of them pretty well," announces the young man.

"Well, that sounds just fine," says Mahler with a laugh.[45]

"I've been appointed chorus director til '96 . . . a colossal piece of luck,"[46] writes Bruno Walter Schlesinger to his parents in Berlin. Mahler soon puts him to the test. "You say you can play anything on sight—even an opera you don't know?" he asks during a rehearsal of *Hansel and Gretel,* the new fairy-tale opera by Engelbert Humperdinck.

"Of course," says Bruno Walter.

"I trust that you know how things happen in a forest—go rehearse the echo for me," orders Mahler, sending him to work with the off-stage chorus.

> Never before had I seen such an intense person [writes Walter], never dreamed that a terse word, a commanding gesture and a will directed solely towards a certain goal could frighten and alarm others and force them into blind obedience.[47]

He is drawn to this man, almost twice his age, like a nail to a magnet, fortified by his unstoppable force. He watches Mahler, sketches him, longs to be like him:

Pale, thin, small of stature, with longish features, the steep forehead framed by intensely black hair, remarkable eyes behind spectacles, lines of sorrow and of humour in the face which, when he spoke to others would show the most astonishing change of expression—the very incarnation of that Kapellmeister Kreisler [in E.T.A. Hoffmann's comic fable]—interesting, demoniac, intimidating.[48]

Walking Mahler home, Walter notes "the irregularity of his walk, his stamping of feet, sudden halting, rushing ahead again."[49] At lunch his sisters Justi and Emma discuss Russian literature. "Who is right, Alyosha or Ivan?" asks Emma, expecting Walter to have read *The Brothers Karamazov.* Mahler throws in quotations from Nietzsche, Schopenhauer (*The World as Will*), and Gustav Theodor Fechner, a philosopher who believes in the soul of all living things, especially plants, and "the comparative anatomy of angels."[50] On a practical note Mahler advises Walter: "Change your name, convert and get your army service out of the way." He needs an underling he can trust while conducting 134 opera nights as well as Bülow's eight Philharmonic concerts. Walter is useful, amusing, a younger version of himself, and—something else. Walter suspects that he reminds Mahler of his younger brother, Otto.[51]

The family has lost track of Otto. After Leipzig he works in Bremen, then returns to Vienna. The last known contact is a draft letter from Justi in October 1894, written with Mahler's authority but perhaps not sent:

Dear Otto
I myself will acknowledge your last letter to G. You certainly cannot expect an answer from *him* to this last letter; he is simply furious about your boundless insolence and has complied with your "request" to leave you alone. . . .

From your last letter [this paragraph in Mahler's handwriting], it is not at all clear what you are thinking of doing and how you will earn your living. . . . If you need money then write to Justine and you will get a monthly allowance as before, so long as you don't have a position that will feed you. After your behaviour you can no longer expect that G will obtain a position for you. See to it yourself as you wish. He asks me to tell you all this.[52]

On February 6, 1895, Otto pays a visit to Dostoyevsky's German translator Nina Hoffmann-Matscheko, an invalid friend of Mahler's. He sits at the foot of her bed, discussing the meaning of life. At four-thirty in the afternoon (according to the police report) he gets up to leave. But instead of going to the front door, Otto enters another room, lies on the divan, produces a revolver, and fires it into his chest. Servants break down the door; a doctor pronounces him dead. Otto, twenty-one years old, has threatened to do "something stupid." "I can still hear him telling me, 'if I don't shoot myself now it will be like blackmail!' " wails Justi.[53] Depressed and aggressive, he has been cut loose by his impatient older brother, abandoned to a terrible end. Where is Mahler's sense of responsibility? Where, indeed, is Mahler when Otto is laid to rest? He gets the lawyer Freund to send the body to Iglau and stays away from the funeral.

"I showed [Otto's] photograph to Gustav," reports Justi, "but now I am sorry because he became so terribly sad."[54] Otto's trunk stands unopened in a corner of Mahler's room. Forty years later it is found to contain Bruckner's Third Symphony manuscript, a brotherly gift of love and hope.

Mahler reacts to Otto's death, as to his mother's, with denial and distraction—the excuse of an imminent premiere. Richard Strauss has booked him for half a concert with the Berlin Philharmonic to perform three movements of his Second Symphony, the ones without soloists and chorus. The concert is sparsely attended, but Mahler is called back to the stage four times. Strauss seems displeased, and the Berlin opera conductor Karl Muck grumbles, "*Scheusslich* [dreadful]." The reviews decry the work's "strangeness," its "incomprehensible form," its "monstrous" effects. A lone critic, Oskar Eichberg in the *Börsen Courier*, detects affinities with Beethoven's Ninth. Mahler writes to him:

If you knew my life of suffering as a creative artist, if you knew the ten years of rebuffs, frustrations and humiliations, if you could see how many works I put in a drawer as soon as they were written, or imagine the incomprehension I have met when, overcoming all obstacles, I managed to find a public—only then will you fully appreciate the depth of my gratitude to you . . . the first and only one in his profession who feels and understands the language I speak and the road I follow.[55]

He sounds close to tears. He writes a resignation letter to Pollini, who does not bother to reply. Exhausted, demoralized, drained of resistance, he occupies his Steinbach cabin in June 1895—and immediately the music takes over.

In the late 1940s an art student in Düsseldorf earns himself a bowl of goulash and a few marks a night playing washboard in a skiffle trio at a restaurant. They must sound pretty good, because one night a guest sends to the hotel for his suitcase. Opening it, he withdraws a golden trumpet and walks up to join the band. This is the night Louis "Satchmo" Armstrong plays freestyle with Günter Grass, a future Nobel Prize winner for Literature.[56]

Grass, in his memoirs, cannot remember what they played, but he thinks it is something out of *Des Knaben Wunderhorn*, a fount of German renewal. In 2003 Grass tours a *Wunderhorn* cycle with his actress daughter, Helene, and a composer, Stephan Meier. The boy's magic horn rings loud in his unconscious. Grass's novel *The Tin Drum* tells of a lad with a round sheet of tin and two wooden sticks, not unlike "Der Tamboursg'sell [The Little Drummer-Boy]," the fifth of Gustav Mahler's *Wunderhorns*. *The Tin Drum* marks the rebirth of German fiction after the Second World War. For Mahler the magic horn awakens him from five years' silence.

6. What Love Tells Me (1895–1897)

THE GREEN GIANT

Summer's marching in," he scrawls at the top of the page. "It's my third symphony," he tells Natalie, who has been readmitted to the summer circle. "One great big laugh at the whole wide world." This symphony "is going to earn me lots of applause and money." Then he changes his mind. "You know, it won't do better than the others! People won't understand its lightness. It soars above the world of struggle and pain in the First and Second. Still, it can only have been produced as a result of them."[1]

Flushed with ideas, he saunters each morning to his cabin on the lakeside lawn, two kittens peeking out of his jacket pocket. The music pulses from him like blood from a severed artery. He covers page after page with little blue-ink notes, completing five movements in ten weeks and leaving the opening section for another year. At one point he toys with a seventh movement, a *Wunderhorn* song, "Wir geniessen die himmlischen Freuden [We enjoy the pleasures of heaven]," only to decide he has gone too far. Even at his most iconoclastic, Mahler never loses sight of a symphony's load-bearing wall: He knows where to stop.

He is out to wreck Haydn's classic form. Apart from Beethoven in the *Pastoral*, few composers have written a five-movement symphony, and none has overrun seventy minutes. Mahler's Third will have six movements and last a hundred minutes. He is pushing the limits of public tolerance. Unable to "do anything about being Jewish, our chief mistake,"[2] he has nothing to lose. If he succeeds symphonic art will never be the same again. And if he fails he will have the satisfaction of not toeing the line. He settles for a two-part structure:

Part one:
   1 Pan awakes: Summer is marching in
Part two:
   2 What the flowers in the meadow tell me
   3 What the animals of the forest tell me
   4 What humanity tells me
   5 What the angels tell me
   6 What love tells me

Drawing on his *Magic Horn* songbook, he uses "Ablösung im Sommer [Summer relief]" as the third movement and "Es sungen drei Engel [Three angels sang]" in the fifth. In between a contralto intones Friedrich Nietzsche's "Das trunkene Lied [the drunken song]" from *Thus Spake Zarathustra*, an unpleasant, supremacist tract Richard Strauss is making into a tone poem. Nietzsche is the pop philosopher of his day, a fount of quotable asperities. Mahler is drawn to his theory of "eternal recurrence," a cyclical fatalism that states that what comes around in nature comes around; all one has to do is wait for the next revolution. Does he really believe in this fatalistic creed? Does he believe anything in Nietzsche? Not for longer than it takes him to compose it. Finished with Nietzsche's song of the Übermensch, the supreme male, he never again professes the superiority of man over woman. Later he will advise his fiancée to throw Nietzsche's works on the fire.[3] Along with the mystic scientist Fechner, whose animal souls infuse the third movement, Nietzsche fulfills a passing need. Mahler has a magpie approach to the world of ideas. He has no fixed belief except in Arthur Schopenhauer's force of will and the existence of a benign Creator.

He ends with a gorgeous finale, a balm of massed strings with a melody that he marks *Langsam, Ruhevoll, Empfindung*: slow, restful, with feeling. He tells Natalie that he has plumbed "the very roots of Nature, which music can reach like no other art or science."[4] The Third is Mahler's *Pastoral* Symphony, "always and everywhere, it is the very sound of Nature."[5] Far from the ceaseless rattle of city noise, it celebrates the simple life against the rush of technology, rustic truth over polished urbanity. It is an ecosymphony, a song of the earth, a yearning for Mahler's nowhere land. But these are just the surface elements, the visible agenda. Beneath the notes, as ironic commentary, other forces are at work.

The symphony's opening theme is—listen carefully—the big tune from the finale of Johannes Brahms's First Symphony. Mahler transposes it into a minor key. Why? Not to pick a fight with Brahms: He needs the old man and cannot afford to offend him. But the theme is not by Brahms. Originally a folk tune, it is now a nationalist student anthem with words by Hans Ferdinand Massman:

Ich hab mich ergeben	[I have given myself
Mit Herz und mit Hand,	With heart and hand
Dir Land voll Lieb' und Leben	To you, land of love and life,
Mein deutsches Vaterland!	My German fatherland!]

When Brahms repeats it in his *Academic Festival* Overture, a British critic calls the theme "insufferable" and "offensive."[6] Mahler has heard it bellowed by student clubs that exclude him as an Untermensch. He opens the symphony with an implied protest against racial discrimination, applying the same technique as in the child's funeral of his First Symphony. First he flips the tune into the minor to darken its mood.*

Snarled out by horns, the tune disintegrates into percussive mutterings, subterranean rustlings, a suggestion of viral invaders within "My German fatherland." Mahler is out to unsettle his audience, to make them uncomfortable in a land that rejects him. Glorious pasture turns gritty and fallow. He tells the tubas and trumpets to play "raw and rude," with a grating roughness. "I need a military band," he says, "that attracts a kind of rabble."[7] He is hinting at mob rule, an anti-Semitic pogrom. This pastoral symphony begins with a warn-

---

* Hear "Ich hab mich ergeben" here: http://www.youtube.com/watch?v=LKGE4GQV6UJ2TM4; Brahms here: http://www.youtube.com/watch?v=FHHb-62BFPL&feature=related; and the Mahler Third opening here: http://www.youtube.com/watch?v=fFfZ1uJPFUg.

ing from history, a foretaste of Nazi violence in an irony so heavy that nobody at the time recognizes its intent. "Only I will be able to conduct [this symphony]," says Mahler in response to initial misapprehensions. "I can't imagine anyone else being able to bring it off . . . at best he will grasp details, never the whole."[8] Perhaps the supreme irony is that he has taken Nietzsche's concept of the Superman and claimed it for the Untermensch.

Before leaving Steinbach he cycles thirty kilometers to visit Brahms in Bad Ischl. The doyen of German music is not in good shape, his full-bearded face jaundiced from liver cancer. During a walk in the woods, Brahms declares that music is finished, over, done with. He detests modern composers, useless the lot of them, Strauss most of all. "Music has come to a dead end," he proclaims. As they cross a bridge over a babbling brook Mahler cries, "Look, Doctor, look down there!"

"What is it?" demands Brahms.

"Can't you see?" says Mahler. "It's the final wave."[9]

Leaving Brahms at his cottage, he looks back and catches sight of him at a kitchen stove, grilling a sausage for his lonely supper. The scene shocks Mahler, warning him that success does not always bring a composer comfort and happiness. He does not want to end his life adulated and alone, like the immortal Johannes Brahms.

FALLING IN LOVE, AGAIN

A new soprano, twenty-two years old, is having her first piano rehearsal in Hamburg when the door bursts open and a small man enters "in a gray summer suit . . . his face burned quite black by the sun." He snaps, "Carry on!" and stands by the door, as if poised for flight, one hand on the doorjamb, the singer recalls.

> The accompanist, still playing, twists his lips for me into an M: so this is Mahler. I closed my eyes. My hands twisted convulsively. All my hopes and yearnings poured into "See, Brünnhilde pleads." It became a prayer, a cry for help in the wretched state to which my shining hopes had shrunk in my first few days at this theatre. The

man at the door stamped violently on the floor, terrifying me. His hat flew onto the piano, then his umbrella. The repetiteur was shoved off his stool with the words, "Thanks, I don't need you any more."[10]

Mahler motions her to carry on. At "See, Brünnhilde pleads," desperate for a word of approval, she bursts into tears. He shouts at her to get on with it. Away from home for the first time, Anna von Mildenburg is unprepared for Mahler on the rampage. Anna is Pollini's new recruit, a substitute for America-bound Katharina Klafsky. Ungainly and not naturally beautiful, with an ash-white complexion and shallow gray eyes, she looks too timid for a Wagner heroine, but her voice is strong and her pedigree good. She is a pupil of Rosa Papier, Mahler's Kassel soloist, who is now married in Vienna to a pianist called Hans Paumgartner, and sleeps with a senior opera official, Eduard von Wlassack. Rosa Papier is a maker and breaker of opera careers.

While Anna sobs, Mahler chews the insides of his cheeks and paces the room. Abruptly he bursts out laughing. "It is good that you cry now," he comforts her. "One day you'll be just like all the rest, ruined by theatrical routines." He takes off his glasses and polishes them. "Accuracy is the soul of artistic success," he tells Anna. "Never prolong a closing note." Her training has begun. He sends her to a gymnastics class to lose weight. She sings a phrase twenty times before he is satisfied. In the dressing room he supervises her makeup and is still wiping surplus paint off her face when her stage call comes. For Christmas he gives her Wagner's writings. Mahler is in love.

It takes him four months to get there. In September 1895 he addresses her as "Dear Fräulein." By October she is "Dear Friend," "My dear Mildenburgle," "Dear Anna," signed "Mahler," collegial and correct. At the end of November he draws a circle above his name, a tentative kiss. Suddenly she is "my dearest, sweetest love,"[11] "Anna, eternally beloved."[12] "My beloved stubborn-head."[13] "I kiss you, a thousand, thousand times."[14] It has been nine years since his last love, and his need is desperate. "Why haven't you written me so much as one word? I am so dreadfully worried about you,"[15] he demands. He has forgotten how to love, all he can do is nag. Anna, young as she is, knows what to do. Groomed by the calculating Papier, she plays hard to get: The more Mahler pours out his heart, the more Anna retreats. "I am suffering to a degree I had not thought bearable," he cries. "To lose the love of a being by whom one believed oneself loved, whose love was almost as precious as life—you can't imagine how terrible that is."[16]

His torment deepens: "Anna! What I have been through these past days, and what I shall go through in future, I cannot describe. Anna! I have never cared for anyone with such a pure and holy love. *And you don't love me!* My God! . . . What have you done to me?"[17]

"Farewell!" he cries. "Farewell, Anna, farewell, farewell"[18]—one word to a line, just as he has done to Josefine Poisl and will do again in his final symphony. Anna has gotten him where she wants him, stamping her terms on the relationship before it begins. Ignoring his request for discretion, she flaunts their liaison all over town and flirts with Mahler's male friends to make him jealous. Chaste until now, Mahler is seduced as much by her physicality as by a recognition that he is molding her into a great dramatic singer. When he makes love to her, he is like a plastic surgeon sleeping with a model whose breasts he has rebuilt. He is in love with his own work and tortured by her flaws. He feels "deep pain" when they are together. His discomfort is eased only by "the blessing of surrendering oneself entirely—'body and soul' to a loved person."[19] He presses himself "bloodily" against her "prickly spines" and implores her, "Will you soon prick me again?"[20] He is in love and in pain, an exquisite dichotomy.

Loving Anna alters Mahler's view of women. He no longer seeks a version of his long-suffering mother, as he did with Marion, nor is he looking for a creative spark. Anna does not inspire symphonies. She is an airhead who prances naked before his prudish eyes. She is prone to hysteria and obtuse to his sensitivities. But she reveres his musicianship and trusts, childlike, in his wisdom. They make plans to escape Hamburg together, onto the world stage. They also discuss marriage. Mahler says he needs to see his sisters settled first, and Anna does not press the point. People start to gossip, and officials in Vienna splutter in their memos that this Mahler fellow is a bit of a lothario, unsuitable for the Court Opera. Mahler, ignoring dangerous undercurrents, finds contentment with Mildenburg. She fills an aching need.

RING OUT THE BELLS

To get through another year of opera drudgery, he persuades two Hamburg friends to finance the premiere of his Second Symphony. Wilhelm Berkhan, a businessman, and Hermann Behn, an ex-Bruckner pupil, shell out five thousand marks. Mahler is grateful, but not for long. Behn, who makes a piano reduction of the symphony, gets on his nerves. "He never stops pontificating about my leitmotivs although, in fact, he understands nothing about me or my music!"[21]

The concert is booked for December 13, 1895, in Berlin. As rehearsals start Mahler realizes something is missing. At the end of the finale,

> I need a chiming bell, something that no musical instrument can deliver. I knew all along I would require help from a bell foundry. Finally I found one, a half hour's train ride away. It is near the Grunewald.
>
> I made an early start. Everything was wonderfully covered in snow. The frost quickened my sluggish system (I didn't get much sleep) and when I arrived at Zehlendorf (that's the name of the place) and tried to find my way through pines and firs . . . sparkling in winter sun, I had left my troubles behind . . . and returned to the peaceful house of Nature. . . .
>
> I was received by an unfussy old gentleman with lovely white hair and beard and such calm, friendly eyes that I felt I was back in the times of the old Masters. . . . He showed me some magnificent bells, one of which, powerful and mysterious, had been made to order for the German Emperor for the new cathedral. I should have liked something of the sort for my symphony, but we have not yet reached the time when only the best and most expensive is good enough for a work of art. I settled for something more modest.[22]

His preparations are medieval in their small-craft concerns. Which composer, other than Wagner, would build a new instrument for his work? In rehearsal Mahler makes the musicians repeat each passage many times over and has a percussionist beat his kettledrum harder and harder until the skin bursts. Horns and trumpets are sent to an upstairs balcony to deliver the *Grosse Appell*—the great summons—after which a flute plays solo onstage and the chorus sings, "Rise again, oh yes, rise again."

He moans that the choir is too small and that he has to sit at dinner with "bovine" critics. He hands out tickets to music students to fill the empty hall. He has to do everything himself. Hours before the premiere, he is struck by a migraine. He "staked his future as a composer on a single card," writes Bruno Walter, "and there, in the afternoon before the concert, he lay with one of the worst sick headaches of his life, unable to move or partake of anything. I can still see him before me on the much-too-high, unstable conductor's platform, deathly pale, mastering his affliction, the musicians, the singers and the audience with a superhuman exertion of the will."[23]

Cellos and basses get the symphony in motion. There is applause after "Totenfeier" and murmurs of appreciation at the guitarlike plucked strings in the Andante. Mahler's friends and family start to believe in a miracle. Justi reports:

> The triumph grew and grew with every movement. Enthusiasm like this is only to be experienced once in a lifetime. I saw grown men weeping and youngsters falling on each other's necks at the end. And at the point where the Bird of Death, hovering above the graves, gives his last extended cry, Mahler said later that he feared for a moment that the long unbroken silence, requiring the whole audience to hold its breath, could not possibly be sustained. But the silence was deathly, no-one dared to bat an eyelid and, when the chorus entered, a shudder of relief shook every breast. The effect was indescribable.

Two conductors—Arthur Nikisch and Felix von Weingartner—rush forward with congratulations and offers to perform his next work. The critics hear "superficial" effects, "brutal ultra-modernism," and a "taste for noise,"[24] but the Berlin press is provincial and of little influence. Bruno Walter dates this night as the start of Mahler's career as a composer. Six weeks later Mahler is still euphoric. "For me, there is no doubt whatsoever that [the symphony] enlarges the *fundus instructus** of mankind," he exults. "The whole thing sounds as if it came to us from some other world. And—I think there is *no one* who can resist it. One is battered to the ground and then raised on angels' wings to the highest heights."[25]

A SYMPHONY AND ITS AFTERLIFE

The Second Symphony defies reason. In hyperinflationary 1923 Berlin, at 4.2 billion marks to one U.S. dollar, it became the first Mahler work to be recorded. Nine years later, in mid-Depression, Eugene Ormandy staged the symphony in Minneapolis, underlining the scherzo's Jewish themes with klezmer clarinets. In July 1967 Leonard Bernstein conducted three movements on Jerusalem's Mount Scopus to celebrate Israel's six-day military victory over Egypt, Jordan, and Syria. "The ancient cycle of threat, destruction and re-birth goes on; and it is all mirrored in Mahler's music—above all, the expression of simple faith—of belief that good must triumph,"[26] he declared. People took the work to mean that nothing is beyond human reach. More than any other symphony Mahler's Second acquired a mythical dimension, defining the lives of those who embraced it. "When I was eleven, my father took me to hear [the Scottish-Russian] George Hurst conduct Mahler 2," related Simon Rattle. "And that was it. That was a completely transfiguring experience. It was the road to Damascus." Six years later, in London, it became the "single occasion that put Simon Rattle on the musical map."[27]

Another transformation took place around the same time in New York, when Gilbert Edmund Kaplan, a Wall Street economist in his twenties, was dragged by a friend to a Saturday rehearsal of the *Res-*

* "Essential furnishings," a Roman term describing the contents of a working farm.

urrection in April 1965 at Carnegie Hall. "It was the American Symphony Orchestra and Leopold Stokowski and I stayed the whole rehearsal, didn't think much of the music one way or another," recalled Kaplan, whose musical involvement had stopped with boyhood piano lessons in a Long Island suburb. That night, however, he could not sleep. He bought a ticket, attended the concert, "and by the final moments I found myself sobbing, absolutely hysterical."[28]

The response was so anomalous to his stable self-image that he had to pursue it further. Kaplan was on the verge of becoming a very big player in the world of high finance. With his life's savings and a loan from the Bronfman distillery magnates, he was about to launch a publication, *Institutional Investor,* that gave the inside track on the biggest money handlers in the world, from megacorporations to national banks. Before he turned thirty Kaplan was on everyone's A-list. Fidel Castro wanted him to know that Cuba's economy was not as weak as Washington made out. Anwar Sadat and Menahem Begin talked to him about Mideast investment. But the more he was sucked into world affairs, the more Mahler's Second "wrapped its arms around me."[29] He bought all seventeen recordings and took his future wife, Lena, on their first date to hear the *Resurrection* at London's Royal Festival Hall. It was she who told him to get a grip on his fixation: Put up or shut up.

So for eighteen months Kaplan took stick lessons from a Juilliard graduate and chased great maestros, swapping fiscal gossip for musical advice. Sir Georg Solti, Chicago's music director, gave him a three-hour tutorial. He flew to just about every performance on earth, as far out as Melbourne, Australia. In Holland he studied Mahler's autograph score at the Mengelberg Foundation. When he thought he knew all it was possible to grasp, he booked the American Symphony Orchestra for rehearsals. The scariest moment "was when I brought the baton down, and nothing happened. I thought: they are not going to play for me. Then the sound came."[30]

For the performance, he forged, like Mahler, a new set of bells. At Avery Fisher Hall in New York's Lincoln Center he solved the innate problem of communicating with the hidden offstage brass by running TV cables up to their balcony; no conductor had thought of doing this before. On September 9, 1982, Gilbert Kaplan conducted

Mahler's *Resurrection* Symphony in an invitation-only performance for members of the International Monetary Fund. Sir Edward Heath, the former British prime minister, and himself an amateur conductor, called it "a very remarkable feat" and Franz Vranitzky, the Austrian chancellor, was warmly appreciative. "I had the feeling," said Kaplan, "that people in the audience were urging me to fulfill my dream because each of them had a secret ambition that they had not attained."

Instead of fulfilling his need, the concert intensified Kaplan's identification with the work. He became the owner of the original manuscript, which he placed on deposit at the Morgan Library and published in a facsimile edition. Orchestras the world over invited him to share his unique, esoteric insights. A recording he made in 1985 with the London Symphony Orchestra topped the all-time Mahler best-seller list with 180,000 sales. Identifying four hundred errors in the printed edition after studying all fourteen extant scores with Mahler's markings, he caused the work to be reprinted and conducted the Vienna Philharmonic in a premiere recording.

Nemesis eventually followed. Lorin Maazel, music director of the New York Philharmonic who had attended Kaplan's Salzburg performance, asked him to conduct the cleansed score on December 8, 2008, a hundred years to the night after Mahler brought the symphony to America. The Philharmonic is an orchestra noted for strong opinions. Several players got murmuring on their cellphones and there was some bad body language in the concert. The *New York Times* critic reported a performance of "sharp definition and shattering power," adding that Kaplan's "every gesture had purpose and impact. The orchestra played with astonishing control and beauty."[31] Barely had these words reached print than a trombone player took to his blog to denounce Kaplan as "an impostor . . . a very poor beater of time who far too often is unable to keep the ensemble together."[32] His gripe was blown up into a *Times* cover story,[33] and the row spilled out online.[34] I found myself wondering why a man consulted by presidents would expose himself to jeopardy at the hands of tin and gut? When I put the question to Kaplan, he said: "I have been driven by a force greater than myself."

Observing his odyssey over a quarter of a century, I came to believe that he had tapped into Mahler's true purpose—that nothing is beyond the human imagination. The Second Symphony questions the value and meaning of life on the cusp of a century in which humanity starts to control the beginning and end of life, one in a test tube, the other by a doctor's signature. Mahler employed music as an arbiter of moral conduct and a test of human courage. Kaplan put his reputation on the line to prove Mahler's faith that nothing was impossible. As the Zionist visionary Theodor Herzl said around the same time: "Wenn du nur es willst, ist es kein Märchen [If you really want it, it needn't be a fairy tale]."

A CHANGE OF CLOTHES

Buoyed by his Berlin breakthrough, Mahler pays for a March 1895 concert of the First Symphony, the *Traveling Apprentice* songs, and "Totenfeier." Taking a Sunday stroll in the Schöneberg district during rehearsals, he sees a man stagger and fall beneath a heavy load, groaning, "God help me." The man has left hospital after a long illness and can find no other means of income. Mahler empties his wallet, rushes back to the Palace Hotel, and collapses weeping in Natalie's room. Natalie, who is there to protect him from the nuisance Behn, offers reassurance. Later, when everyone has gone to bed, she comes to his room, takes his hand, and presses it to her lips. "Natalie, what are you doing?" he cries, backing off from carnal complications.

The concert is a failure, overlong, ill attended, and sporadically booed, but for Mahler it is a wake-up call to take control of his life. He gives Pollini a year's notice and begs Rosa Papier to find him a job in Vienna. "You cannot imagine how happy I would be to work in my own country at last," he writes.[35] Papier gets to work on her lover, Wlassack, an administrator at the Opera, where the music director, Wilhelm Jahn, is half blind, the chief conductor, Hans Richter, plays cards when he should be rehearsing, the sets are archaic, and the repertoire stale. Singers are past their peak, and nepotism is rife: Jahn relies heavily on his nephew who, in addition to being his amanuensis, is also the chorusmaster. The Opera urgently needs a shakeout, but Papier warns Mahler that he needs to get a foot in the door before he can rise to the top. She tells him to apply for fifth conductor, behind Jahn, Richter, Johann Nepomuk Fuchs, and the ballet specialist, Josef Hellmesberger.

Mahler, leaving nothing to chance, mobilizes his contacts book. Lipiner, librarian of Parliament, commends him to the Opera executive director, Freiherr Josef von Bezecny. From Budapest, Mihalovics describes Mahler as "one of the best and noblest human beings I have ever met."[36] Nina Hoffmann intercedes with Countess Kinsky, sister of the controller of state theaters, Prince Lichtenstein. Brahms, with months to live, lets it be known that he favors Mahler. A nephew of the composer Karl Goldmark, a "stupid but good-natured"[37] journalist called Ludwig Karpath, gets wind of the push and is sworn to secrecy by Mahler in exchange for future scoops.

None of these efforts is enough. In January 1897 Mahler is told that "under present circumstances it is impossible to engage a Jew for Vienna."[38] "Everywhere," he bemoans, "the fact that I am a Jew has at the last moment proved an insurmountable obstacle."[39] But he does not despair, having made arrangements to remedy his deficiency. On February 23, 1897, at Hamburg's Little Michael Church, Gustav Mahler is baptized into the Roman Catholic faith.

He is the most reluctant, the most resentful, of converts. "I had to go through it,"[40] he tells Walter. "This action," he informs Karpath, "which I took out of self-preservation, and which I was fully prepared to take, cost me a great deal."[41] He tells a Hamburg writer: "I've changed my coat."[42] There is no false piety here, no pretense. Mahler is letting it be known for the record that he is a forced convert, one whose Jewish pride is undiminished, his essence unchanged. "An artist who is a Jew," he tells a critic, "has to achieve twice as much as one who is not, just as a swimmer with short arms has to make double efforts."[43] After the act of conversion he never attends Mass, never goes to confession, never crosses himself. The only time he ever enters a church for a religious purpose is to get married. His wife calls him a "Christ-believing Jew,"[44] but the prayers he offers in mortal anguish, scrawled in his final score, are only to God the Father. Mahler, officially a Catholic, remains a Jew. He is a relic of an unending persecution, a kind of *marrano*, like one of thousands who went underground for centuries in Spain after Ferdinand and Isabella started burning the Jews in 1492. And to Viennese anti-Semites, he is the archetypal Jew.

At the end of March, Papier tells him the ruse has worked. Prince Lichtenstein is forcing Jahn to retire, and Wlassack has enlisted the veteran critic Hanslick to endorse Mahler as someone who "would give our opera new life without violating its classical tradition."[45] Mahler is called to Vienna on April 1, 1897, to sign a one-year contract as fifth conductor. Brahms dies two days later, and Mahler stays for the funeral.[46] On April 7 it is announced that Jahn will go on indefinite sick leave.

Before leaving Hamburg, Mahler tells Anna von Mildenburg that he cannot take her along as his mistress. She has hysterics at the breakup, and, according to Alma Mahler, begs him to visit her one last time. As he enters her bedroom, she pulls back a curtain to reveal a Benedictine monk, Father Ottmar, who is waiting to marry them.[47] Like many of Alma's tales, this is fairy dust. Mahler, leaving Hamburg, plays Anna along with a promise of reunion. "Goodbye, dear, much-loved Annie. . . . Our future separation will only be a physical one. The bond we have joined together can never be broken. I am yours, my love, and remain true to you."[48] Later he specifies: "I ask you dearest Anna: have you the strength to work with me in Vienna and—at least for the first year—to renounce any relationship and any form of favour from me? I hope you realise it will be *no less difficult for me* than for you."[49] For Mahler work must come first. Mildenburg cheers herself up by seducing Hermann Behn. If she can't have Mahler she will work her way around his friends.

Jahn introduces him to the Opera orchestra on May 10, 1897, and he conducts Wagner's *Lohengrin* the following night, allowing "no dragging or distortion." Max Kalbeck, Brahms's trusted biographer, calls him "one of the elect." He puts a routine revival of *Magic Flute* through ten rehearsals, returns to work with a high fever after having two abscesses lanced in his throat, radiating, as one writer puts it, "energy, will power and a desire to forge ahead."[50] On October 8, aged thirty-seven, he is promulgated by imperial decree as artistic director of the Vienna Court Opera.

7. A Taste of Power (1897–1900)

THE STATE OF ILLUSION

At the end of three decades of Ring construction, the tune that pumps out of beer gardens is Johann Schrammel's "Wien bleibt Wien." Vienna remains the same. The population may have trebled, the economy diversified, and the facilities improved, but the city clings to a lazy assumption that nothing will ever change. Vienna basks in "a world of *Sicherheit*," a state of blithe confidence, a belief in the steady betterment of life. "One began to believe more in 'progress' than in the Bible," reflects the writer Stefan Zweig.

> At night, the dim street lamps of former times were replaced by electric lights, the shops spread their tempting glow from the main streets out to the city limits. Thanks to the telephone, one could talk at a distance from person to person. People moved about in horseless carriages with a new rapidity. . . . Hygiene spread and filth disappeared. People became handsomer, stronger, healthier.[1]

Zweig's *Sicherheit* applies, however, only to the middle classes, excluding a huge underclass. A police permit is required to live in Vienna. Thousands live unlicensed, ten families to a cellar, among rats and disease, disenfranchised and unseen. This is the domain where Adolf Hitler, arriving in 1906, acquires his political education.

Vienna is a city of grand illusions. One of its grandest edifices is the Parliament building, with 516 members from thirty different parties. Each member has the right to give speeches in his native tongue, but no translators are provided. When debates get over-heated, Parliament is suspended, sometimes for years on end. The assembly, writes the sardonic novelist Robert Musil,

> made such vigorous use of its liberty that it was usually kept shut; but there was also an Emergency Powers Act by means of which it was possible to manage without Parliament, and every time when every-one was just beginning to rejoice in absolutism, the Crown decreed that there must now be a return to parliamentary government. . . . In the breathing-spaces between government and government, every-one got on excellently with everyone else and behaved as though nothing had ever been the matter. Nor had anything real ever been the matter.[2]

Franz-Joseph, emperor for half a century, is a ramrod ruler who sleeps on an iron cot and rises at dawn. He is a decent, dutiful man who never ventures any opinion stronger than "That's nice" for fear of breaching the fragile peace. Bloodshed is never far from the sur-face of the *Sicherheit* society. In September 1897 the Austrian prime minister, Count Badeni, offering language concessions to Czechs, is shot and wounded in a duel by a Germanist MP. The empress Elisa-beth, known as "Sisi," is stabbed to death the following year by an anarchist in Geneva. The nation mourns with its emperor, although everyone knows he is estranged from Sisi and consorts with a Burgtheater actress, Katharina Schratt.

Artifice in Vienna transcends reality, *Schein über Sein* is the catch-word. Appearance matters more than existence: Better to be seen than to be. In a city built on delusional lines, and in the absence of meaningful politics, the arts provide an alternative reality. The plays of Schnitzler, the poems of Hugo von Hofmannsthal, the paintings of Gustav Klimt, and the lieder of Hugo Wolf afford relief from a life of make-believe. The arts attain such social impor-tance that the influential daily *Neue Freie Presse* allocates half of its front page to a cultural essay. It is known by the French term *feuilleton* (little page) and edited by the polemicist and playwright Theodor Herzl. In the absence of reality, art becomes life, as Zweig describes.

Whereas in politics, in administration, or in morals, everything went on rather comfortably and one was affably tolerant of all that was *slovenly*, and overlooked many an infringement, in artistic matters there was no pardon; here the honour of the city was at stake. . . . This knowledge and the constant pitiless supervision forced each artist in Vienna to give his best, and he gave to the whole its marvellous level. Every one of us has, from his youthful years, brought a strict and inexorable standard of musical performance into his life. He who in the Opera knew Gustav Mahler's iron discipline, which extended to the minutest detail . . . is rarely satisfied by any musical or theatrical performance.[3]

Slovenliness—*Schlamperei* in local dialect—is Mahler's first target at the Opera. "Tradition is Schlamperei" he is quoted as saying. What he actually says is: "What you people call tradition is nothing other than your own comfort and sloppiness."[4] Art demands hard work, he declares. The only tradition worth preserving is precision. His goal is to achieve a perfect performance. He knows it will not be easy. He knows, too, that the forces of darkness are rallying to plot his downfall.

On April 8, 1897, the day of Mahler's promulgation, Karl Lueger is elected mayor of Vienna. It is the fourth time he has won, and each time the emperor has refused to ratify his appointment. Lueger is a militant anti-Semite. Known as *Der schöne Karl*—"handsome Karl"—for his erect posture and square blond beard, Lueger appeals to the "little man," canvassing in taverns and promising a free cab ride home for "every citizen who has caroused through the night."[5] Under threat of riots, and after a week's deliberation, the emperor finally awards him the chain of office.

Lueger proves to be an outstanding mayor, efficient, transparent, and tech-savvy. He introduces electric trams, takes gas and other utilities under municipal control, creates parks and recreation spaces, dresses his staff in a green uniform, and makes sure his name is carved on all new edifices—"built under Dr. Karl Lueger"—encasing Franz-Joseph's Ring in his own stone legacy during the first decade of the twentieth century. At mass rallies, "he transfers his will onto others in an almost supernatural way."[6] His racism, selective and at times quiescent, can be whipped up at will against the "money and stock exchange Jews," the "beggar Jews," the "ink Jews" (intellectuals), and, perpetually, the "press Jews." Under Lueger, Vienna becomes the first modern city to make hating Jews municipal policy.

Right-wing commentators view Mahler's appointment as a political counterweight to Lueger's, one of the checks and balances of a bumbling constitution. The *Deutsche Zeitung* wonders why it "is opportune to appoint *a Jew* to the German Opera of a city [with] a strong movement against *Jewification*."[7] The *Reichpost* warns that it will not be long before Mahler "starts his Jew-boy antics on the podium."[8] Mahler's advent is dressed up as an insult to Hans Richter, whom Mahler tries to mollify: "From my earliest youth you have been the model I have tried to emulate. . . . When in doubt I ask myself, what would Hans Richter do?"[9] Wagner's acolyte huffily assures Mahler that "you will not find me a hostile colleague . . . once I am convinced that your work will benefit the imperial institution and advance our noble art."[10] Mahler dubs him "honest Hans" and determines to get rid of him.

That summer, fed up with Steinbach, he scurries around the Tyrol and the rain never stops. He returns to work on August 1 and, finding himself the only conductor in the house, leads *Lohengrin, Faust, L'Africaine, Bartered Bride,* and *Marriage of Figaro,*[11] while blowing off "the dust of Schlamperei and inaccuracy" that "lies finger-thick"[12] over Wagner's *Ring.* The production has not changed since 1877, but with Mahler in the pit the drama feels recharged. There is urgency to the acting, extra brilliance to the sound, and an integrity to the text. "In this *Ring* one could hear things that nobody had heard before, things one had given up all hope of hearing," exclaims Hugo Wolf.[13] Mahler, though, is dissatisfied. He hears flaws in the orchestra and is furious when a timpanist whom he rehearsed to precision is absent at a key downbeat. Told that the man left early to catch the last train, Mahler orders a pay increase for his players so that, like Lueger's drunkards, they can afford a cab home after late finishes.

Leasing an apartment at Bartensteingasse 3, he is at his desk at nine, rehearses all morning, walks home at lunchtime, takes a nap, followed by a stroll, and returns to work to sign papers and conduct the night's show, aware of the physical and creative cost of his commitment. "My job absorbs me completely and seizes me body and soul," he confides.[14] "I am swamped as only a theatre director can be. . . . All my senses and emotions are turned outward. I am becoming more and more a stranger to myself. . . . Remember me as one usually remembers the dead."[15]

THE BIRTH OF ART

A third upheaval shakes Vienna in the week of Mahler's and Lueger's ascendancy. On April 3, 1897, forty artists quit the establishment Künstlerhaus that controls major exhibitions to form a Secession group, open to foreign and modern ideas. Their leader is Gustav Klimt, a painter of decorous nudes and shimmering lakes. Together with Carl Moll and Josef Engelhardt, and the wealthy art critic Berta Szeps-Zuckerkandl, Klimt hires the polemicist Hermann Bahr to write a breakaway manifesto. "We are not arguing for or against tradition," states Bahr. "We have no tradition. It is not a struggle between the old art and the new . . . it is art itself we are fighting for."[16]

At the inaugural exhibition, opened by the emperor, Klimt sketches a square building on a scrap of paper and hands it to an architect, Josef Maria Olbrich. Six months later the Secession gallery is ready for occupancy, an airy space with a crown of golden thorns and a lintel motto: "To each age, its art; to art, its freedom." Defining the new Jugendstil (youth style), the Secession imports Seurat, Munch, Whistler, and Charles Rennie Mackintosh, among a host of current trendsetters. It also embraces commercial architects, furniture designers, and printmakers, among them Otto Wagner, Josef Hoffmann, and Koloman Moser. Klimt aims to abolish the distinction between fine and applied arts, aiming for a visual parallel to Wagner's *Gesamtkunstwerk*, a union of all the arts. Mahler senses a kindred spirit at work in the Secession. In a city whose ideology is introspective, racist, regressive, and smug, Mahler and Klimt represent a progressive, liberal alternative, an escape from the all-pervasive unreality.

Unlike Klimt, Mahler does not bother with committees. He tears into the Court Opera with terror tantrums, screaming at colleagues until he obtains a satisfactory response. "Mahler is a vampire: he sucks the blood out of our veins," writes a singer.[17] "An elemental catastrophe," is an orchestral musician's impression. "An earthquake of unprecedented intensity and duration shook the entire building from the foundation pillars to the gables. Anything that wasn't very strong had to give way and perish."[18] "I see him at rehearsal: angry, twitching, screaming, irritated, suffering at all the inadequacies as if in physical pain," reports Stefan Zweig. "I see him again brightly chatting in the street with a natural, childlike cheerfulness. . . . He was always somehow swept along by an inner force, always totally animated."[19] Mahler tells friends that his rages are calculated: They are the only way to get rid of *Schlamperei.*

On his first day as director, he abolishes the claque—a group of cheerleaders who receive free seats and small fees from singers in exchange for exaggerated applause. The claque exists in most houses, adding a whiff of sulfur to dull nights when guest performers are booed. Mahler rules that the claque "brings the Opera into discredit and prevents us from attaining our artistic goals." He orders singers "to give me your word of honour that you will abstain from any contact with the claque and will cease all payments and distribution of free tickets."[20]

Ushers are instructed to lock all doors the moment a performance begins, keeping latecomers in the lobby until the end of the first act. "And I thought that going to the theatre was meant to be enjoyment," sighs the long-suffering Franz-Joseph, but Prince Lichtenstein congratulates Mahler on his measures. "It has taken you no time at all to make yourself Master at the Opera House," says the theater commissioner. "You're a real success. All Vienna is talking about you and the things you do. They say there's always something happening now at the Opera, like it or not."[21] Lichtenstein's number two, Prince Alfred Montenuovo, gives Mahler unfailing support against the Opera administrators, Baron Plappart, and his deputy, Wlassack. "I am banging my head against the wall," says Mahler, "but the wall is getting a hole knocked in it."[22] Bahr sees him "living in a fantasy world, a man with not even an inkling of reality,"[23] but Mahler knows exactly what needs to be done.

He shakes out the timeservers, replacing a third of the orchestra. "I was the youngest in 1897," records the composer Franz Schmidt. "By 1900, I was already the longest-serving active cellist."[24] New singers are recruited wholesale and dismissed if unfit. Theodor Bertram, of Bayreuth, is gone after eighteen days. Jenny Korb sings just four times: "Appearance without charm and lacks personality,"[25] notes Mahler. By trial and error he assembles the most cohesive ensemble ever seen, a gallery of singers that resonates through time on gramophone recordings. Leopold Demuth, Bayreuth's Hans Sachs, shares roles with the veteran Theodor Reichmann. Two Czechs, Berta Förster-Lauterer and Wilhelm Hesch, arrive from Hamburg. Marie Gutheil-Schoder, a thrilling Carmen, is a mezzo of such dramatic flair that Mahler employs her part-time as a stage director. Hermine Kittel is a fine contralto, Selma Kurz a coloratura with the longest trill on earth. Erik Schmedes and Leo Slezak are Wagner heroes. Mahler signs up Georg Maikl, Richard Mayr, Margarethe Michalek, Anton Moser. Lucie Weidt, a supercharged soprano, is recommended by Anna von Mildenburg.

And then there is Mildenburg herself, whom Mahler hires at a salary higher than his own. In her first season she suffers stress and sings only twenty-five times, but Anna goes on to give Mahler her best singing years and causes him no serious discomfort, other than by flaunting her affairs with (among others) Behn, Lipiner, and the bisexual Ludwig Karpath; she finally marries, in 1909, the busy writer Hermann Bahr. No longer mentor and debutante, man and mistress, Mahler and Mildenburg enter the annals of opera as partners in a golden age.

Mahler expects singers to be creative. "He never came to rehearsal with a finished, worked-out directorial concept," reports Gutheil-Schoder. "Possibly he pictured in his mind one important scene that was the focal point of an entire act, but he would also leave room for individuality to find expression. 'Just do that . . . very pretty, I like that. . . . That mood, I want to sustain.' This way he intensified everyone's parallel or receptive inspiration."[26] "Rehearsal was marvellous," remembers Selma Kurz. "He forced everyone to give of their best and their last gasp and he, too, was totally exhausted and wrung dry."[27] "He was a martyr to the consuming flames of work and he expected us to be the same," writes the happy-go-lucky Slezak. "It would never have occurred to any one of us to leave the room if Mahler was rehearsing a few scenes in which he were not involved. His way of rehearsing brought everything out of a singer that he could possibly give. . . . If we did pull it off, Mahler . . . would come up to us on the stage and congratulate us and start handing out twenty-heller coins."[28]

Alert to individual nuance, he treats each singer on merit. When Slezak requests leave of absence so that he can earn big fees at public concerts, Mahler hits the roof.

"What, are you crazy? You've only just been away!"

"No, you are mistaken, it's been weeks. . . ."

On his desk there was a panel with roughly twenty-five or thirty buttons. . . . Mahler lunged irately at it and slammed down about twelve or fifteen buttons at once with the flat of his hand. . . .

Doors opened on all sides. . . .

Secretary Schlader, stage managers, people from props, all rushed up, even the fire officer had got the signal and appeared in full regalia all set to man the pumps. The only one whose button had not been hit was Wondra [the schedule keeper]. One argument is countered by another, matters come to a head, my patience snaps and fuming I quit the scene. . . . [Some hours later] we are in the auditorium, he is sitting at his desk and conducting and all the gall and irritation just disappear like the snows of March in spring sunshine. This scenario would be repeated several times a year, or a month, or a week, so things weren't exactly pleasant.[29]

With Reichmann, less rambunctious, Mahler grants a leave request "with pleasure," affirming "my readiness to be of service to such an outstanding artist." Reichmann, a relic of the Jahn regime, responds to Mahler's encouragement until, past fifty, his voice loses power and Mahler terminates his contract. But hearing that Reichmann is in a clinic, seriously ill, he sends a new contract to arrive before the singer dies.

These swings from despotism to collegiality, calculation to improvisation, characterize Mahler's management style. He devotes an inordinate amount of time to personnel matters. Of the thirty to fifty letters that he writes or dictates on an average day, most are to do with singers. He also supervises the orchestra and chorus, monitors the box-office returns, and balances the eternal conflict for stage time between opera and ballet. Nothing escapes his attention. It is said of Mahler that he has eyes at the back of his head—and not only his own eyes. He has informers and enforcers. Some, like the concertmaster Arnold Rosé, abuse their clout to the detriment of independent-minded players like the cellist Franz Schmidt. "I vegetated for fully ten years more in the Vienna Court Orchestra," gripes Schmidt. "It wasn't exactly a bed of roses."[30]

THE WORM IN THE APPLE STRUDEL

In his inaugural season Mahler conducts 111 performances of 23 operas, of which four—Smetana's *Dalibor*, Tchaikovsky's *Eugene Onegin*, Bizet's *Djamileh*, and Leoncavallo's *Bohème*—are new to Vienna. In each of the next two seasons he conducts ninety-nine times, taking charge every two or three nights.[31]

> When the house grew dark, the small man with sharply chiselled features, pale and ascetic looking, literally rushed to the conductor's desk. He would let his baton shoot forward suddenly, like the tongue of a poisonous serpent. With his right hand he seemed to pull the music out of the orchestra. . . . He would stare at the stage and make imploring gestures at the singers. He would leap from the conductor's chair as if stung. Mahler was always in full movement, like a burning flame.[32]

Mahler is leading from the front, making sure every work is presented to his immaculate standard. His excessive schedule is, however, a reflection of conductor drought. Richter, unwanted, departs for the Halle Orchestra in England. Johann Nepomuk Fuchs drops dead, and his successor, Ferdinand Löwe, drops out. Mahler hires Franz Schalk, a reliable Bruckner pupil, but he needs a young conductor of high vitality. "What's all this beating about the bush?" he berates Bruno Walter. "I need an adjutant here, one who carries his marshal's baton in a knapsack (at present, I'm conducting everything myself and I am, by now, *exhausted*). What on earth does it matter whose successor you are? . . . I need you here before 1900 because I shall be dead by then if things go on like this."[33] Walter, fearful of vanishing into Mahler's vortex, procrastinates. He is developing an identity as a composer with pleasant song cycles and a symphony in D minor. Mahler, sensing his anxiety, puts their personal ties above his professional need. "We're friends again, aren't we?"[34] he checks. When Walter finally arrives in July 1901, Mahler cuts his own conducting nights by half.

Alongside the Opera he takes another job. In September 1898, Vienna Philharmonic players ask him to replace Richter as chief conductor for their cycle of concerts at the Musikvereinsaal. This is a cynical maneuver. The Philharmonic, founded in 1842, is owned by members of the Opera House orchestra, whose day jobs depend on Mahler. Eager to conduct symphonies, he promises innovation. At the first rehearsal players find the scoring of Beethoven's *Coriolan* Overture has been thickened in parts for added emphasis. Some of them contact the racist *Deutsche Zeitung*, which, under the headline "Jewish Power at the Vienna Court Opera,"[35] flays Mahler for insulting a German god: "It seems Beethoven had a flawed gift for orchestration because he wrote the overture without an E-flat clarinet, so Mahler has to write it in for him. . . . If Mr. Mahler wants to make corrections, let him tackle Mendelssohn and Rubinstein—the Jews will never allow that—but let him leave our Beethoven in peace. We enjoy and admire him as he is, without the E-flat clarinet, and without Mahler."

Trust between conductor and orchestra is ruptured from this moment. Mahler, in three seasons, conducts two dozen concerts of seventy-nine works, twenty-six by Beethoven,[36] including his own massed-strings arrangement of the Eleventh String Quartet, op. 95, and a Ninth Symphony with textural revisions, doubling the woodwind section and adding extra horns and trumpets. The players continue to grumble and refuse to play most of the new works he proposes. In April 1899 they perform Mahler's Second Symphony as a fund-raiser for their pension kitty, selling out the house to an "almost exclusively Jewish audience" with a work that is received with "shameless enthusiasm on the part of young Israel"[37]—or so the Lueger press reports it. Everything Mahler does with the Vienna Philharmonic is tinged with an undercurrent of anti-Semitism. Contrary to the modern myth of a "Mahler tradition," orchestra and conductor endure a three-year marriage of convenience that produces no creditable issue.

The one occasion when players agree to perform a work of Mahler's in their prestige series, in November 1900, audience members bray with laughter during the Funeral March of the First Symphony. After this debacle the Philharmonic refuses to play another Mahler work unless its fees are paid by a commercial promoter. Mahler, for his part, adds one leaf of glory to the Philharmonic record by giving the orchestra international status. In June 1900 he leads the Philharmonic to Paris, its first foreign tour, a junket organized by Alexander Rosé, the concertmaster's brother.[38] The organization is inept, the halls are half empty, and the orchestra runs out of funds, forcing Mahler to beg the fares home from Baron Albert Rothschild. But while the players mutter, Mahler finds an unexpected source of support.

It is six years since Capt. Alfred Dreyfus, a Jewish artillery officer, was charged with spying for the Germans, stripped of his rank, and shipped to Devil's Island, off the coast of French Guiana. Efforts to uncover the right-wing plot behind these false charges are brutally suppressed. France's head of counterintelligence, Col. Marie-Georges Picquart, is sent to Africa and later arrested for revealing awkward evidence. After the publication of his pro-Dreyfus essay, "J'Accuse!" (in a newspaper owned by Georges Clemenceau), Émile Zola is tried for criminal libel and flees to England. Anti-Semitic riots break out in French cities, and xenophobia is still rampant when Mahler comes to Paris in June 1900. Among the year's popular songs are "À bas les Juifs [Down with the Jews]," "Vos Gueules, Judas [Shut your mouth, Judases]", "Dreyfus über Alles," and "La France aux Français [France for the French]."[39] Picquart finally nails a plot leader, Maj. Hubert-Joseph Henry, who is found dead in his prison cell, but six more years will pass before Dreyfus is cleared—and a century before a French president offers an apology.[40]

Mahler, in Paris, finds himself adulated by music-loving Dreyfusards who attend his concerts—Colonel Picquart himself, along
with Georges Clemenceau, his brother, Paul, and Paul's wife, Sophie
Szeps, sister of the Viennese art critic Berta Zuckerkandl. Sophie
brings along her lover, the mathematician Paul Painlevé, who gave
scientific evidence in Dreyfus's defense. After Beethoven's Fifth Symphony at the Théâtre du Châtelet, Painlevé takes the party backstage. Mahler is struck by Picquart's "strong personality, integrity,
exceptional class."[41] The Dreyfusards gather around, sensing kinship. They become Mahler's greatest fans, attending his performances whenever possible and championing his work as a moral
cause.

A DIFFERENT SET OF JINGLE BELLS

He moves to a third-floor apartment in an Otto Wagner building—
clean white lines and no "eyebrows" on the windows—at Auenbruggergasse 2, a quiet side street close to the Belvedere Gardens, a
twelve-minute stroll from the Opera. He no longer needs all ten
rooms, as his sister Emma is marrying the cellist Eduard Rosé,
Arnold's older brother, eighteen years her senior, and is off with him
to Boston. Arnold, a notorious womanizer,[42] starts an affair with
Justi. Natalie, catching them together, is sworn to silence in
exchange for more time with Mahler. Natalie, nearing forty, has
not given up on him. Mahler has felt flutters of love for three
singers—Gutheil-Schoder, Rita Michalek, and the lovely long-
trilling Kurz[43]—but he is far too busy to pursue any serious
romance.

Four days after Emma's wedding, in June 1898, he enters hospital
for a second hemorrhoid operation ("my subterranean troubles").
The pain disables him all summer. The most he can manage is two
more *Wunderhorn* songs, and he fears he is drying up. The next summer, 1899, he goes with Justi and Natalie to a village near Linz, only
to find their booking canceled. They move to Alt-Aussee, twenty
kilometers from Steinbach, where the weather is wretched. He
cranks out another song, "Revelge," which he plays to Natalie, Justi,

and Arnold on July 7, his thirty-ninth birthday. "These past three summers," he grumbles, "I've been like a swimmer making a few strokes just to show he can still swim."[44] The next morning the sun comes out, and he complains of the noise of a passing band. He goes upstairs and, in ten days, writes two movements of a fourth symphony.

Reinvigorated like an athlete on a sugar rush, he decides to build a house of his own beside a lake where he can compose undisturbed all summer long. Anna von Mildenburg recommends the Wörthersee, where she lives. The railway line runs along the north side of the Carinthian lake. Mahler finds a plot on the undeveloped southern bank at the foot of a forested hill in a spot called Maiernigg. In the thick of the woods he erects a brick cabin with a lane cleared through the trees so that all he can see from his desk is the glistening lake below. In his new composing hut, on August 5, 1900, Mahler finishes the Fourth Symphony. Having planned six movements, he condenses it into four. It lasts less than an hour, with a normal-size orchestra. The Fourth is his classical symphony, reminiscent of Haydn in its jocularity and of Beethoven's Ninth in the plangency of its adagio. Some analysts, like the Marxist Adorno, regard this symphony as a step backward, a concession to convention. But Mahler, though he needs a popular success, does not give up on changing the world. He just buries his subversion that bit deeper.

The jingling sleigh bells that open the symphony are as dangerous as a runaway car on a mountain pass, driving conductor and orchestra to near chaos. "It begins as if it can't count up to three," says Mahler, "and then it goes straight into the full multiplication table until finally it's calculating dizzily in millions upon millions."[45] He marks the passage *"Bedächtig—nicht eilen—Recht gemächlich* [Deliberate, don't hurry, really leisurely]," in direct contradiction to its anarchic content. "Childlike, simple and wholly unselfconscious"[46] is another Mahler description, a wicked deception. He is back to his old ironic tricks, conveying two meanings at once, in constant opposition.

No fewer than seven original melodies are "shuffled" (Adorno's apt verb)[47] in the opening movement, interwoven contrapuntally "with the greatest, almost pedantic regularity,"[48] before the section blazes out in a symmetrical rattle of fool's bells. The English music critic Neville Cardus points out that this is the first Mahler symphony "which can be appreciated in a completely musical way"[49] without ulterior thoughts. To do so, however, would be like eating lettuce salad without a dressing, tasteless and forgettable.

What the Fourth Symphony does is extend Mahler's narrative of the simple life in two directions—attacking prejudice on earth and cruelty in heaven. At the start of the second movement, the concert-master is asked to lay down his expensive violin and take up a two-bit fiddle tuned one tone higher, "so that it screeches and sounds rough."[50] Mahler has asked for rough playing before, in the Funeral March of the First Symphony. Here he wants the refined concert-master to forget his airs and graces and play like a ragged Gypsy, member of an "inferior" race, alien to the concert hall.

Not entirely unknown, however, since Liszt, Brahms, and Dvořák have all made hay of *Zigeuner* melodies, but where they dress up Gypsy music for family consumption—Brahms drenches it in Italian sauce, "alla zingarese"—Mahler presents it in the raw, jaunty and contemptuous. He confronts civic society with its greatest fear, the untamed classes outside the law, and he exacerbates the threat by treating Gypsy music not as a primitive sound to be colonized by an educated composer but as an art with a vitality and integrity all its own, art that tunes at a different pitch from the norm, played along another scale. The scherzo of Mahler's Fourth Symphony is arguably the first multicultural work in Western music, and he is cer-tainly the first before Béla Bartók to treat indigenous music with respect and admiration as an equal form of art.

Mahler, aware that he is on dangerous territory, covers his tracks with a crackle of diversionary ironies. He calls a jolly episode "Death strikes up a dance," and remarks that "St. Ursula stands by, smil-ing,"[51] aware that the fourth-century Ursula is the most solemn of saints. He is making Yiddish jokes at the church's expense. "Don't try to understand the work as a story," explains Bruno Walter on Mahler's behalf. "It's pure music . . . open to anyone with a subtle sense of humor."[52] The smile gets wiped off near the end of the sec-ond movement, and again at the close of the sumptuous adagio, by echoes of Mahler's Second Symphony. Death is never very far from the children who play in his meadows. Cardus remarks, acutely, that Mahler here is both man and boy.

The symphony ends with an 1892 *Wunderhorn* song, "We enjoy heaven's joys." Mahler wants it sung "with a childlike, cheerful expression," "ohne Parodie," without parody, in contrast to all the preceding ironies. The righteous are in heaven, reaping their just rewards. Angels bake bread for their lunch. Saint Martha cooks the vegetables, grim Saint Ursula laughs aloud, the wine flows freely. A little lamb, "innocent and lovable," is released from the fold and carefully marked. Then it is killed for the pot. Saint Luke slaughters an ox, Saint Peter catches fish. Mahler, a former vegetarian, is making a case for animal rights. This is no heaven for God's tender creatures, unless they happen to belong to the human race. Is that what God wants? Or is it man's will, his perpetual urge to kill? Even without parody, Mahler's heaven is unnerving.

With its classical dimensions and compact form, the Fourth Symphony secures a rapid premiere in Munich, where on November 25, 1901, with Rita Michalek as soprano soloist, the reception is fiercely xenophobic. "Jewish wit has invaded the symphony, corroding it," writes a Swiss aesthete, William Ritter. Others complain about this "restless, nervous work."[53] "Nothing but Viennese corruption, carnival," growls the poet Karl Wolfskehl. "No trace of spontaneity, not a single autonomous idea, no original feeling," notes the Berlin periodical *Die Musik*.[54]

In Vienna there are boos between movements and cries of "Shame!" Critics attack the "false naiveties" and a vision of heaven "that is more like hell." Max Graf, in the *Neues Wiener Journal*, notes that, since the song in the finale was sketched first, the symphony "needs to be read *from back to front*, like the Hebrew Bible."[55] Graf, a lawyer by training and a member of Sigmund Freud's inner circle, knows from his bar mitzvah that Hebrew is written right to left. *"From back to front"* is a pejorative judgment, asserting that Christian literacy is superior to Jewish antiquity. Hearing Mahler turns the intelligent Freudian Graf into a Jewish anti-Semite.

Yet, in each and every performance, Mahler changes someone's life and mind. Ritter, a tutor to Bavarian royalty and an avowed anti-Semite, cannot sleep after the Munich premiere. He writes to Mahler, who sends him proofs of the symphony. Later he introduces Mahler to his lover, a young Slovak, Janko Cadra. Mahler, comfortable with unconventional couples, sends warm regards to Janko in his letters to Ritter. Inclusivist and nonjudgmental, he bears no prejudice against any racial and sexual minorities. The multiculturalism of his Fourth Symphony is not an empty gesture. Mahler, ahead of his time, welcomes the outsider into the fold.

THE ENEMY WITHOUT

He is not the first composer to have trouble with critics, but Mahler's attitude to the press is unhelpful. As a newspaper writer and editor in another place and time, I can see with 20/20 hindsight every mistake he makes long before he makes it, but no amount of well-meant advice would have deterred Mahler from a preset collision. To understand his dilemma one needs to grasp the diversity of Viennese media and the modesty of their circulation, aimed for the eyes of an elite. In the center stand the Jewish-owned *Neue Freie Presse* (45,000 readers) and *Neues Wiener Tagblatt* (65,000).[56] The *NFP* music critics are Hanslick (till 1904), the operetta composer Richard Heuberger, and Julius Korngold, father of the child prodigy. The *NWT* has Max Kalbeck as chief critic, Ludwig Karpath as second string.

At the far right are the *Deutsche Volksblatt* (25,000; critics Camillo Horn, Hans Puchstein), the *Deutsche Zeitung* (10–15,000; Theodor Helm), the clerical *Reichspost* (6,000; Fritz Gaigg von Bergheim), and the *Vaterland* (Richard Kralik and his sister, Mathilde). Helm and the Kraliks do not necessarily toe the racist line.

In between are the *Neues Wiener Journal* (60,000; Albert Kauders, Max Graf, Paul Stefan), *Illustriertes Wiener Extrablatt* (40,000; Josef Königstein), and two government newspapers, *Fremdenblatt* (21,000; Ludwig Speidel) and *Wiener Abendpost* (9,500; Robert Hirschfeld). Speidel, along with Gustave Schönaich in the *Reichswehr*, wages Wagner's cause against the Brahmsians Hanslick and Kalbeck. "We had the feeling of being in the tent of great warriors and generals after a victorious battle," writes Graf.[57] There is also a socialist *Arbeiter Zeitung* (24,000; Josef Scheu).

It does not take much for a charismatic conductor to bring critics and editors to his side. A warm smile and a gourmet lunch usually do the trick. He doesn't need to meet them often; that's what press chiefs are for. Mahler, however, relies on Lipiner for press strategy[58] and treats critics as either lackeys or enemies. A lackey does as he's told. Mahler orders Karpath to write a puff piece on the Dresden conductor, Ernst von Schuch. "You know what to say. *Distinguished conductor.* Outstanding man of the theatre. High honours and decorations. Champion of dramatic art and its modern exponents."[59] When Karpath writes an inconvenient review Mahler threatens him with violence. "Don't forget the respect you owe me as Director of the Opera," he yells, shaking a fist in the critic's face. "If you try to undermine my authority, I'll show you!"[60]

Enemies are treated with disdain. Mahler is unable to conceal his feelings. When he sees a hostile critic, he lets fly. He calls critics *die Herren Vorgesetzten*, "the superior gentlemen." A man of infinite subtleties, sensitive to most human foibles, Mahler cannot fathom the workings of press freedom and refuses to recognize the legitimacy of criticism. His obduracy is puzzling, unless one considers that he may already have earmarked the press as a convenient scapegoat for his eventual, inevitable downfall.

8. The Most Beautiful Girl in Vienna (1901)

At the start of 1901 he is preparing Wagner's *Rienzi*, his own *Song of Lament*, two big concerts with the Philharmonic, and a bevy of plans with Richard Strauss, while suffering from a sore throat, migraines, stomachaches, and bleeding hemorrhoids. He takes two days off in bed, supervising rehearsals by telephone. Schmedes and Mildenburg call in sick. Mahler roars back to work and the show goes on. Verdi dies; a moment's silence is observed. The pressure is relentless.

On February 24, a Sunday afternoon, Mahler conducts the Viennese premiere of Bruckner's Fifth Symphony, working from a text that has been mangled by editors. He leaves the concert looking pale and unwell. That night he conducts *The Magic Flute* on its hundredth anniversary. Any other musicians, faced with two big shows in a day, would take it easy through the familiar work. Mahler, being Mahler, fires up three hours of Mozart with customary incandescence. "He looked like Lucifer: a face as white as chalk, eyes like burning coals,"[1] writes a young audience member, thinking: "He can't take much more of this."[2]

He awakes in the middle of the night, his sheets drenched in blood from a burst hemorrhoid. Justi calls a doctor who puts him in an ice-water bath. When the bleeding persists, he summons a surgeon who, delayed in traffic, tells the patient that "half an hour later would have been too late." Professor Julius von Hochenegg is a pupil of Professor Theodor Billroth, a pioneer of abdominal surgery and a friend of Brahms. He has a rectal ulcer named after him, and students from all over the world.

Hochenegg subjects Mahler to an excruciating procedure, inserting a large instrument into his rectum and probing around until the polyp is found and tied off. Surgeon and patient are soiled with blood and fecal mucus. Mahler tells Strauss that he lost two and a half liters of blood.[3] "Hovering on the border between life and death I wondered whether it would not be better to have done with it at once," he says, "since everything must come to that in the end. Beside, the prospect of dying did not frighten me in the least . . . and to return to life seemed almost a nuisance."[4] He adds: "I thought my last hour had come."

How true is that? Death from hemorrhoids is unusual, and Hochenegg may be scaring him. Nevertheless Mahler seems to recognize that this is a crossroads in his life, a moment to assess past achievement and plan a different future. He agrees to go under the knife and is gratified to hear that the emperor has written to Hochenegg, commanding him to take good care of his Opera director. Prince Montenuovo raises Mahler's salary by 16 percent and doubles his expenses allowance. Heartened, Mahler undergoes surgery on March 4 and, during convalescence, reads a new Bach edition. Bach, he tells Natalie, "reminds me of those gravestones that show the dead sleeping with hands folded over their remains. They seem to hold on to life, even beyond this existence."[5]

His sepulchral imagery resembles that of the hallucinations of the recovery room, where patients are kept after general anesthesia, a place where the boundaries of life and death can blur in a patient's mind. The situation is personally familiar. Coming around after gallbladder surgery at Saint Mary's Hospital, Paddington, I hear a nurse speaking in an unusual French accent. When I ask where she is from, she names a village down the road from my mother's Alsatian origin, in Bischheim. I have no memory of my mother, who died when I was a baby. The connection between her voice and the nurse's is drawn from another realm, from the kind of existential vestibule that Mahler describes after his brush with mortality. In his case the mood persists for months. On a pre-Easter break to Abbazia, on the Adriatic coast, he sees my mother, my brother Ernst and I standing one evening by the window of the sitting room [in Iglau, when] . . . the sky filled with yellow smoke, the stars began to move, and flew together, or engulfed each other, as if it were the end of the world. Suddenly, I was in the marketplace below. The fiery vapour followed me and as I looked back I saw coming out of it a huge figure—the eternal Jew. . . . His right arm rested on a tall staff that bore a golden cross. . . . [He] tried to force me to take his staff. I woke with a scream of terror.[6]

Ernst and his mother rebuke him for the sin of following the golden cross, forsaking his Jewish faith. In another dream Death grips him by the arm in a ballroom and says, "Come with me." Like Joseph in the Bible and Freud at Bergstrasse 19, Mahler is struggling to interpret ethereal dreams.

While he is recovering, the Vienna Philharmonic shares his concerts between Franz Schalk and the ballet conductor Josef "Pepi" Hellmesberger, Jr. *Schlamperei* makes a welcome return. Pepi is praised by Hirschfeld for his "lack of wilfulness" and by Graf for his "lack of initiative." Players tell the press that Mahler will be deposed. Mahler, preempting their vote, resigns. *Fesche Pepi*, or Dandy Joe, a lover of pubescent girls, conducts the Philharmonic for three years until a street brawl with the father of a very young dancer gets him fired from the Opera. The Philharmonic begs Mahler to return, but he has the dignity to decline.

That summer in Maiernigg, Mahler takes out his student-era poetry book and composes three death-of-children songs, along with four more poems by Rückert, a last *Wunderhorn* lied, and half of a fifth symphony. Prolonged rest and self-contemplation have eased the flow of music, and his delight in the new house is uncontained. "It's too beautiful," he sighs, leaning from his attic balcony. "I don't deserve it."[7] Tourists on a passing steamer call out, "It's Mahler! Hooray for Mahler!" He runs indoors, blushing but not displeased. He is, says Justi, "beside himself with happiness" as he sits down to write about the death of children.

Out of 430 poems in the Rückert cycle, he picks five. Why these and no others? The opening lines reveal his state of mind:

1 Now will the sun rise just as brightly
  As though no disaster struck last night. . . .
2 Now I can see clearly
  Why dark flames leaped out at me from your eyes
3 When your little mother
  Comes in through the door
4 Often I think they are just out walking
  They won't be long, they'll soon return
5 [Final couplet]: The hand of God protects them:
  They rest as in their mother's house.

The first song evokes his near-fatal nocturnal incident, the others his dream of mother and boys. The children could be Ernst and Gustav. Morbid as the title may sound, *Kindertotenlieder* is not a requiem for the dead but a survivor's meditation. The set is written for baritone; underlining its autobiographical intent, he never conducts it with a female singer. *Kindertotenlieder* is Gustav Mahler first person singular.

The tinkle of a glockenspiel behind the opening stanza turns the heaven of the Fourth Symphony into an unfriendly place, somber and forbidding. In the closing phrases the children's souls find uncertain repose amid a morose plucking of harps. The afterlife has lost its appeal; Mahler does not want to go there. He closes the Resurrection chapter in his life, never bothered again about what happens in the great beyond. What matters to Mahler, in his second life after surgery, is the here and now.

Five more songs by Rückert form an ode of love around a midnight meditation, *Um Mitternacht*. One song in particular, "Ich bin der Welt abhanden gekommen," frames Mahler's state of mind:

I have left the world behind,
The world on which I squandered so much time;
It has known nothing of me for so long
  It might as well believe I'm gone.
Not that I'm much bothered
If it takes me for dead:

> I cannot contradict it
> > For I am really and truly dead to the world.
> Dead to the world's hubbub
> > And at peace in a still stretch of land:
> > I live *alone in my own heaven,*
> > > *In my own love, in my own song.*[8]

The song contains both self-analysis and self-concealment. It proclaims, and feigns, indifference toward a world that rejects his music: toward a trivial, ephemeral society that cannot see beyond superficial beauty and must be shunned if he is to be the composer he wants to be. Coming close to death has allowed him to shake off the expectations of the living. He can write now with confidence for a time unborn, a time when everyone he knows will be long dead and only his song endures.

The heartache opening on harp and cor anglais (reminiscent of Verdi's "Willow Song" for Desdemona in *Otello*) and the harp twangs beneath a moaning wind at the close ache with an irreducible sense of solitude. Mahler is alone in the world. He needs to find a home, *"in my own love,"* somewhere he need not feel so utterly forsaken.

The Rückert set, unlike the death-of-children songs, has neither running order nor fixed number. Five appear in 1905 with two *Wunderhorns* as *Seven Recent Songs (Sieben Lieder aus letzter Zeit),*[9] and posthumously as *Seven Last Songs.*[10] The last time he plays them[11] he ends with "Ich bin der Welt." "It is me, myself,"[12] he tells Natalie as the summer ends.

They are alone on the romantic lake. Justi has gone with Arnold Rosé for a health cure (does Mahler notice nothing?) and Natalie waits until they are back in Vienna before lunging at Mahler, pressing her desperate mouth on his. He fends her off. She demands to know why he won't marry her. "I can't love you," says Mahler. "I can only love a beautiful woman." "But I am beautiful," wails Natalie. Mahler avoids seeing her again.

AT FIRST SIGHT

Sophie Clemenceau is in Vienna to see Mahler conduct. Her sister, Berta, throws a dinner party on November 7, 1901, at Nusswald-strasse 20, in the suburb of Döbling, with Mahler as guest of honor. First to arrive are Klimt and Carl Moll, the leading Secessionists. Moll brings his wife, Maria, and her daughter, Alma Schindler. Twenty-two years old, fair-haired, and with a figure that turns heads in the street, Alma sits between Klimt and the ex–Burgtheater boss, Max Burckhard, eminent older men, both of whom have kissed her. Others present are Berta's husband, the anatomist Emil Zuckerkandl, and Friedrich Viktor Spitzer, a photographer member of the Secession.

Mahler arrives with Justi. Hearing laughter at the girl's end of the table, he calls over, "May others join the fun?" Someone arrives late from a concert by the Czech violinist Jan Kubelik, conducted by Alexander von Zemlinsky. Alma declares she does not like flashy virtuosos. "Nor do I!" cries Mahler. Eager to impress, he tells a story about throwing out a letter from an archduke who wanted him to engage a girl he fancied.

Over coffee the artists raise the question of physical beauty. "The head of Socrates is beautiful," declares Mahler. "I find Zemlinsky beautiful," says Alma provocatively. Zemlinsky, her teacher, is famously ugly.

"Why don't you perform his ballet, *A Heart of Glass?*"[13] she demands of Mahler. "You've kept him waiting a year for an answer."

"The ballet's worthless," says Mahler. "How can you defend such rubbish?"

"It's not rubbish, you've probably never looked at it properly," shrills Alma.

Mahler faces such special pleadings every day. He has just rejected an operetta by the critic Heuberger, turning him into an adversary. But he tells Alma: "I like the way you support your teacher. I'll send for Zemlinsky no later than tomorrow."

This is what Berta Zuckerkandl sees and hears.[14] Alma's version is more vivid. Mahler, she says, cannot understand Hofmannsthal's plot for Zemlinsky's ballet. "I'll explain it," Alma offers. "I'm all eager-ness," smiles Mahler, baring strong white teeth.

> We had long ago drawn apart from the rest, or else they had left us alone [writes Alma]. There was a magic circle around us that quickly encloses those who have found each other. I promised him to come one day [to the Opera], when I had something good to show him. He smiled ironically, as though to say that he would have a long time to wait, and then invited me to the dress rehearsal next morning of *Tales of Hoffmann*. Madame Clemenceau and Frau Zuckerkandl came up at that moment and he invited them also.[15]

He offers to walk her home. She declines, joining her parents in a cab. Mahler says he expects to see her at the Opera. "Ein Mann, ein Wort!" he calls after her—"I'll hold you to your word!"

"I liked him *immensely*—although he's very restless," she tells her diary that night. "He stormed about the room like a savage. The fel-low is made *entirely* of oxygen. When you get near him, you get burnt. Tomorrow I shall tell Alex *some* of this."[16] Alex is Zemlinsky, her lover—almost. "I shall never forget the touch of his hand on my most intimate parts. . . . One little nuance more and I would have become a *god*. . . . I would like to kneel before him & kiss his loins—kiss *everything, everything*. Amen!"[17] Her mother dislikes Alex, who is half Jewish. Alma threatens to kill herself if the lessons are stopped.

Next morning she accompanies Berta and Sophie to the Opera. Mahler is pacing the corridor, waiting for her. He takes Alma's coat, ignoring the two ladies. "Fräulein Schindler, how did you sleep?" he demands.

"Very well. Why shouldn't I?"

"I didn't sleep a wink all night," says Mahler.

He goes into the pit and conducts *The Tales of Hoffmann*, which has not been seen in Vienna since its second night in December 1881, when 400 people in an audience of 1,760 died in a Ringtheater fire. There is a pause when Gutheil-Schoder comes on in a gown slit up "to the waist"[18] and Mahler, affronted, sends her to get it sewed up. In the break, "Mahler came twice to the railing & spoke to us—really kind," writes Alma.

Soon after (some pages are missing from her diary[19]), the mail brings her a love poem:

> *Dan kam so über Nacht!*
> *Hätt ich's so nicht gedacht*
> *Dass Contrapunkt und Formenlehre*
> *Mich noch einmal das Herz beschwere.*
> It happened overnight:
> I would never have imagined
> That counterpoint and music theory
> Would disturb my heart again. . . .

The last stanza discloses its authorship:

> *Ich hör's: Ein Mann—ein Wort!*
> I still hear it: *I'll hold you to your word.*
> It rings in my ear all the time
> A canon of some sort.
> I glance at the door—and wait.

Alma's mother demands to know who wrote the poem. Alma, disingenuous, says she is not sure. They go to see Gluck's *Orfeo ed Euridice*, conducted by Bruno Walter. Bored, she looks up at the director's box and catches Mahler's eye. In the interval he is presented to her mother and pours them tea in his private room. "You live on the Hohe Warte?" he asks. "It's my favorite walk." Frau Moll invites him to drop by. Mahler reaches for his diary. Saturday is agreed.

He does not wait for Saturday to come around. On Thursday, November 28, he is at her door, a semidetached Josef Hoffmann house on a hill overlooking the city. Next door lives the graphic artist Koloman Moser; two more villas belong to the Secession photographers Spitzer and Hugo Hennenberg.[20] Ushered in for tea, Mahler chats with the Molls until, looking at the clock, he asks to use the telephone. Told that they don't have one yet, he asks Alma to walk him to the post office. It is snowing, and there is a biting wind. Moll and Moser walk behind as chaperones. Alma hears

Mahler tell his sister on the phone that he won't be home for dinner. "Then he told me how much he had been thinking about me & how worried he was because his life was preordained. Only his art—and now his thoughts are of other things."[21] He explains that Justi organizes his life, giving him space to compose. If he had someone else, things would change. What if that person had an artistic sensibility? asks Alma. Mahler, ducking the question, stays for dinner.

The next day Alma shows Zemlinsky the songs Mahler has sent her. She finds them simplistic but, seeing Zemlinsky grimace, she sings them all weekend. On Monday afternoon Mahler climbs the Hohe Warte once more. "He told me that he loved me—we kissed each other. He played me his pieces—my lips are sealed. . . . His caresses are tender and agreeable. If only I knew. He—or the other."[22] Zemlinsky is thirty years old, full of promise. Mahler is her mother's age. "What if Alex were to become famous?" she wonders.

At the opening night of *Tales of Hoffmann*, Mahler, looking round from the pit with that searching glare, catches her flirting with an architect, Felix Muhr. "I've lost him!" wails Alma. On Saturday, December 7, Mahler rings the doorbell. "We kissed each other over and over again. In his embrace I feel so warm."[23] He calls her "Almschi," a pet name. He is off to Berlin, telling her: "I hear nothing but this one voice, stronger than all else. May it never fall silent in my heart. A voice that knows but one word and one note: I love you, my Alma! . . . Mine, mine, your Gustav."[24]

"I simply can't work," records Alma. "I pace around the room, go over to his picture, reread his last letter—I love him!"[25] But when Felix drops by she plays piano with him for hours. The architect asks if he stands a chance. Alma tells him she is in love with Mahler. After politely threatening to kill himself, Muhr says he has heard from a doctor that Mahler is dying of an incurable disease.

Alma cannot sleep. Clearing the decks, she dumps Zemlinsky. "Alex," she writes, "You know how *very* much I loved you. You have fulfilled me *completely*. Just as suddenly as this love arrived, it has departed—been cast aside. [Another] love has taken command of me with renewed force! On my knees I beg forgiveness for the evil hours I have given you. Some things lie beyond our control."[26]

She meets Justi for tea at the Zuckerkandls' and wishes she could ask about Mahler's health. "I feel really sorry for him. . . . But his love is so *touching*." For distraction she flirts "outrageously" through five hours of *Meistersinger* with "young Doctor Adler whom I find tremendously attractive."[27]

Mahler's love letters from Germany are mingled with irritated exhortations:

> Dearest girl do try to write more clearly. Separate the letters more clearly and shape the consonants more precisely. Why don't you use German script, as I do? You write that you spent a difficult afternoon with a handsome, rich, well-educated and musical young gentleman. Almschi! Almschi! Just think! My God, what kind of substitute would that be? . . . So there he stood, pale and trembling and was even prepared to kill himself on your account! I would never dream of that! How I would love to run my fingers through your dear tresses—even though I prefer you without them, just a simple hairstyle.[28]

Burckhard warns her off Mahler, "saying that when two strong personalities come together they usually fight until one of them is forced into submission." Then Zemlinsky drops by.

> He came into the room, paler than usual and very quiet—I went to him, drew his head against my breast and kissed his hair. I felt so strange. Then we sat down and talked seriously, only of matters concerning us both—side by side—we whose bodies had coiled in love's wildest embrace. He, a little sarcastic as ever, but otherwise kind, touchingly kind. . . . Today I buried a beautiful love. Gustav, you'll have to do much to replace it for me.[29]

Mahler complains that she is always writing about "the virtues of some young man" and suggests that Justi finds her manipulative. "He's a sick man," explodes Alma. "His position is insecure, he's a Jew, no longer young and as a composer . . . deeply in debt. So where's the calculation on my part? . . . I love him and will stand by him. . . . My Gustav! I long for him *disgracefully*."[30]

She flirts "madly" again with Louis Adler. "The fellow is so damned good-looking. And Muhr was watching." Alma is socially bifocal, seeing herself and, at the same time, how others see her. Appearance, *Schein über Sein*, matters as much to Alma as actual experience. Her fatal attraction is a physical magnetism that, more than youth, beauty, and piercing blue eyes, outshines "all the nonsense"[31] she spouts. Men fall at her feet. The last of her husbands describes her, not altogether fondly, as "one of the great sorceresses."[32] It is this magic that kindles Mahler's love and desire, quelling his qualms about their age difference and her willfulness. He knows she will never be easy to live with, but he wants her as much for adventure as for love. She is the antipode of his submissive mother, the seal upon his past.

He conducts his Fourth Symphony in Berlin and heads off to hear his *Resurrection* in Dresden, where, on arrival, Mahler sits down in his hotel room and writes Alma the longest letter of his life, "probably the most important one I ever had to write." Weighing every word, he makes his case in two statements, written either side of a general rehearsal. "I know I must hurt you," he warns Alma, "but I have no choice."

He starts by ridiculing the men who chase her. "All these Burckhards, Zemlinskys, etc., possess no true individuality," snorts Mahler. They are a pack of "mutual admirers" who flatter to seduce. Many of the things she tells him "are not your ideas, thank God, but those of others." Her artistic identity is unformed, and he will not tolerate her presumption to be a composer.

> In your letter you write of "your music" and "my" music. *Forgive me but I cannot remain silent.* On this point, my Alma, we must set things straight and I mean *right now*, before we meet again. . . . Let me speak in general terms. A husband and wife who are both composers: how do you envisage that? Such a strange relationship between rivals: do you have any idea how ridiculous it would appear, can you imagine the loss of self-respect it would later cause us both? If, at a time when you should be attending to household duties or fetching me something I urgently needed, or if as you wrote you wish to relieve me of life's trivia—if at such a moment you were befallen by "inspiration": what then?
>
> Don't get me wrong! I don't want you to believe that I take that

philistine view of marital relationships which sees a woman as some sort of diversion, with additional duties as her husband's house-keeper. Surely you wouldn't expect me to feel or think that way? But one thing is certain: if we are to be happy together, you will have to be "as I need you"—not my colleague, but my wife![33]

He goes on to say such blustery things as "you have only one pro-fession: to make me happy," and "this makes me suffer just as much as you," affording future feminists all the ammunition they need to depict Mahler as a brute and Alma as his victim. Starting with a tendentious biography by the French politician Françoise Giroud, Alma and her thwarted creativity will be cited as an admonitory case history in the future academic study of "feminist aesthetics." Mahler, however, is not asserting male dominance. He specifically denounces "Nietzsche's utterly false and brazenly arrogant theories of masculine supremacy,"[34] assuring her that he is not seeking a sub-missive wife. On the contrary, he loves her combative nature. What he seeks to avoid is a professional rivalry that might offer his ene-mies a chink of vulnerability. There can only be one composer in this marriage. If there were two, her work might be vaunted at his expense, and he might be attacked for promoting, or suppressing, it. If both composed, both would lose and the marriage would fail.

These are not unreasonable considerations, given the disparity of their achievements. Mahler is a famous composer. Alma has written ninety-five songs, piano pieces, and sketches, none of them pub-lished or performed.[35] She is not by any reckoning a professional composer, nor is she convinced that this is what she was born to do. He does not forbid her to compose. What he demands is that she should not compete.

Mahler's aim is to negotiate a prenuptial accord with a young woman who is headstrong, desirable, and, by her own account, superficial. His final demand is that she

surrender yourself to me *unconditionally*, make every detail of your future life completely dependent on my needs, in return you must wish for nothing except my love. And what that is, Alma, I cannot tell you—I have already spoken too much about it. But let me tell you just this: for someone I love the way I would love you if you were to become my wife, I can forfeit all my life and all my happiness.

Taking Mahler at his word—in a letter that is not revealed until 1995, by which time feminist prejudices are set in stone—he offers to "forfeit all my life" for Alma. He, too, will give up composing, and life itself, if that is what is required to keep her love. He asks no more of her than he himself will give. Little does he imagine that his pledge will be tested, someday, to the limit.

His long, closely argued letter strikes Alma like a death sentence.

My heart missed a beat . . . give up my music—abandon what has until now been my life. My *first* reaction was—to pass him up. I had to weep, for then I understood that I loved him. . . .

Mama and I talked it over until late at night. She had read the letter. . . . I find his behaviour so ill-considered, so inept. It might have come all of its own—quite gently—but like this it will leave an inevitable scar.[36]

She has a decision to make, and a deadline, for Mahler is due back. "Yes—he's right," she decides. "I must live *entirely* for him, to make him happy. And now I have a strange feeling that my love for him is deep & genuine. But for how long?"[37] Mahler returns to Vienna and sweeps her into his arms. "I long to bear his child," she writes. "If he has the strength. He hopes so." She prays that his health "will not let me [sic] down," and that she won't find him one day dying in a pool of blood.

Two days before Christmas he buys her a ring, and a week later she takes him to bed. "Today we all but joined in wedlock," she records. "He let me feel his masculinity, his vigour & it was a pure, holy sensation, such as I would *never* have expected. He must be suffering *dreadfully*. I can gauge his frustration by mine."[38] On New Year's Day, she calls at his apartment. "What I have to write today is terribly sad. . . . He gave me his body—& I let him touch me with his hand. Stiff and upright stood his vigour. He carried me to the sofa, laid me gently down and swung himself over me. Then—just as I felt him penetrate—he lost all strength. He laid his head on my breast, shattered—and almost wept for shame. Distraught as I was, I comforted him."[39] On January 3, 1902, they achieve consummation. "Bliss upon bliss!" exclaims Alma.

Is Mahler aware that his every intimacy is on paper? He knows Natalie has been keeping a diary, but she is someone he has trusted since he was fifteen. Alma he met the month before last. He knows little about her except that she lives in a good neighborhood and mingles with fine artists. He assumes that she has received a conventional upbringing and has solid loyalties. He could hardly be more mistaken.

THE ABSENT FATHER

Alma's story starts with a bankruptcy. In 1871 a brewer in Hamburg goes bust and, with whatever cash he can muster, sends his hazel-eyed daughter to Vienna to become a singer. She catches the eye of Emil Jakob Schindler, a well-dressed painter, and marries him—only to find that he is penniless, sharing a Mayerhofgasse apartment with a fellow struggler, Julius Victor Berger. Three months pregnant, Anna keeps house for both men. Alma is born on August 31, 1879. Schindler finds childbirth "despicable" and leaves on borrowed money for a long health cure. While he is away Anna sleeps with Berger, their landlord, conceiving a second daughter, Margarethe, known as Grethe.

Schindler takes a paying pupil, Carl Moll, and they all move to a castle, Schloss Plankenberg,[40] where Alma grows up in "an artistic Eldorado." In August 1892, while with Moll and his brother on the holiday island of Sylt, Schindler dies of a ruptured appendix.[41] Alma is two weeks short of her thirteenth birthday. Schindler, she will write, was "my *Führer*. . . . All I ever did was done to please him. All my ambition and vanity was satisfied by a twinkle of his understanding blue eyes."[42] The lost father, idealized by Alma, sets her in pursuit of creative, extraordinary men.

Her mother, in a *Hamlet* twist, marries Moll in 1895 and bears his daughter, Maria. An easygoing fellow, emollient to a fault, Moll sells his own work for good prices and acts as middleman for bigger artists. President of the Secession, he marries off Grethe to one of his pupils, Wilhelm Legler, and is seeking a match for the resentful Alma. "I want to do something really remarkable," she tells her diary. "To compose a really good opera, something no woman has ever achieved. In a word, I want to be a somebody. But it's impossible— and why? I don't lack talent but my attitude is too frivolous for my objectives, for artistic achievement. Please God, give me some great mission, give me something great to do! Make me happy!"[43]

Gustav Mahler is the answer to her maiden prayer. Mahler is an artist, a genius, esteemed by the emperor, handsome, and powerful. But he has sensitive hands and a bohemian scorn for wealth. He is a great man, whom her love can make greater still. The resemblances to Emil Jakob Schindler are unerring. "I must rise to meet him," she writes of Mahler. "For I live only in him."[44] Mahler loves a girl who misses her father, as he has yearned for his mother. Her middle name is Maria. He asks her to use it. She starts signing herself Alma Maria.

On January 5, 1901, Mahler gives a dinner to introduce Alma and the Molls to his friends. The guests are Lipiner and his wife, Clementine, her brother Albert Spiegler, his wife, Nina (Lipiner's ex), Anna von Mildenburg (Lipiner's mistress and Mahler's ex), Justi and Arnold Rosé, and, for some reason, the Molls' neighbor, Kolo- man Moser. The gathering is fusty and incestuous. Alma is in a petu- lant mood, talking only to her mother and to Mahler. When Mildenburg asks if she likes Mahler's music, Alma replies, "I haven't heard much, and what I've heard I didn't like."[45] She feels as if she is on trial.

"His friends . . . all conspicuously Jewish," she notes. "I amused myself by stunning them with unprecedented impertinence."[46] She walks out with Mahler and barely bids the guests good-bye. When Lipiner complains, Mahler replies, "She's still young." The librarian follows up with an attack on Alma's "impudence" and "superficiality" and Mahler's "contempt" for others. "You don't consider anyone," snarls Lipiner. "We're all just objects to you." Alma gets what she wants, separating Mahler from "people he has been dragging behind him like shackles around his feet ever since his youth."[47]

As the director's fiancée, she shares a box with Richard Strauss and his wife, Pauline, during his opera *Feuersnot*. She finds Pauline a shrew and Richard "an unashamed materialist."[48] Mahler agrees. "Strauss creates such disillusion around him," he tells her. "You were spot-on in your comments about him. . . . The time will come when people will separate the wheat from the chaff. My time will come when his is past."[49] This is liberating for Mahler. Alma has freed him of tact and allowed him to redefine himself vis-à-vis his rival. "My time will come" is Mahler's claim to a place in history. "When his is past" differentiates him from a man whose eye never strays from the main chance. Once Mahler described himself and Strauss as "two miners who dig a shaft from opposite sides and finally meet underground."[50] Now, thanks to Alma, they are set on separate paths.

The wedding is set for March 9, a Sunday, at the green-domed Karlskirche, across the Ring from the Musikvereinsaal. Just before 1:30 Mahler, in a gray suit, enters the empty church with his witnesses, Moll and Rosé. It is pouring, and he wears galoshes. Alma, her mother, and Justi arrive by cab, their footsteps echoing on the marble floor. "When it came to kneeling down," writes Alma, "Mahler misjudged the hassock and found himself on the stone flags; he was so small that he had to stand up again and make a fresh start. We all smiled, including the priest."[51]

Picture the scene: Anxious little Jew about to marry blond bombshell, trips over his prayer stool and falls flat on his face, ha-ha, no one laughing louder than the priest, Josef Pfob. Is this what really happens? My scrutiny of the spot suggests an ulterior scenario. Above the altar is a Baroque sunburst with four Hebrew letters at its center—*yod, heh, waw, heh*—the tetragrammaton that is the unpronounced Jewish name for God. Gustav Mahler looks up as he sinks to his knees, misses his footing and falls. Alma thinks he trips because he is so short. But Mahler has just seen the God of the Jews. Guilt and betrayal clog his gullet. He needs a moment to collect himself before he takes Christian vows. He falls over to gain time. Alma and the priest giggle at his discomfiture. He does not belong in church.

At the wedding feast Alexander Rosé's child, Eleanor, is sent home for being naughty. What did you do? I ask her, eighty-five years later. "I mimicked Mahler's walk." She smiles and shows me how.[52]

The next day Justi marries Arnold Rosé. On Tuesday night the Mahlers head for St. Petersburg, where he arrives with a migraine, sore throat, and chilblains, while Alma—ten weeks pregnant— throws up with morning sickness. Mahler's cousin Gustav Frank, a czarist official, greets them in temperatures thirty degrees below zero Celsius. They go to the Hermitage to see the Rembrandts, and Alma lectures Mahler on painting techniques. He conducts concerts for much of their honeymoon. Alma recognizes that love with Mahler will come second to work. "I knew once and for all," she writes, "that it was my mission in life to move every stone from his path and to live for him alone."[53]

THE TRUTH, AND NOTHING BUT

The love story of Gustav and Alma will become the stuff of novels, movies, songs, feminist theory, and popular myth. Most of it is founded on Alma's three books—a volume of letters that she edited in 1924,[54] a memoir of Mahler she wrote in 1940 (English edition, 1946),[55] and her 1960 autobiography, in differing versions, English and German.[56] None of these texts can be trusted.

Alma's motives were noble, up to a point. She wanted to enshrine Mahler's memory and herself as his muse. That required adjusting some inconvenient facts. The letters she issued were cut and sometimes changed. Of 159 published letters, only 37 appear verbatim; a further 200 were suppressed;[57] many more were burned.

Her memoirs play fast and loose with truth. She claims to have seen Mahler conduct *Magic Flute* on the night of his hemorrhage, looking "like Lucifer," when her diary shows she was home all evening.[58] In her memoirs, Mahler's "demand that I instantly give up my music"[59] is augmented by invented quotes. Strauss, reading Alma's account of their *Feuersnot* night, scribbled in his copy: "Completely implausible. At any rate an utter fabrication . . . the inferiority complexes of a dissolute woman."[60]

Alma's distortions are part memory lapse, part malice. Of her wedding day she notes, "There were six of us at the wedding breakfast," when the invitation that Eleanor Rosé showed me proves that extended families were invited. Alma claims they left for St. Petersburg that same night, March 9, implying that Mahler did not stay for his sister's wedding. A study of the Vienna rail timetables by the Danish scholar Knud Martner shows that there was no train to St. Petersburg before Tuesday, March 11.[61] Mahler saw Justi married, and Alma lied about it.

Nothing she writes can be accepted without corroboration, but she cares enough about posterity to leave one truthful source: The one place Alma never lies is in her diaries, which are kept (with two thousand boxes of her papers) in the Charles Patterson Van Pelt Library of the University of Pennsylvania. To Alma's undying credit, she loved Mahler enough to leave a reliable paper trail.

9. Small Interludes of Happiness (1902–1906)

All of a sudden everything starts to go right. The Secession puts on a Beethoven exhibition and asks Mahler to conduct the Ninth Symphony. The exhibition's centerpiece is Max Klinger's half-naked bust of Beethoven, placed in a Josef Hoffmann room, walled by a new Klimt triptych. One of its panels shows a knight in armor confronting hostile powers. The knight is unmistakably Gustav Mahler.

The show is curated by Alfred Roller, a professor at the School of Arts and Crafts, whose mural, *Sinkende Nacht* (*Night Is Falling*), hung behind the Beethoven bust, quotes *Tristan und Isolde*: "O sink hernieder, Nacht der Liebe."[1] Roller is seeking fusion between music and visual imagery. Mahler, for his part, is trying to get a grip on art. Like every other Jew, he has three millennia of inhibitions about graven images, prohibited in the Ten Commandments. The taboo runs very deep. Man is made in the image of God, who is unseen. Any portrait of man breaches God's invisibility. Jewish boys like Mahler are taught to shun such things for life.

The only picture that hangs on Mahler's wall is *The Concert*, attributed to Giorgione, in which the monk at the keyboard looks a bit like him. He needs to understand art if he is to modernize the Opera. Alma is teaching him all she knows, and he admires the Secession, but Klimt is not a man he can talk to, and Moll is too mercantile. He gets Moser to make Alma a silver jewelry box with a rose-petal motif for Christmas,[2] and Hoffmann to forge her a ring. But it is with Roller, a man his own age from Brno (Brünn) in Moravia, that he finds affinity. Roller tells Mahler he hates his Wagner sets. Mahler asks for alternatives. Roller dashes off a sketch on the Molls' tabletop. "I'm going to hire him," Mahler tells Alma on the way home. Alma is exultant. Newly wed, she is becoming a light at the Opera.

She joins her husband for the premiere of his Third Symphony at Krefeld, at a convention of German musicians under Strauss's chairmanship. After the first movement Strauss strides the length of the aisle up to the stage, yelling acclaim. The Dutchman Willem Mengelberg invites Mahler to conduct in Amsterdam. The publisher C. F. Peters requests the privilege of printing his next work. Alma, in tears, decides her husband is "a great genius." At dinner, for some reason, Strauss snubs them.

They head on to Maiernigg, where Mahler does not vary his summer schedule—up at six, compose all morning, swim at noon, light lunch, a long hike or a row on the lake, a little sunbathing, dinner, and early to bed. Alma hates the place, is listless and bored. "Why can't he include me in his work?" she demands.[3] There are visits from his Opera secretary Alois Przistaupinsky, his "dull, obtrusive" lawyer, Emil Freund, and from Anna von Mildenburg, who lives nearby. One night she gets Mahler to walk her home in a thunderstorm. Alma, furious with jealousy, feels insecure. August is a black month for her, the month her father died.

Mahler, on the eve of that anniversary, slips a new song into her *Siegfried* score for her to find. They sit at the piano singing, "Liebst du um Schönheit, O nicht mich liebe [If you love for beauty, don't bother to love me]." It ends: "Love me forever, I'll always love you."

There is more to come. Days before her birthday he takes her to his hut and plays her the Fifth Symphony. To be the first to hear a new work is an indelible privilege. Alma, not quite twenty-three, is overwhelmed. She finds the symphony "magnificent" and wonders how much of it is affected by her. More, in fact, than she imagines. Mahler has changed his technique.[4] This is his first symphony that does not quote precomposed songs from his notebook, and the first for fifteen years to dispense with the singing voice. It is, says Bruno Walter, pure music, cleansed of "extra-musical thoughts or emotions."[5]

In three sections and five movements, lasting seventy minutes, its mood, according to Walter, is "one of optimism"[6]—yet it opens with a funeral march. The initial trumpet call, a repeated triplet and minim, hints at Beethoven's Fifth. But where Beethoven knocks at fate's door expecting it to open, Mahler's call is distant, stuttered and forlorn, joined by a bleak roll of drums. There is a hint of a *Wunderhorn* song, "Der Tambourg'sell," but the clear resemblance is to the third tune in Felix Mendelssohn's fifth book of *Songs Without Words*, op. 62,[7] a theme played at Mendelssohn's funeral. Is Mahler aware of the connection? Unlikely. He has little respect for Mendelssohn, accusing him of "missing the point"[8] and bracketed with him too often as musical Jews. This theme states their significant difference. Where Mendelssohn turns his tune into a musical fairy tale, Mahler blows it into elemental, explosive conflict. He is not afraid of giving bad news.

The second movement is marked "storm-tossed, with the greatest vehemence," and the Scherzo is a quick-slow alternation of waltzes and *Ländler* (country jigs) that reminds Mahler of Goethe's poem "An Schwager Kronos," in which Time is a coachman rattling down the road of life's sunset. No optimism here.

The Adagietto melds Eros and Thanatos, love and death, the elusiveness of one, the inevitability of the other. Mahler marks two passages *morendo*—Italian for "dying away"—and a wisp of the Gaze motif from *Tristan und Isolde* (mm 67–71) implies love until death. But which is it, love or death? According to Mengelberg, Mahler is pledging undying love to Alma. "Instead of a letter, he sent her this in manuscript form; no other words accompanied it," reports their Dutch friend. "She understood and wrote to him: He should come!! (*both* of them told me this)."[9]

But the Adagietto is not a simple eternity ring. Its first and last phrases are identical to Mahler's signature song, "I Am Lost to the World." He is not so much vowing love to his wife as withdrawing into unreachable solitude. Better still, he is doing both. The Adagietto is about love and the renunciation of love. It raises musical ambiguity to a degree of sophistication in which the same few notes convey love and loss, commitment and retraction, the life force and death. It is an apotheosis of ironic opposites in which the meaning depends on how it is performed, how a conductor shapes and

stretches the movement. In manuscript Mahler reckons the Adagietto should last seven and a half minutes. On a printer's proof he
writes nine minutes, which concurs with his own performances.
Mengelberg (recorded 1926) and Walter (1938) take seven and eight
minutes respectively, rushing perhaps to cram the music onto two
record sides.[10] Later interpreters take much longer: Georg Solti ten
minutes, Leonard Bernstein and Pierre Boulez eleven, Klaus Tennstedt thirteen, and Bernard Haitink five seconds under fourteen—
almost twice as long as Mahler's first estimate. The longer the
Adagietto, the sadder it sounds. With any other composer, halving
the tempo would amount to a distortion. Mahler, though, wants
conductors to decide, as he instructed: "If, after my death, something doesn't sound right, then change it," he orders Otto Klemperer.[11] The Adagietto is every maestro to himself, a challenge to
the conducting profession.

It fades, without pause, into a horn call that yields, in turn, three
new themes. A churchlike chorale near the end is dismissed by Alma
as "hymnal and boring." What about Bruckner? retorts Mahler. "He
can do it, not you," she snaps,[12] implying that a born Catholic can
write better church music than a convert like him. She volunteers to
prepare a fair copy for the publishers, sparing him a winter chore.
Strauss, hearing the symphony, tells Mahler his pleasure is "slightly
dimmed by the little Adagietto—but as this is what pleased the audience most, you are getting what you deserve."[13] Strauss is aiming for
the jugular, accusing Mahler of naked populism. Mahler knows full
well that the hinted marital intimacies of his Fifth Symphony are a
world apart from the thumping literalisms of Strauss's *Symphonia
Domestica*.

A CHILD IS BORN

On November 3, 1902, as Mahler stomps up and down the Auenbruggergasse corridor, Alma gives birth to a baby girl. They christen
her Maria, and Anna after Alma's mother, squidging the name into a
Viennese endearment, "Putzi." Mahler cradles the baby in his arms,

soothing her in rich, paternal tones. Alma, slow to recover, suffers postnatal depression. They sleep at either end of the long corridor. When he strokes her hair, she rebuffs him. "He disgusts me so much that I dread him coming home," she tells the diary.[14]

Mahler vents his frustration on his sister. "I have seen 'something' has been bothering you. . . . I sense the same thing from Arnold, too. . . . This sensitivity, I would think, you really could leave to those with a 'Jewish nature.' "[15] Anxiety, pain, and self-doubt—Mahler's "Jewish nature"—are brought to the fore by Alma's physical rejection.

He plunges into an oblivion of work. Over lunch at his apartment, he appoints Alfred Roller head of stage design, starting with *Tristan und Isolde*. Roller sweeps the stage of clutter and presents every scene in a different light, attuning it to time of day and musical "color." Each Roller setting[16] advances the plot in a way that is at once real and surreal, from an orange-yellow dawn to an empurpled night. Overriding Wagner's directions, he sets Tristan's ship on the diagonal, the better to contrast the captain on deck with Isolde below. The split-screen effect accentuates character development.

Up in the lighting turrets, Roller experiments with colored discs and optical aids, graduating the mood shifts. "When [King] Mark[e] returned to find Isolde in Tristan's arms, it was not the usual idiotic stage dawn that filled the sky but an excruciating greyness that made you shiver," notes the Graz critic Ernst Decsey.[17] Many of the effects, Mahler tells Decsey, are conceived "over cups of black coffee." In rehearsal Mildenburg resists the innovations. Mahler asks Roller to explain things to her at home; Mildenburg takes the taciturn professor to bed and proclaims him a genius.

At seven in the evening on Saturday, February 21, 1903, with nationalists warning of an anti-Wagner "outrage," opera production enters the modern age. "The mysterious delicacy, the lashing impetuosity of the strings, contrasting storm and calm, are controlled by Mahler as perhaps never before." Tristan is sung by tall Erik Schmedes, Isolde by Mildenburg in a Klimt-like costume. Richard Mayr is King Marke; Hermine Kittel sings Brangäne, Isolde's maid. "Breathless stillness draws the eye to the stage. The curtain divides. . . . The music becomes almost visible, grows plastic in its indescribable perfection, as if transported into another world."[18]

After the second act Mahler collapses with a migraine. "If only someone else could take over," he moans. His sister Justi, in a misplaced attempt at Jewish humor, tells Alma, "I had him young, you've got him old."[19] Mahler returns to a sustained ovation, a roar that does not abate until he breaks his rule and takes a personal bow. The opera ends just before midnight. In the morning the Wagnerite Schönaich leads a chorus of praise, endorsing Roller as "a man with a true vocation."[20] The Brahmsian Kalbeck praises the "great graphic harmony," and Julius Korngold the "painted Tristan music."[21] Mahler's aim, says Hermann Bahr, is "to remedy the insufficiencies of a single art, which no longer satisfies our increased dramatic demands, with resources from the other arts."[22] In a century of motorcars and manned flight, of socialism and psychology, the public will no longer accept static, monolithic stagings. Mahler and Roller have achieved Wagner's alliance of the arts.

"My dear Herr Roller," writes Mahler after the premiere,

How you put me to shame! For days I have been wondering how to thank you. . . . And I've come to the conclusion that, instead of trying to put anything into words, I should simply remain silent.—I know we are similar in one respect: in our completely unselfish devotion to art, even if we approach it by different roads. And I was also fully aware that you would not think me unappreciative or undiscerning if I did not try to [express] what you have achieved and what you have come to mean to me. . . . Could you not dine with us on Friday?[23]

They go on to reconfigure *Fidelio, Falstaff, The Flying Dutchman, Lohengrin* and the *Ring*, five Mozart operas, and Gluck's *Iphigénie en Aulide*. In five years at the Vienna Opera, Mahler establishes a benchmark of consistency. In the next five years, with Roller, he creates an aesthetic that places Vienna in the vanguard of modernism. Where Paris embraces abstract art, Vienna drives fusion and fission across all the arts. Klimt, Moll, and Roller quit the Secession as a thing of the past. Hoffmann and Moser found the Wiener Werkstätte.

Arnold Schoenberg breaks through to atonality. Hugo von Hof-
mannsthal versifies Elektra's taboo love; Arthur Schnitzler's text for
Reigen (La Ronde) is banned; Theodor Herzl's early death triggers a
Schnitzler novel, *Der Weg ins Freie*, about a composer facing Viennese
anti-Semitism. All these sparks and more fly out of and around the
Mahler-Roller collaboration.

Roller provides some of the clearest glimpses of Mahler, at work
and at play. "Please don't think I was really angry," he tells the
designer after a rehearsal tantrum, "being fierce is the only weapon I
have for keeping order."24 Roller visits Mahler at the lakeside and
observes him in the nude. "In the course of my profession," he writes,

> I have seen a great many naked bodies of all types and I can testify
> that at the age of forty [-four] Mahler had the perfect male torso,
> strong, slim, beautifully made. . . . His lips were classically shaped
> and their immediate area had that multiplicity of detail which is pro-
> duced by the habit of very carefully articulated speech. They were
> thin and, when he was wearing his customary sober expression, usu-
> ally closed. It was only when he was listening intently that they
> stayed slightly open. But if Mahler was disgruntled, angry or out of
> sorts, he would pull his mouth out of shape, taking half his lower lip
> between his teeth, wrinkling his brow and tightening the folds of his
> nose. Pulled about like this, his face took on such a distorted grimace
> that he really did become "the nasty Mahler."

He defines Mahler as "a combination of robust goodwill and triumph [over] adversity," and he detects "Christ-like" qualities in this
"infinitely modest" Jew. They are as close to each other as two
partners in art can be, sharing the same ideals and, at different times,
the same lover. But art is short and life is long, and when the wind
changes, Roller swears fealty to another leader.

On May 8, 1906, a teenager from Linz cadges a ticket and
squeezes into the standing section to see Mahler conduct *Tristan und
Isolde*. He returns a year later, hoping to study with Roller, but he is
too timid to knock at his door with a letter of introduction. In February 1934 Adolf Hitler summons Roller to his Chancellery to regret
his callow shyness and reminisce about that revelatory *Tristan und*

Isolde, recalling every last detail: "in the second act, the tower to the left, with the pale light."[25] Neither man mentions Mahler, who is being written out of the record. Roller accepts a commission to stage *Parsifal* at Hitler's Bayreuth.

"I DON'T COMPOSE: I AM COMPOSED"[26]

In five summers at Maiernigg, Mahler writes four symphonies, leaving only for a four-day excursion to Toblach in the Dolomites as relief from the "stifling" lakeside heat. Alma finds him at his most "approachable, human and devoted"[27] during these Maiernigg summers. Yet it is amid this idyll of family tranquillity that Mahler writes his bleakest symphony, "the product of a decidedly pessimistic turn of mind."[28]

The Sixth is Mahler's prophetic heart of darkness. It crashes on the ears with a tramp, tramp, tramp of marching armies and rams home its verdict like a hanging judge at a treason trial. Gone are the gaudy, jaunty training marches of his garrison boyhood. These armies threaten the destruction of civilization. Alma calls this work *anticipando musiziert*, seeing the future through music. Mahler feels he is being "raised by inspiration to a higher, anticipatory level of experience."[29]

He marks the opening *allegro energico*, an unstoppable force. The middle sections, a scherzo and andante moderato, are interchangeable. Mahler conducts them in either order, leaving conductors to settle which comes first (see pp. 230–32). In the finale he tinkles pastoral cowbells and crushes them with a road hammer. Three massive blows (at mm 336, 479, and 783, the final one later deleted) toll annihilation: This is the way the world ends, for Mahler, for you, for me, for us all, with a bang, not a whimper.

Mahler is Jeremiah, the prophet of doom. Where others in Vienna—Herzl, Freud, Trotsky—proffer utopias, he sees no hope. In rehearsal at Essen in May 1906 he is seen "sobbing, wringing his hands, unable to control himself."[30] What has come over Mahler that a work of his hands should tip him into such despair?

The clues are in the chronology. He writes three movements in summer 1903, after his *Tristan* triumph. In June 1904, six days after the birth of his second daughter, Anna Justine ("Gucki"), he goes to the lake to finish the symphony, insisting, "I dare not give up any of my summer."[31] Missing his family, he digs a sandpit for the children and frets about water snakes. "I'm pining away,"[32] he tells Alma, who is undergoing a gynecological procedure. He thinks of visiting her, but cannot tear himself away from the work. He worries that she may prefer younger men and remembers how, after their first child was born, she said, "You disgust me."

Alma, in Vienna, has a bad dream. "A large green snake with long legs suddenly forces itself inside me. I pull at its tail. It won't come out. I ring for the chambermaid. She pulls with all her strength. Suddenly she gets hold of it. It slides out with all my inner organs in its mouth. Now I am hollow and empty like a wrecked ship."[33] She knows about Freud and the significance of snakes. She fears she has married only half of Mahler—man and musician, artist and director, Christian and Jew—whose snake is tearing her apart. There are problems in this marriage as Mahler composes the Sixth.

When Alma finally joins him, he leads her ceremonially up to his hut and shows how she is portrayed in a soaring allegro theme and their children in the andante. The deadly hammerblows are, he tells her, for himself, "the last of which fells him as a tree is felled." Both of them weep, "but at the same time he was serene. He was conscious of the greatness of his work. He was a tree in full leaf and flower."

He then plays her the final two death-of-children songs. "Don't!" she shrieks. "Don't tempt Providence!"—or so she claims. Of all the perjuries that Alma commits, this is by some margin the ugliest. She accuses Mahler of endangering their children by anticipating their death, of placing his music above their lives. It is a terrible charge, repeated ad infinitum in concert notes, television documentaries, theater plays, and feature films—Alma's revenge for a thought crime that he does not commit. She does.

Chronology once more reveals the wretched truth. The dates that Alma gives for the incident are skewed. On the page in her memoirs where she accuses him of composing infanticide, she goes on to describe "the two little children tottering in zig-zags over the sand."[34] Maria, at this time, is two years old and Anna newly born. The Sixth Symphony and *Songs on the Death of Children* are finished before he sees children puttering in the sandpit. Nothing is further from his mind than harming his adored daughters.

The one who has murderous feelings toward the children is Alma. Years later, in July 1920, she confesses in her diary:

> As a young woman—very lonely next to the much older husband—I saw . . . Putzi [Maria] . . . at the window pressing her endlessly beautiful dark hair against the glass as Gustav and I drove by below. Gustav gave her a loving wave.
>
> Was that it? I don't know—but suddenly I KNEW: this child must go. . . . At once.
>
> Away with the thought! Away with the accursed thought.

But the child was dead after a few months.[35]

And there lies the terrible trauma behind the worst of Alma's lies. Alma is jealous of Mahler's delight at the little girl. She wishes her dead and, horrified at her own mind, transfers the guilty wish onto her blameless husband. Mahler never contemplates the death of his own children; Alma does. A fame-seeking fabulist, she knows what the world would like to believe and invents a fictional subtext for Mahler's music that clings to him like coral to a reef: sharp, submersed, immovable by bare hands.

THE ELIXIR OF YOUTH

His power at the Opera reaches the point where he is able to take time off to fulfill a growing demand to hear his contentious symphonies. In October 1903 he conducts a week of concerts with Mengelberg's orchestra, at the Concertgebouw in Amsterdam. The Dutch demand to hear his Fourth Symphony twice, before the intermission and after, the better to appreciate it. "I know of a musical city where I am completely understood—by the conductor by the orchestra, by the public: Amsterdam,"[36] exults Mahler. In 1904–5 he travels to Heidelberg, Mannheim, Prague, Cologne, and Leipzig with his Third Symphony; Mainz with his Fourth; Cologne, Hamburg, Trieste, and Breslau with his Fifth.

The absences mount up. There is a jaunt with Alma in May 1905 to Strasbourg, capital of German-occupied Alsace-Lorraine, where Mahler gives his Fifth Symphony in the first half of a concert, and Strauss his *Symphonia Domestica* in the second. Walking down a shopping street, they enter a piano showroom, where Strauss plays selections from *Salome*, his opera of Herodian sadism and sexual perversion. Mahler, captivated by post-Wagner sonorities and para-Freudian taboos, declares that Strauss has made "the unbelievable believable" and promises to stage the work in Vienna. He then dines with Dreyfusards—Picquart, Painlevé, Paul and Sophie Clemenceau, and their friend Gen. Guillaume de Lallemand. Georges Clemenceau can't make it to Strasbourg. He is plotting to become prime minister.

Back home, Alma tires of Mahler's admirers and seeks company her own age: "I must begin another life, I can't bear this one any longer. . . . My dissatisfaction grows hour by hour. What a misfortune not to have any friends. . . . If only Hans Pfitzner lived in Vienna. If only I had the right to see Zemlinsky! Schoenberg interests me too. I've been thinking a lot. . . . It must all change."[37] Mahler responds quickly to her simmering discontent. "Dear Herr von Zemlinsky [he writes], Won't you drop by some time? We should discuss our project face to face. Would you care to have coffee with us this afternoon? If so, come around two. . . . Possibly with Schoenberg."[38]

The project is a premiere of Mahler's songs by the Association of Creative Musicians Zemlinsky has founded with Arnold Schoenberg, his bald-headed brother-in-law, composer of a scandalous sextet. In *Verklärte Nacht (Transfigured Night)*, a woman tells her lover she is pregnant after casual sex with a stranger. Schoenberg, like most young men, has sex on his mind most of the time—but in a clinical way, searching for a music that can convey its extreme dimensions. He scorns Mahler as a nineteenth-century composer, a dinosaur. "He could not do much with his first symphony, why should I bother with his fourth?" is Schoenberg's response to a concert invitation.

Over coffee Zemlinsky is muted, not wanting to seem as if he is after a job at the Opera (which he is). Schoenberg, sloppily dressed, is confrontational. He declares tonality to be on its last legs. Mahler demurs. Schoenberg interrupts his counterargument. Voices are raised and Schoenberg rushes out into the Auenbruggergasse shouting, "I shall never set foot in there again!" Mahler tells Alma: "I don't want to see that conceited pup in my house."

But within a fortnight he is asking, "Why don't those two young fellows come by anymore?" He finds *Transfigured Night* "bold, interesting and significant" when played by the Rosé Quartet, and advises Schoenberg to make a version for string orchestra that might be more widely performed. Knowing the headstrong radical is married, penniless, and dependent on private pupils, Mahler helps him out with discreet sums of money. He can hear him pushing against the limits of tonality and is intrigued to see where Schoenberg might be taking the music of the future. Schoenberg, for his part, finds a searing honesty in Mahler's music.

My dear Director [he writes in December 1904]

I must not speak as musician to musician but as one human being to another if I am to convey the incredible impression made on me by your (third) symphony. The thing is, I saw your very soul, naked, stark naked. It was laid out before me like a wild, mysterious landscape, full of frightening chasms and abysses, and beside them, serene and smiling, sunlit meadows, havens of rest. . . . I believe I felt your symphony, I shared the battle against illusions, ached with the pain of disillusionment. I saw the forces of good wrestling with evil; I saw a man in torment, struggling for inner peace; I felt a personality, a drama, *truth*, the most uncompromising truthfulness!

I had to get this off my chest, forgive me. I cannot feel by halves. With me it is either one thing, or the other.

Devotedly, Arnold Schoenberg[39]

By this process of mutual appreciation, and through Alma's insistence, Mahler becomes a patron of the "new music," a beacon of the avant-garde. Art is renewing itself ever faster. In Paris, Gauguin and

Rodin are yesterday's men, overtaken by Pablo Picasso, Blue and Cubist. Klimt in Vienna is under attack from the simplifying zeal of Otto Loos and the furies of Oskar Kokoschka. Alma puts Mahler at the crest of the new wave, the heartbeat of her generation.

The Seventh Symphony is finished in summer 1905, built around two interludes of "Night Music," evocative of the countryside in darkness. The work appears to look backward, sharing a bucolic atmosphere with the Third Symphony and an opening phrase with the Fifth, its raps at the door reduced to ironic susurration. Like the Fifth it has five movements, hinged on a middle Scherzo of escalating drama that Mahler marks "wild" and, enigmatically (in a sketch at New York Public Library), *Belfast*.[40] Dabs of color from a guitar and mandolin are splashed in the second interlude. The finale is fast and eclectic, with mocking references to Franz Lehár's operetta *The Merry Widow*, the Lutheran hymn "Eine Feste Burg," and Mahler's own Second, Third, and Fourth Symphonies. It could well be read as a commentary on his past works, abstruse and, for all its fanfares, self-absorbed.

On August 15 he informs Guido Adler in schoolboy Latin: "Lieber Freund! Septima mea finita est. Credo hoc opus fauste natum et bene gestum. Salutationes plurimas tibi et tuis etam meae uxoris. G. M. [Dear Friend! My Seventh is finished. I believe it is well conceived and favourably born. Best regards to you and your wife from me and mine]."[41] Then he shoves the score into a safe for three years. Bruno Walter dislikes it. Adler responds with a dusty academic analysis. Only one musician grasps the work at first hearing. "I am now really and entirely yours," declares Arnold Schoenberg:

Which movement did I like the best? Each one! I can make no distinction. Perhaps I was somewhat hesitant at the beginning of the first movement. But in any case only for a short time. And from then on I grew warmer and warmer. From one minute to the next I felt better and better. And there was not a moment's relapse. I was in tune to the very end. And it was all so transparently clear to me. In short, at a first hearing I felt so many subtleties of form, and yet could follow a main line throughout.[42]

Unfathomable to the conservative Walter yet "transparently clear" to Schoenberg, the symphony becomes a sourcebook for modernists. Schoenberg's first atonal full score, *Five Orchestral Pieces* (1909), takes the pentagram form of Mahler's Seventh. His twelve-tone *Serenade*, op. 24 (1924), employs guitar and mandolin; the Second Chamber Symphony of 1938 contains a quotation from Mahler's "Night Music." There is a mysterious transaction at work: Either Schoenberg is imitating Mahler, or Mahler has anticipated several landmarks of the post-tonal sound world.

Schoenberg's pupil Alban Berg segments each act of his opera *Wozzeck* (1925) into five Mahlerian movements, using guitar and two retuned fiddles. Anton Webern, using mandolin and guitar in *Three Orchestral Songs* (1913), calls Mahler's "Night Music" "nothing but love, love, love."[43] Schoenberg, ferocious in his convictions, will fire a rocket in 1949 at the music editor of the *New York Times*, Olin Downes, berating him for a disrespectful remark about Mahler's Seventh Symphony. "One who writes as unfoundedly about Mahler, will certainly also be wrong about Schoenberg," rages the dying revolutionary. "If you would study the orchestral score you could not overlook the beauty of this writing. Such beauty is only given to men who deserve it."[44] For Schoenberg, as for Mahler, music is a reward for the righteous.

BRING ME THE HEAD OF THAT MAN ON A PLATE

Alma is sexually restless. Hans Pfitzner, in Vienna for his opera *Die Rose vom Liebesgarten*, makes a pass at her. "We were alone in the sitting room. I was pleased. I felt my skin prickling as it hasn't done for a long time." On a solitary stroll she finds, "with longing and satisfaction," that a young man is trailing her. She tells Mahler, who is "grumpy and terse . . . deep down, we've become strangers to one another."[45] Mahler, when he visits her for love, is brusque and perfunctory.[46] Afterward he is silent. When she asks what's wrong he says, "Read the *Kreutzer Sonata*"—Tolstoy's novella of marital breakdown. She tells her diary: "With Gustav I often can't find anything to talk about. I know in advance every word he's going to say. The last weeks have been so murderously hot I haven't felt like doing anything. I could long for a man—*for I haven't got one*—but I am too lazy even for that."[47]

Disconsolate, Mahler intensifies his musical friendships. A Berlin conductor, Oskar Fried, is detained for the day for a wide-ranging conversation; his assistant, Otto Klemperer, becomes the last of Mahler's acolytes. Fried and Mahler chat

> like two old friends to whom nothing is worse and more banal than wasting time and showing off. . . . He was a God-seeker. . . . He saw himself bearing a sacred trust. It suffused his whole being. . . . But from time to time he would doubt this heavenly mission and worry momentarily whether he had the ability to carry it through. . . . In such moments he needed . . . a servant, a disciple on whom he could test the reality and validity of his religious mission.[48]

Fried, ahead of Freud, zones in on Mahler's need—his acute neediness—for intellectual stimulus, emotional support, and spiritual affirmation, none of which are fulfilled by a fickle wife and a repetitive job at the Opera.

Strauss's *Salome* rekindles his enthusiasm for new work. In eight years Mahler has introduced some twenty operas to Vienna, none of them epoch making:

Smetana's *Dalibor*
Tchaikovsky's *Eugene Onegin* and *Pique Dame*
Bizet's *Djamileh*
both *Bohème*s (Leoncavallo's and Puccini's)
Charpentier's *Louise*
Rezniček's *Donna Diana*
Goldmark's *Prisoner of War*
Siegfried Wagner's *Bärenhäuter*
Rubinstein's *Demon*
Zemlinsky's *Once Upon a Time*
Strauss's *Feuersnot*

Pfitzner's *Rose vom Liebesgarten*
Wolf's *Corregidor*
Delibes' *Lakmé*
Wolf-Ferrari's *The Curious Women*

His single great omission is the gritty Czech realism of *Jenufa*, by Leoš Janáček, which Mahler refuses to consider without a German text. *Salome*, on the other hand, makes a blazing, edgy noise and violates sexual and religious taboos. "It's your best, so far," he tells Strauss. "Every note is right!"[49] He agrees with the censor to change some biblical names—Jochanan to Bal Hanaan, for instance—but press leaks arouse a blasphemy furor, and the opera is banned. "These accursed newspaper hacks (heaven knows who they got the story from, I told no-one) have completely spoiled things again,"[50] he tells Strauss. The hacks, for their part, blast Mahler. "He is being hounded, hounded, hounded," writes Hermann Bahr. "Why do they hate him so?"[51]

After its premiere in Dresden on December 9, 1905, where the soprano Maria Wittich refuses to strip in the Dance of the Seven Veils and is replaced by a ballerina, *Salome* is staged in Graz the following May. Mahler has a picnic on performance day with Alma, Pauline, and Strauss and joins an audience that is reputed to have included Schoenberg, Puccini, and Hitler. Much has been made of that night in Graz as a seminal moment, an event that (in the words of *The New Yorker* critic Alex Ross) "illuminated a musical world on the verge of traumatic change."[52] But *Salome* in Graz is no breakthrough, and Strauss is no revolutionary. After his next opera, *Elektra*, he reverts to stroking bourgeois ears with *Der Rosenkavalier*. Strauss is preparing to forsake shocking novelty, while Mahler craves it ever more.

Ten days after *Salome*, he conducts his Sixth Symphony in the industrially blackened Ruhr town of Essen. Strauss calls it "overinstrumented,"[53] reducing Mahler to tears. In a press interview he lashes back, describing Strauss as a populist and himself as an idealist. "I am, in Nietzsche's expression, 'a man not of his own time.' . . . The timely one is Strauss. That is why he can enjoy immortality while he is still alive."[54]

By the time he reaches his summer hideaway he is completely drained. Then, "on the first morning, I went up to my shack resolved to take it easy (for I was in dire need of rest). . . . As I entered that all-too-familiar room, the Creator Spiritus took possession of me."[55] In eight weeks he composes the gargantuan Eighth Symphony.

It is a work in two halves, the first an eighth-century Pentecost hymn, "Veni Creator Spiritus," and the second the closing scenes of Goethe's *Faust*. The two sections are held apart, rather than conjoined, by an interlude of instrumental balm (a device taken up by Benjamin Britten in the "Sea Interludes" of his isolationist opera, *Peter Grimes*). For reasons beyond reason, Mahler equips the work with the biggest force ever gathered in a symphony hall—huge orchestra, two adult choruses and a boys' choir, seven vocal soloists—a symphony of one thousand performers. The acutely practical musician seems to be making his symphony unperformable—unless he has simply become lost to the world, detached from its inhibiting realities.

Mahler relates that he writes the symphony "as if it were dictated to me,"[56] that he "surrendered himself" to a celestial message. One incident illustrates his illusion of predestination. While composing the "Veni" hymn he writes more music than words, "like water spilling over a full basin."[57] Frantically he writes to the classicist Fritz Löhr, begging for an authentic text. "Please reply *at once, express*! Otherwise it will be too late. I need it both as Creator and creatus [created]!"[58] Löhr's early edition contains a lost verse that exactly matches the extra music he has written.

Safe in its tonal relations, the Eighth Symphony is remarkable chiefly for its gigantism. But beneath the roar of voices, the orchestral music—I attended Klaus Tennstedt's rehearsals in 1991—is a synoptic synthesis of Mahler's first seven symphonies, a summary of his life in music, a closure of sorts. "It makes all my other works seem like preparatory efforts," he tells the writer Richard Specht, in Salzburg.[59] In fact it draws a line under Mahler's past. He has nowhere obvious to go.

Mahler is in Salzburg to conduct *Marriage of Figaro* in Mozart's 150th birthday year. Walking past the Hotel Bristol, he sees Roller sitting at a table with the critic Korngold and leaps through an open window to join them. Korngold has brought his son, Erich Wolf-gang, who wants to be a composer. "A genius!" cries Mahler (accord-ing to his father). "Take him to Zemlinsky . . . he will learn all he needs."[60] Erich, nine at the time, will become Hollywood's most suc-cessful sound tracker. Zemlinsky is about to join Mahler as third conductor at the Court Opera. His latest work, *Der Traumgörge (Görge the Dreamer)*, depicts Alma as the Dream Princess and quotes Mahler's theme song, "I Am Lost to the World," in its opening chords.

Mahler opens his tenth season at the Opera with a week of unpar-alleled intensity. The Dreyfusards are in town, and Mahler tells them, "I'll make a secret festival . . . no one except us will know."[61] He conducts *Fidelio, Figaro, Abduction from the Seraglio,* and *Magic Flute.* Picquart relates how, "tortured and dishonoured" in jail, he swore he would one day see Gustav Mahler conduct Wagner's *Tristan und Isolde* in Vienna.

On the night of *Tristan* he is mounting the grand staircase at the Opera when Berta Zuckerkandl rushes up with a telegram from Paris: "Please tell General Picquart that I have made him Minister for War. He must return tonight. Clemenceau." The lion of the Dreyfus case is being asked to purge the French army of its crime. Berta expects him to rejoice. Picquart, however, is enraged. "You should have kept this from me until morning," he scolds her. "A real friend would not have hurt me so deeply." He stays for the first act of *Tris-tan,* thanking Mahler "for the rare artistic treat."[62]

THE PAINTER'S REVENGE

In the hallway of my house hangs a canvas copy of a late portrait by R. B. Kitaj. It is an unusual Kitaj, a side-on head shot of Gustav Mahler, copied from a photograph and augmented by scarlike fur-rows that run from the edge of the left eyebrow up into the receding black hair. The furrows form a K, the artist's initial. Kitaj always said a painting had to mean more than what you see at first glance.

I got to know him while he was working on the portrait, his Chelsea studio stacked with packing cases, ready for his return to America. "The School of London is now closed,"[63] said Kitaj, winding up the group he formed with Francis Bacon, David Hockney, Lucian Freud, Frank Auerbach, Leon Kossoff, and Howard Hodgkin. His reason for leaving was a mauling by British critics of his 1993 Tate exhibition, an onslaught on which he blamed the death soon after of his wife, Sandra Fisher, from a brain aneurysm. What the critics hated was Kitaj's lines of comment and explanation on his paintings. Kitaj accused them of anti-Semitism. "Was it a coincidence that I was the only Jew who put the Jewish drama at the heart of my paintings?" he demanded. "Was it a coincidence that I was the only exegete among painters?"[64]

"You've caught me at a terrible moment," he said when I turned up to talk about Mahler. "I really didn't welcome intrusions this past year. But Mahler I couldn't refuse." He had felt a kinship with Mahler since he studied in 1950s Vienna, seeing hatred in the eyes of his landlady, his tutors, the shopkeepers. "The streets I walked on I could have been hauled off just a few years before," he said. Kitaj equated anti-Semitism with antimodernism. "Jewish brilliance," he said, "made the modern world." Jews like Mahler and Kitaj were agents of change, architects of human unease.

His Mahler portrait would be hung ceremonially in an intermission hall of the Vienna Opera. At the unveiling there were sniffs of disapprobation—not at the likeness of Mahler, which was inoffensive, but at the Attersee backdrop, which Kitaj painted in weird colors, a dark blue mountainside, pink-and-yellow lake, a pitch-black conifer and its shadow falling bloodred onto the water. Why? I asked. Kitaj shrugged. Art is art, and color is just shades. Each of us sees Mahler in a different light, he seemed to be suggesting. Each of us makes the Mahler he deserves. A fierce, warm man and a passionate friend and father, Kitaj took his twelve-year-old son, Max, home to California that winter. He died there in October 2007, by his own hand.

10. Three Hammerblows (1907)

The end comes out of an ice blue sky. On New Year's Day 1907 the racist *Deutsche Volksblatt* attacks Mahler for releasing the singers Hermann Winkelmann and Sophie Sedlmair and raising ticket prices. Other papers run follow-ups, and the *Extrablatt* notes that the director is off again to conduct his symphonies in Berlin, Frankfurt, and Linz. Before he leaves, Mahler's Sixth Symphony is received with stridently unpleasant reviews. Hirschfeld writes that Mahler lacks "true inner creative strength." Kalbeck calls him "a prosaic noise-maker," and Korngold rates the symphony his weakest. As soon as he is gone *Die Zeit* runs a full-page cartoon, captioned: "Director Mahler is unavailable."

Prince Montenuovo, disturbed by press unrest, orders Mahler home, but he finishes the tour, telling Alma, "I am pursued by a pack of dogs. But I'm not the person to give up half way. . . . When my suit gets splashed with ordure, I brush it off. . . . Just as well we've got 50,000 and an annual pension of 5,000 to fall back on. It's time to tighten our belts."[1] It reads as if he can see what is coming.

"Mahler's neurotic regime has brought disorder," cries the *Extrablatt* on his return. "Is Herr Mahler Tired of His Job?" asks the socialist paper. Mahler asks Montenuovo for a statement of confidence. The prince tells him to silence rumors the way he does best—with a stupendous performance. Mahler conducts Roller's staging of *Die Walküre*, dark and slow paced, its tenebrous shades adding numinous depth. Mildenburg, Schmedes, the baritone Friedrich Weidemann, and Förster-Lauterer are outstanding. Hirschfeld calls the production "an inspired improvisation"; Kalbeck hails it as a climactic event.

On February 5 Mahler attends the Rosé Quartet's premiere of Schoenberg's String Quartet, op. 7, a work that runs forty-five minutes without a break or the relief of a catchy tune. Some listeners object, whistling into their front-door keys. "How dare you whistle while I'm applauding?" shouts Mahler. "I whistled at your filthy symphony, too!" cries a heckler. "I'll box your ears," says Mahler. He is pulled away. Three days later, during Schoenberg's *Chamber Symphony*, Mahler tells restless audience members to shut up. At the end he applauds long and hard. "I don't understand his music," says Mahler, "but he's young and maybe he's right." That night Guido Adler warns Alma that "Gustav made a spectacle of himself today. . . . This could cost him his job."[2]

Roller excels himself in Gluck's *Iphigénie en Aulide,* outfitting the chorus in white tunics and black wigs against a yellow set. Mildenburg is a vengeful Clytemnestra, Gutheil-Schoder a delicate Iphigénie, Schmedes a leonine Achilles. "I have put everything I am and everything I am capable of into *Iphigénie,*" says Mahler. "It is my final confession." Emil Zuckerkandl finds him on the morning of the premiere staring at a billboard. "I can't take my eyes off the poster," exclaims Mahler. "I can't believe that . . . this very evening these singers and this orchestra will be taking their cue from me. It makes me so happy!"[3] The anatomist tells his wife that, at this moment, there is "something holy" about Mahler.

But more trouble is brewing. For Auber's opera, *The Mute Girl of Portici,* Roller hires a guest dancer, Grete Wiesenthal. The balletmaster, Josef Hassreiter, protests. Montenuovo reprimands Mahler, his second rebuke in a month. Someone tells the lord chamberlain that Mahler will be in Rome the day after Easter, when he ought to be in Vienna. Montenuovo summons Mahler again to tell him that his absences are unacceptable. Mahler, incensed, offers to resign. Montenuovo, used to defusing such threats, tells him to prepare severance terms. Mahler strolls among Roman ruins with Alma and conducts the Orchestra of Saint Cecilia. Their luggage gets lost in transit, and he performs in borrowed clothes. On his return he finds that Montenuovo has reinstated an aged tenor he dismissed. Meyer-beer's *Prophète* is almost canceled for a shortage of singers. The press, sniffing blood, turns isolated incidents into a running crisis. "One called them 'affairs,' " explains Julius Korngold, "which gave the flimsiest event a semblance of importance. One manufactured 'affairs' and threw up one's hands in indignation over one's own product."[4]

Korngold, interviewing Mahler, finds him "alive and vital, [doing] his work as if he were going to be director for the next fifty years." He announces a bold season for 1907–8 with Debussy's *Pelléas et Mélisande*, Goldmark's *A Winter's Tale*, and Zemlinsky's *Traumgörge*. But one day he hauls Walter out of rehearsal and, walking down the Ringstrasse, tells him: "In ten years at the Opera I have completed my circle."[5] In the last week of May, eminences led by Schnitzler, Klimt, Bahr, Hoffmann, and the piano maker Ludwig Bösendorfer sign a tenth-anniversary tribute to Mahler. "If I want to stay on my seat, all I have to do is sit back," says Mahler. "But I am not offering resistance and will end up sliding off."[6]

Lilli Lehmann, a veteran of the 1876 Bayreuth *Ring*, finds Mahler during the second interval of *Tristan* "taking some tea and talking animatedly with at least thirty other persons." A stage manager pokes his head around the door of his dressing room to report that Schmedes is losing his voice. Mahler cuts some of his lines. The official returns, saying that Mildenburg, in sympathy, cannot sing. "Mahler exploded from his calm like a jumping devil out of a box, hopped about the room as though possessed." Lehmann, fifty-eight years old and long out of the role, offers to stand in. Mahler, tears of gratitude in his eyes, says: "You may fetch me out of my grave if you ever need me, Lilli, and I will conduct anything where and what you like."[7]

As the season ends and asparagus blooms in lunchtime cafés, Mahler goes to Berlin to see a man from the Met, Heinrich Conried by name. New York is at war, divas drawn. Oscar Hammerstein, a cigar oligarch, has signed Nellie Melba and Luisa Tetrazzini for his Manhattan Opera Company. The Metropolitan Opera holds on to Caruso, but it needs a big conductor to boost public confidence. Conried, an Austrian Jew, manages the Met on behalf of its stock-holders and is Caruso's personal agent. Slippery and philistine, he is the kind of employer Mahler abhors, but Conried needs a maestro and Mahler needs a well-paid job.

All winter Conried has been tempting him with "the highest fee a musician has ever received"—125,000 crowns ($75,000) for six months' work, four times his Vienna salary. Messages are shuttled through a middleman, the Opera costumier Rudolf Winternitz. By the time Mahler meets Conried in Berlin, the fee is fixed at $15,000 a month, and all that remains to discuss is the details. Mahler, exhausted, does not want to work more than two nights a week. Conried, a stroke victim who gets around on canes, demands three. They part without agreement. Fearing he has lost the job, Mahler cables Conried on his way home: "I shall prove to you in America that I am placing my ability and my whole being at your disposal." Conried tells the *New York Sun* that he has just signed "Europe's most famous conductor." Mahler contacts Hammerstein to see if he can get a better deal.

His resignation is confirmed in a newspaper interview with Karpath. "I have not been overthrown," says Mahler. "I am leaving of my own free will because I want to have full independence. Also, *and this is the main reason,* because I have come to realize that opera, of its very nature, is an institution that cannot be maintained indefinitely at the same high level."[8] Karpath, after talking to Mahler, runs errands for Montenuovo to Felix Mottl, the first-choice successor. But Mottl cannot get released from Munich, and Montenuovo makes a final bid to persuade Mahler to stay. With a satisfied grin, Mahler quotes back to the prince his own statement that "he had no use for a director who spent his time on concert tours, promoting his own music." They agree, with dignity, that his time is up.

Much ink has been spilled over the reasons for Mahler's departure, and the press is widely held to blame for an anti-Semitic "campaign." My own day-by-day reading of the Viennese newspapers in the first half of 1907 shows, to an editor's eye, no sign of a witch hunt. What one reads is an outbreak of why-oh-why journalism in a dull news period. The papers feed off one another's stories but there is no competitive zeal to topple a faltering leader, and the anti-Semitism is no different from before: There is no "spike" in Mahler's last six months.

Mahler himself gives the reason for his departure, a reason that is inconvenient for opera fans and has therefore been downplayed. Put simply, he has lost his faith in the improvability of opera. Korngold, in an unpublished typescript, quotes him as follows: "If I felt like leaving my post it is (1) not the fault of the naughty journalists (though I leave them without regret), (2) not 'that I want to devote myself to composition' (I am always ready if composition will devote itself to me)—but only the realization that the theater in its present form is an inartistic institution and that all conflicts that develop for a person (like me) develop from its very character. For this reason, I could blame no one . . . not even myself."[9] He is leaving because he can do no more. In a manner rare and exemplary among chief executives, he has taken a long, hard look at his work and found himself wanting. He has nothing more to give, so he quits. Few in his profession will ever show such clarity and courage.

On June 21, witnessed by Roller and Winternitz,[10] he signs a contract with the Met. His child Anna has scarlet fever, so he spends the last nights of the season sleeping at the Imperial Hotel. Then he takes a train to Maiernigg, sharing a carriage with Anna von Mildenburg and the last of her lovers, the all-purpose Hermann Bahr.

ONE BLOW AFTER ANOTHER

Alma and the girls have gone ahead. He arrives, on the last night in June, to hear that Maria, five years old, is out of sorts. On the third day they call the district doctor, Carl Viktor Blumenthal. He diagnoses scarlet fever with the dreaded complication of diphtheria, a disease that clogs up the respiratory system until the patient suffocates. Maria is too infectious to be admitted to the hospital. Treatment, limited and ineffectual, is attempted at home.

Mahler runs in and out of the little girl's room, taking "leave of her in his heart."[11] Three days after Mahler's forty-seventh birthday, the child cannot breathe. Alma and the English nanny, Miss Turner, lift her onto a table, where, under general anesthetic, Blumenthal performs an emergency tracheotomy, opening an airhole into the child's windpipe above the collarbone. Mahler is confined to his room. Alma runs along the lake, shrieking with grief and fear. At five in the morning, the doctor is finished. The child survives, fighting for breath, living another day. "Mahler, weeping and sobbing, went again and again to the door of my bedroom, where she was; then fled away to be out of earshot of any sound. It was more than he could bear," writes Alma. On the morning of July 12 Maria, known as Putzi, dies.

"We telegraphed to my mother, who came at once," records Alma. "We all three slept in his room. We could not bear being parted for an hour. We dreaded what might happen if any one of us left the room. We were like birds in a storm and feared what each moment might bring—and how right we were!"[12] Alma's harrowing account, written thirty years later, depicts Mahler as peripheral and useless. "He fled: he could not bear to hear the death-rattle."[13] This may be true—he evaded his mother's death and Otto's—but these are different circumstances, and he is a different man. Nothing is so devastating to a parent as a child's torment. The injustice of it affronts belief and undermines relationships. It attacks the intellect and all emotions. No parent is left unchanged by a child's illness. Mahler, haunted from boyhood by child deaths, faces as a father the most terrible of losses. It is hard to believe that he does nothing other than weep and flee, the more so since he comports himself with great responsibility in the next stages of the darkening saga. It is Alma who blanks out, huddled with her mother and husband, oblivious to her younger child, Anna, who is left to believe she carried the germ that killed her sister.[14] Alma's grief is real and wrenching, but her response is to transfer her guilty feelings onto Mahler and little Anna.

An avuncular cousin of Alma's, the neurologist Richard Nepallek, arrives from Vienna to deal with formalities. Temporary burial is arranged in the parish churchyard. On the funeral morning, Mahler sends Alma and her mother for a walk by the lake. Anna Moll, who has a heart condition,[15] complains of palpitations. Alma, dipping a handkerchief in the water to make a cold compress, looks up the hill and sees Mahler, his face contorted with distress as the coffin is loaded onto the hearse—the sight he has tried to prevent her from seeing. She gives a cry and falls down in a faint.

Dr. Blumenthal is called out again. He examines Alma and, diagnosing "extreme exhaustion of the heart," prescribes complete rest. Mahler, trying to lighten the atmosphere, makes a little joke and says, "Come along, doctor, wouldn't you like to examine me, too?" He lies down on the sofa, and Blumenthal, kneeling beside him, puts a stethoscope to his chest. "Well, your heart is nothing to be proud of," he says, rising with what Alma describes as the mock cheerfulness that doctors adopt when they deliver bad news. Mahler, says Blumenthal, is suffering from a severe cardiac insufficiency. He could drop dead at any moment. There is a shocked silence. This, writes Alma, is "the beginning of the end for Mahler."[16]

Nepallek bundles Mahler onto the Vienna train and takes him to Friedrich Kovacs, chief cardiologist at a major city hospital. Professor Kovacs confirms a contraction of the mitral valve on the left side of Mahler's heart. The heart is damaged, either from birth or—more likely—from early rheumatic fever, the condition that killed Ernst. Stenosis, a narrowing of the valve, and mitral incompetence, a leakage from it, is his diagnosis. Mahler is at risk from infections of the mouth and throat, which can bring on valve failure. Even brushing his teeth can yield fatal results. Kovacs restricts him to short walks at a gentle pace, a semi-invalid existence. He must give up hiking and swimming and reduce the efforts he makes in conducting. This is bad science, though the best available. A century later Mahler would have been advised to adopt a healthy diet and exercise regime, and the damaged valve could be repaired surgically.

"Mahler did as he was told," writes Alma. "Watch in hand, he accustomed himself to walking and forgot the life he had lived up to that fatal hour."[17] He resumes their vacation in the Dolomites, beside the Toblach lake. "Our suffering drove us apart," writes Alma. Mahler reads a book of Chinese poems given to him by Theobald Pollak, a Jewish friend of Alma's father, a senior official in the state railways. (This was thought to be a proof copy of Hans Bethge's translation, published October 1907. But a newly deciphered note in Alma's diary shows that he reads Hans Heilmann's text, given him by Pollak in July 1905.[18])

In the third week of August, Mahler, still director, goes back to the Court Opera while Alma shuts up Maiernigg and leaves the keys with an agent, never to return. There is smallpox in Vienna. Going for his jab, Mahler asks the doctor for an opinion on valvular deficiency and is told not to worry. "He said I could most certainly follow my profession and I should live an absolutely *normal* life except that I should avoid *over-exerting* myself. The strange thing is that he actually said the same as Blumenthal, but his whole manner had something comforting about it. I have lost my fear of conducting."[19] He forgets to buy Alma a present for her twenty-seventh birthday.

An hour before dawn the full moon squats on the lake like a sunken life buoy, fat and vaguely comical. I stare across the Wörthersee, thinking that this is the hour Mahler used to rise, pulling on woolen clothes and thick boots in midsummer to climb through the woods to his composing warren. My side of the lake is thick with tourists. His side, forested and forbidding, has been taken over by politicians, bankers, and German film stars. A television soap opera, *Ein Schloss am Wörthersee*, accentuates the snob distinction. Mahler's house juts out on a slight promontory.

On my first visit my guide was a Nazi hotelier who had spent time in South America. He asked me why the Allies had not linked arms with Hitler to defeat Communism. Politically the region was poison. Many Carinthians yearned for the promises that Hitler made, and the state governor, Jörg Haider, was a charismatic racist of the Karl Lueger kind who died in a high-speed car crash in October 2008. The lovely Wörthersee is pleasure island, nonjudgmental, never look back.

Our friends Annina and Felix drive us around the lake and up a hill road to the forest entrance, where, deep within, Mahler wrote four symphonies and songs on the death of children. The composing cabin has been whitewashed on the inside, its walls hung with photographs and facsimiles of Mahler's creative occupancy. One exhibit catches my eye, a snapshot of the dedicated Blumenthal, country doctor. "What ever became of him?" I ask.

"His son taught me German literature at school," says Felix.

"Good teacher?"

"He was banned after the war. The usual reasons."

SLIPPING AWAY

In September, Felix von Weingartner becomes director of the Vienna Opera, and Mahler is free to leave. One by one he conducts all his favorite operas—*Don Giovanni, Figaro, Magic Flute, Walküre,* and *Iphigénie en Aulide*—to low attendances. His time is past. On October 15, ten years to the day since he became director, he conducts a last *Fidelio* and, with its closing chorus, "Never can we over-praise / the saviour of her husband's life," pockets his baton, and leaves the pit.

He has two concerts to give in Russia and one in Finland. In St. Petersburg he sleeps in his honeymoon suite and dines with the pianist Ossip Gabrilowitsch, who lusts after the absent Alma. In Helsinki the painter Axel Gallen-Kallela takes him on a boat around the archipelago, a three-hour trip in icy autumnal winds. They pull in at a cove where, in firelight, Gallen-Kallela paints a contemplative portrait of Mahler, one finger supporting his cheek, eyes shut, glasses glistening. Jean Sibelius takes him for a walk. Although Mahler calls his *Spring Song* "a standard piece of kitsch served with nordic harmonies as a national dish," he finds the Finn "extremely sympathetic."[20] They discuss the future of the symphony. Sibelius, who has finished his Third, extols structural severity. Mahler disagrees: "No, the symphony must be like the world. It must embrace everything."[21] For the next century composers will split between those who prioritize technical immaculacy and clarity of form (Stravinsky, Debussy, Bartók, Boulez) and those who try to reflect the whole messy world in a genre of expanding relevance (Berg, Prokofiev, Shostakovich, Schnittke). At a crossroads on their walk, Mahler and Sibelius have defined the symphonic dichotomy.

He has three farewells to perform in Vienna. In the foyer of the Opera, Secession photographer Moritz Nähr is set up to take his portrait. Mahler, bristling, never looks at him. Only in the last of eight exposures, glancing left, does he pay attention. The portraits are commonly held to represent Mahler at the peak of his power. As the lens clicks, he longs to be elsewhere.

Franz Schalk, whom he has treated badly, offers him a concert with the Vienna Philharmonic. Grumbling that the players are his enemies, Mahler cannot resist a last-ditch *Resurrection*. The hall is packed, the atmosphere electric. Alban Berg writes to his fiancée: "My darling, I have been unfaithful to you. . . . In the finale of the Mahler symphony I felt a sensation of complete solitude, as if in all the world there was nothing left but this music—and me listening to it."[22] Berg learns what it means to be lost to the world.

At the artists' entrance of the Opera, Mahler posts a final directive. "The hour has come to end our work together," he writes:

> I leave this place of work which has meant so much to me and I bid you all farewell. Instead of the whole, the complete creation that I dreamt of, I leave behind something fragmented and imperfect—as man is fated to do. It is not for me to judge the value of my work . . . but at this moment I am entitled to say of myself: I was honest in my intentions and I set my sights high. . . .
>
> In the press of battle, the heat of the moment, there have been wounds and errors on both sides, yours and mine. But when a work succeeded, when a task was accomplished, we forgot all troubles and sorrows and felt richly rewarded. . . .
>
> Vienna, 7 December 1907   Gustav Mahler

The letter is ripped off the notice board during the night and left shredded on the floor. "I am aware that what I leave behind is bits and pieces," Mahler tells Emil Zuckerkandl. "Dear friend," says the anatomist, "you achieved what no-one else did—and only by refusing to compromise."[23]

Three Schoenberg pupils and the critic Paul Stefan circulate a private invitation:

> The admirers of Gustav Mahler will gather to take leave of him on Monday 9 December before 8.30 a.m. on the platform of the Westbahnhof. . . . Since this demonstration is intended to surprise Mahler, it is vital that no one connected with the Press should be informed.

Two hundred people turn out on a gray winter's morning. Pollak, the railway official, ushers them onto the platform. Rosé's quartet is there, Schoenberg with his pupils, Zemlinsky, Roller, a few Philharmonic players. Mahler moves among them, shaking hands, exchanging words. Alban Berg presents his fiancée, Helene, who picks up a glove that Mahler drops. He rewards her with a look so gentle that she remembers it to the end of her days. Mahler and Alma board the train. The guard blows his whistle, and the engine starts to puff. As the train disappears around a bend in the line, Gustav Klimt has the last word. "Vorbei," he says: It's over.

And so it was. Weingartner demolished Mahler's legacy with a vengeance. He cut chunks out of operas, mangled Roller's sets, and got rid of Mahler allies. In two and a half years he restored *Schlamperei*. After Weingartner, directors, more or less rigorous, came and went—Richard Strauss (1919–24, with Schalk), Clemens Krauss (1929–34), Herbert von Karajan (1956–62), Lorin Maazel (1982–84)—but *Wien bleibt Wien*, always taking the easy way in the end.

Mahler's perfectionism took root elsewhere. Zemlinsky transferred it to Prague, Walter implanted it in Munich, Klemperer in Berlin, before all of them took it into exile. The Mahler manual for managing an opera house remained the benchmark for excellence and efficiency more than a century later.

"The authority of the director is very clearly defined," Lorin Maazel told me in January 1983, tipping back his chair in an office he thought was once Mahler's. "I take the decisions. You only get intrigues when the direction is uncertain."[24] A year later Maazel was gone, driven out by a hail of attacks from racists, opportunists, and café dwellers, fueled by a self-important press. *Wien bleibt Wien*. I asked Maazel how many nights he conducted; Twenty-five a year was his reply. Mahler, I reminded him, conducted more than a hundred. "I love to conduct," said Maazel, "but as a form of recreation. I can't see it that way if I'm grinding out eleven operas in fifteen nights. I'm not born to be a hack."[25] And Mahler was?

In the bowels of the Opera, in charge of the scores, I found Peter Poltun, an American nuclear-disarmament diplomat who gave up vodka chasers with Soviet generals to curate orchestral parts in Vienna. He named every current musician whose ancestor played for Mahler, and showed me a copy of *Tristan und Isolde* with Mahler's furious pencil marks in blue and red, as vivid as if it had been conducted the night before.

Leaving the Opera, I paced out Mahler's homeward walk. His apartment, restored after 1945 bombing, was occupied by a Norwegian pianist who assured me that the bathtub was from Mahler's time. I resisted the invitation to take a dip. Walking around the Ring, Mahler's Seventh Symphony playing in my headphones, I counted stone memorials to Haydn, Mozart, Beethoven, Schubert, Johann Strauss (father and son), Josef Lanner, Bruckner, and, in the city park, Alma's father, Emil Jakob Schindler. Nowhere was there a monument to Mahler. His only mark on the city is a formerly seedy Mahlerstrasse, named in 1919 and now fringed by a fashionable shopping mall.

I returned many times. Vienna is impossible to judge on first impression, or tenth. *Schein* prevails over *Sein*, illusion over substance. During one Vienna Festival I discovered Otto Wagner's 1903 construct of a mental asylum, parish church, and small theater, an attempt to heal damaged minds with faith and art. The hospital was used by the Nazis for killing sick children; the concert hall remains active. Deconstructing Vienna is a frustrating task. *Wien bleibt Wien.*

One November morning on the Kärntnerring, I awake to the voice of a muezzin calling the faithful to prayer. The brain whirs. Where am I? Isn't this the city that stopped the advance of Islam in 1683? Is Western civilization again under siege? The hotel receptionist tells me that there are fifty-three mosques in Vienna. About 4 percent of Austria's population is Muslim, many of them refugees from Balkan wars, some resident here for five generations. This city was always, innately, multicultural.

I stroll a silent Ring. It is All Saints' Day, a public holiday, when business shuts and everyone visits cemeteries. Life stops and death rules for the day—"a fearful torment past, and sweet dreams over," in the words of Schubert's "All Souls' Song." Eros and Thanatos, love and death, are Vienna's everlasting Ring-around. What Mahler left behind was, in his own words, "bits and pieces," the most any of us can do in a short life span, a humbling object lesson on our mortal limitations. Why Mahler? It's a question I've never had to ask in the dying cadence that is Vienna.

11. Discovering America (1907–1910)

New York, not yet a wonderful town, is having a year of record influx, 1.25 million immigrants, 11,745 on a single day. The population hits 4 million. A telegraph link is established to Ireland, allowing newcomers to wire home. The first electric train service runs out of Grand Central Station. The first taxicab plies for trade. The Plaza Hotel opens on Central Park, and the store windows on Fifth Avenue are a theater of dreams. It is a year of limitless diversions. Florenz Ziegfeld introduces his *Follies*. Sholem Asch sells out Yiddish theaters with *God of Vengeance*, the tale of a Jewish brothel keeper. The songs on every lip are "School Days" and "I'm Afraid to Come Home in the Dark." The *New York Times* reports from Vienna—"by Telegraph to Clifden, Ireland; thence by Wireless"—that the best singers are "deserting" the Court Opera for the wealth of Manhattan.[1]

Suddenly prosperity turns delusional. The Knickerbocker Trust Company's involvement in a fraudulent bid to corner the copper market brings a clamor of depositors to its doorstep, at Thirty-fourth Street and Fifth Avenue. On October 24, in the panic of 1907, bank shares dive and Wall Street trembles. Financiers John Pierpont Morgan and John D. Rockefeller save the day. "If people will keep their money in the banks, everything will be all right," declares Morgan as the Knickerbocker president, Charles T. Barney, shoots himself. Ten days later a leading firm of brokers cannot pay its bills. On Saturday morning Morgan gathers fifty bankers in his library and, through the weekend, hammers out a deal, which President Theodore Roosevelt okays seconds ahead of the Monday opening bell. The knife-edge tension leads to the creation of a Federal Reserve to monitor monetary stability. But nothing is fixed. Nothing ever is.

New York, neither pretty nor clean, is governed from Tammany Hall by Charles F. Murphy, a millionaire Irishman who coins the phrase "honest graft" to cover a kickback culture that pervades public service, from policing to waste disposal. Much of the population lives in what the novelist Theodore Dreiser calls "conditions which would better become a slum section of Constantinople."[2] Many immigrants earn no more than twenty-two cents an hour, maybe four hundred dollars a year. A dentist makes two to three thousand. A lady can spend that much in an afternoon's shopping on the Avenue of Dreams.

A singer's daughter recalls "great sumptuous dinners and receptions planned and executed with cold magnificence . . . the preferred entertainment was the private musicale after dinner, in the ballroom with its ranks of little gilt chairs, where the greatest artists of the Metropolitan and the concert world sang or played for perhaps half an hour each, for a fee possibly as high as $2,500."[3] The Metropolitan Opera, ruled by J. P. Morgan and his friends, separates the city's moneyed heads from its milling masses. Its aim, writes Edith Wharton in *The Age of Innocence*, is to "compete in costliness and splendor with those of the great European capitals."

Situated on Thirty-ninth and Broadway, the Met veers from Italian opera to German and back again. Conried, manager since 1903, has to fend off competition from Hammerstein and interference from his own stockholders. Morgan makes him cancel *Salome* after his daughter is offended by the dance. Conried's last gambit is a conductor who will restore music as the company's chief priority.

Gustav Mahler disembarks from the *Kaiserin Augusta Viktoria* before noon on December 21, 1907. An Ellis Island official registers his name as "Mohler," inflates his height to five feet eight, and gives his occupation as "Musical Dr." On subsequent arrivals he is five feet two and "Band Master."[4] Newsmen cluster. Mahler denies rumors of irascibility: "I am the most amiable man in the world, but I expect my people to do their duty and to do it quickly."[5] An Austrian Embassy official and the Met's conductor of German repertoire, Alfred Hertz, take him to the Hotel Majestic at West Seventy-second (now 115 Central Park West), where a *New York Times* man is waiting. "I have been looking forward with pleasure to my engagement in America," says Mahler. "I am thoroughly in sympathy with the season which Mr. Conried has planned and I hope to be able to contribute something in an artistic way."[6] His platitudes sound the more ponderous in translation. He refuses, even in America, to speak English.

Lunch is at Conried's apartment, where they find the manager reclining on a divan, next to an antique suit of armor lit from within by red electric bulbs. Mahler has nothing to say to a man of such poor taste. He goes to see *Tosca*, with Enrico Caruso, Emma Eames, and Antonio Scotti. The next morning he starts work on *Tristan* with the Munich tenor Heinrich Knote and a Lilli Lehmann pupil, Olive Fremstad. Moments into the Prelude, he pulls up. "All other rehearsals in this theatre must be stopped," he says. "I can't hear my orchestra."[7] After forty-five minutes Mahler shuts his score. While he rehearses, Alma is alone at the hotel. "Often," she writes, "I sat on the stairs on our eleventh floor merely to catch some sound of human life below."

On Christmas she weeps all day. Toward evening there is a knock at the door. Maurice Baumfeld, director of a German theater on Irving Place and a "good Schlemiel" (Alma's Yiddish term for a well-meaning fool), takes them out to a party where they meet a "raddled" old actress called "Putzi." The name of their dead child causes Alma to faint. Mahler telephones for a doctor, then another. Diagnosed with "weakness of the heart and nervous collapse,"[8] she is given strychnine and told to rest. Mahler tends to her with solicitude.

On New Year's Day 1908 he treads on Alma's train as they leave the hotel and she, "half-naked," darts upstairs to sew her dress together. The Met calls. Mahler refuses to leave without her. A car is sent. As the first-night audience fidgets in its seats, Mahler visits each singer's dressing room before entering the podium to conduct the *Tristan* of his life. Knote, chubby and weak chinned, makes up in vocal strength what he lacks in heroic stature. Fremstad, regal and serene, surmounts high C's and Louise Homer, as Brangäne, is a homegrown gal who sings her heart out. It is one of those Met nights when everything clicks. Two retired Isoldes, Lilian Nordica and Johanna Gadski, lead the ovations. The triumph, writes Alma, is "immediate," adding airily that "Americans are very critical and do not by any means receive every European celebrity with favour. They really know something about music."

An eighteen-year-old student in the top gallery hears, for the first time, Isolde's every word.

My eyes turned to Mahler to find a reason. He was "riding" the orchestra with the calculated sureness of a master trainer, at one moment curbing it to a crafty balance between it and the voice on stage, at another giving it its head as it raced alone. Perhaps at certain climaxes he was too solicitous for the voice. Though I heard the words and the voice, I was sensible of the reins on the orchestra, and I did not feel the thrill and elation of a great fusion of both, which I had expected. Nevertheless it was an entirely new Tristan for me. Now at last I knew how Wagner should sound. [Alfred] Hertz had misled us. Wagner could be as clear, as understandable, as lucid as Aida.[9]

The critics are bowled over. "Comparable to the best that New York has known," writes Richard Aldrich in the *Times*. "Mr. Mahler did honor to himself, Wagner's music and the New York public," agrees the *Tribune*'s Henry Krehbiel. The *Sun* reports a full house, "as large as it might have been on a Caruso night." After the prejudice and egotism of Vienna, the astuteness and objectivity of the New York critics seem heaven sent. There are about twenty daily newspapers in New York, of which seven cover the arts. The Big Five critics, "the most unmerciful in the world,"[10] are Krehbiel, Aldrich, Henry Theophilus Finck (the *Post*), and William James Henderson and James Gibbons Huneker on the *Sun*. Krehbiel, the doyen, is built like a football player, with the looks of a film star. Tetchy, opinionated, and dedicated to improving public taste, he is revered by readers and ignored in the opera boardroom. The balance between press and power is altogether healthier than in Vienna.

Which is not to say that New York's press is any less combative than Vienna's. It scrabbles for wisps of dinner-party rumor and, days after Mahler's debut, reports that he is to be Conried's successor. The story is not altogether without substance. The board has told Conried his time is up, and a stockholder is on his way to Milan to hire La Scala manager Giulio Gatti-Casazza, with his conductor, Arturo Toscanini. Fearing Italian dominance, the incoming chairman, Otto H. Kahn, proposes that Mahler should control the repertoire. Kahn, German-born and a British citizen, is everything J. P. Morgan fears and loathes—a polyglot Jew, with links to European banks. A Jew cannot buy or even rent a box in the Met's Diamond Horseshoe. Kahn, however, has paid off the company's $450,000 deficit and is in a position to call the tune. He asks Mahler to run the next season. "I quite decisively refused," reports Mahler.[11]

"Anxious to work away from the German atmosphere and the Jew (Mahler is a J.),"[12] the rest of the board endorses Toscanini's appointment, and Mahler begins to fear he will be pushed out. His application intensifies. After five *Tristan*s in New York and two more in Philadelphia and Boston, he devotes fifteen rehearsals to *Don Giovanni*, in which Fyodor Chaliapin sings his first Leporello, Antonio Scotti is the Don, and the women are Emma Eames, Marcella Sembrich, and Johanna Gadski. The singing, he finds, is "almost unsurpassable."[13] Rehearsing *Die Walküre* he addresses his attention to chorus morale. "Ladies," he begins. "Never before have I heard such voices assembled for the Valkyries, not even in Vienna." A twitter of delight shivers through the ranks. "And now, ladies," he continues, "finding that you are possessed of such wonderful voices, I must ask you to use them."[14] Their triple forte almost disturbs trading on Wall Street.

Fremstad, strained in *Walküre*, shines in *Siegfried*, and he closes with *Fidelio*—Berta Morena, Karel Burrian, and Anton van Rooy—inserting the *Leonore* no. 3 overture after the dungeon scene to heighten dramatic tension. Mahler calls it "a total success, completely altering my prospects from one day to the next."[15] Otto Kahn presents a new contract, allowing him to conduct concerts as well as opera. At Kahn's, Mahler meets a physician, Joseph Fränkel, who practices the art of *Augenblickdiagnose*, identifying a patient's condition as he or she enters the room. "He was a genius both as a man and as a doctor and we both fell in love with him,"[16] writes Alma. Mahler is enjoying

America. It "is altogether different from Europe. One feels there first and foremost a human being, with no-one above you. If you want, you can greet the President, 'Good morning, Mr. Roosevelt.' And if you don't want to, you don't."[17]

One image from this first trip sticks in his mind. Alma, chatting in their hotel suite with a young woman, a student of Roller's, is disturbed by a noise in the street below:

> We leaned out of the window and saw a long procession in the broad street along the side of Central Park. It was the funeral cortège of a fireman, of whose heroic death we had read in the newspaper.[18] The chief mourners were almost immediately beneath us when the procession halted and the master of ceremonies stepped forward and gave a short address. From our eleventh-floor window we could only guess what he said. There was a brief pause and then a stroke on the muffled drum, followed by a dead silence. The procession then moved forward and all was over. The scene brought tears to our eyes and I looked anxiously at Mahler's window. But he too was leaning out and his face was streaming with tears. The brief drum-stroke impressed him so deeply that he used it in the Tenth Symphony.[19]

NOT A NINTH SYMPHONY

He dares not write a ninth symphony. It is a fatal number. Beethoven died after nine symphonies. So did Schubert, Bruckner, and Dvořák. Mahler, if he wants to live, must avoid the number 9. So he pretends he is writing a song cycle and puts a fake title on the opening page— *The Flute of Jade*—or so Alma explains. Mahler may have other reasons. It is four years since he has written a song, and two since his last symphony. He has lost the habit and needs to refresh his technique to cope with the shattering changes in his life. A different location might help.

Cupped in a high, green valley, Toblach is where Mahler has fled the lakeside heat for the last four summers. Alma and her mother find "a large, isolated farmhouse with eleven rooms"[20] in an outlying hamlet, Alt-Schluderbach. The farmer, Sebastian Trenker, occupies the ground floor. There are chickens in the yard and goats in the meadow. Mahler is delighted. He puts two grand pianos in the farmhouse and an upright in the wooden shack he is having built in a hillside copse. Alma refers to it crudely as his earth closet. At six in the morning the farmer's daughter, Marianne, brings him breakfast—tea, coffee, butter, honey, eggs, rolls, fruit—and poultry. "A full-sized stove furnished the little house," she recalls. "He would light it himself and prepare his meal on it. . . . He often told us how, as a child of a poor, large family, he had only a piece of bread to live on all day long in order to pay for his studies."[21] One day a hawk flies into his shack, chasing a jackdaw. "The peaceful abode of musical absorption had become a battleground."[22]

He stares out, frustrated, at a slope he is forbidden to climb. "I am told to avoid any exertion, keep a constant eye on myself and not walk much. At the same time, the solitude in which my attention is more turned inward makes me feel all the more distinctly everything that is not right with me physically. . . . For the first time in my life, I am wishing my holidays were over."[23] He feels, he says, like a morphine addict who cannot get his fix. He is forcing his mood as low as it can go: "If I am to find the way back to myself again, I must surrender to the horrors of loneliness."[24]

Over the next six weeks he composes with unremitting concentration, through a stream of visitors—the Molls, the Korngolds, Roller, Fried, the banker Paul Hammerschlag, an American piano salesman, and the lovelorn pianist Gabrilowitsch, who kisses Alma on the mouth in a moonlit meadow. On September 1, Mahler finishes *Das Lied von der Erde (The Song of the Earth)*. He has "no idea" how to describe it. He tries "symphony for a tenor and an alto voice and orchestra,"[25] and "a Symphony in Songs"[26] before realizing he has created a new form. "It is the most personal thing I have done,"[27] he tells Bruno Walter, and it bears no apparent relation to anything he has done before. The summer of three blows has bred a new Mahler.

He takes seven out of eighty-three Chinese poems and turns them into six movements:

1 The Drinking Song of Earth's Sorrow
2 The Lonely Man in Autumn

3 Of Youth
4 Of Beauty
5 The Drunkard in Springtime
6 Farewell (Der Abschied)[28]

Poems 1, 3, 4, and 5 are by Li Bai (also known as Li Po, or Li Tai Po), a bibulous writer who, according to legend, drowned while reaching for the moon's reflection in a river. "Reaching for the moon" implies an erotic lunge. Li Bai (701–62), it is said, committed suicide out of unrequited love. Mahler knows no more of him than what he reads in Hans Bethge's fanciful essay: "He poetized the turbulent, windswept, inexpressible beauty of the world, the everlasting pain and mystery of existence. All the world's grim melancholy nested in his breast; even in moments of high joy he could not shake off the earth's shadows."[29] Could this be Mahler himself?

Li Bai is taught to every preschool child in China.[30] "When I read his poems, I can feel the power and compulsion," writes a twenty-first-century Shanghai academic. "Knowing his personality and his tragic end makes the feeling even stronger."[31]

"The Lonely Man in Autumn" is by Qian Qi; the "Farewell" conflates two works by Meng Haoran and Wang Wei. None of the texts is close to the Chinese. What Mahler uses is a reworking by the poet Bethge from Heilmann's literal German translation of French renditions by the Marquis d'Hervey-Saint-Denys (1862) and Judith Gautier (1867). Mahler, using the material at fourth hand, takes the liberty of rewriting the last two stanzas in "Of Youth" and the last three in "Of Beauty," as well as adding several lines.

Why is he drawn to poets who lived a millennium before his time and half a world away, to a tone system based on five notes? As a boy, desperate to be elsewhere, he wrote a school paper on the influence of the Orient on German literature. Now he is looking to escape the fear of death. He writes a perfect pentatonic scale, C–D–E–G–A,[32] perhaps trying, like Schoenberg, to break out of European tonality. Alternatively the reduced tonal options may reflect a physical constraint, his restricted mobility. Two drunken songs belong to his father's tavern. Throughout he dwells on fellowship and farewell, the love that connects one person to another and the death that parts them forever. "Dark is life, is death," is Mahler's refrain, uniting the state of being with that of being gone.

He opens with horns, a large orchestra, and a high tenor at the top of his range, reaching for one last drink to a reproving Jew-ish clarinet. The second song sighs woodwind regrets: Summer is gone and the sun ain't gonna shine anymore. In the song "Of Youth" the poet sees youngsters in their Sunday best chatting away and writing verses while he, old and impotent, peeps into their green-and-white porcelain pavilion. Beauty, in the fourth song, finds boys and girls at play beside the water, a posse of horseback riders (with a blast of the Russian national anthem); one maiden throws the poet a meaningful glance but, though spring comes in the fifth song, drink is now his best companion.

The "Farewell," introduced by low instruments and an alto sunset, lists what we leave behind at the close of life—a twitter of birds, a rustle of leaves: "The brook sings loud and sweetly in darkness, the flowers pale, the earth breathes deep in rest and sleep." Poet and friend, artist and life, are ready to part, but just as the separation seems final and irrevocable, Mahler injects a verse of Wang Wei and some lines of his own in a consolation unlike any other.

After the words "O world, drunk on everlasting love and life," the music starts to disintegrate, flaking off like a mind in dementia until memory runs out. When it reaches standstill, the man mounts his horse. "I am going to the homeland, my resting place," writes Mahler, three times homeless. His closing text dredges hope out of the acceptance of loss. The last phrase "Ewig, ewig," repeated, over and over again in pairs, means "forever and ever":

> The beloved earth blossoms everywhere in spring
> And turns green again.
> Everywhere and forever, the far horizons are blue and bright.
> Ewig, ewig. . . . Ewig, ewig.

Showing the score to Walter, he demands: "Is it endurable? Won't people want to do away with themselves after hearing it?" He follows up with a nervous joke. "Any idea how this is to be conducted? I haven't."[33]

• • •

How does Mahler pack so much emotion into so trite a word? The "Ewig" enigma resisted me for years until a chance sighting at a 1988 exhibition in Vienna cracked a subconscious code. It was the fiftieth anniversary of Hitler's Anschluss, and among the artifacts was a photograph of a railway station festooned with a banner: "Der Ewige Jude," the eternal Jew. Of course. "Ewig" has a specific connotation in the German mind. It is the eternal Jew, who killed Christ and is condemned to wander the beloved earth, a touchstone of Christian theology. In 1940 Joseph Goebbels makes it the title of a film whose purpose is to justify genocide. "Ewig" and "Jew" are linked in the German mind. "Ewig" in *The Song of the Earth* is the Jew in Gustav Mahler, the *alter* ego, the old, real Mahler he manages to rediscover as his life enters its closing phase. It is the sound of catharsis, for Mahler and for all who listen to *The Song of the Earth*.

Its healing power cannot be overstated. One summer, most of it spent at the bedside of a sick child, I flew to Edinburgh for the festival, only to be told on arrival that there was a problem at home. "Wait half an hour," said my wife, when I offered to fly back. By the time she called again the crisis was over. I stayed on, in a wretched state. There was a sold-out concert that night of *The Song of the Earth*, just what I needed. Talking myself into a manager's seat, I sat through an uneven performance—missed tops from the tenor and too hot in the Usher Hall for the strings to stay in tune—but when the "Ewigs" came around the effect was irresistible. Life, I knew, would go on. My child would overcome her condition. Mahler had tapped determinedly into our human resilience, our infinite capacity for self-renewal.

BROTHERS IN MAHLER

Three days after writing the last "Ewig" he is in Prague, rehearsing his Seventh Symphony. The venue, a temporary structure, doubles as a banquet hall. While Mahler works with the Czech Philharmonic, waiters set tables. After rehearsal "he took all the parts back with him to the hotel and made improvements. There were a lot of young people there and we wanted to help him but he wouldn't let us."[34]

Friends converge—Arnold Berliner from Hamburg, Oskar Fried from Berlin, Walter and Berg from Vienna, followed by Justi, Guido Adler, Zemlinsky, Gabrilowitsch, and Pollak. Street photographs show Mahler sharing Walter's umbrella on an afternoon stroll.[35] "He was relaxed and extremely amusing," relates Otto Klemperer, "holding forth uninhibitedly and rather loudly about his successor in Vienna."[36] Mahler takes a shine to young Otto, perhaps in memory of his dead brother.

His letters to Alma are, contrarily, morose. "I'm wondering how I can transform sausage cauldrons into timpani, rusty watering-cans into trumpets and a public bar into a concert hall."[37] When she arrives he sends Berliner to meet her at the station. Their marital unease is becoming visible. The Swiss writer William Ritter sees concupiscent males hovering around Alma, sensing sexual availability.

At the dress rehearsal Mahler throws the orchestra a little joke. "Dear friends," he says, smiling. "Take care. Today you play for me and will do what *I* want. Tomorrow you play for the public and will do what *you* want." The musicians, writes Ritter, are charmed. "By the end, there were neither Czechs nor Germans, neither Christians nor Jews. We were all brothers in music and in Mahler's art."[38]

The premiere, on Saturday, September 19, 1908, is "not a success."[39] Janko Cadra, Ritter's lover, hears Slovak tunes in the first "Nachtmusik," and a quiet kind of loving in the second. What strikes him is an affinity to Klimt, "the same colors but with Mahler more passionate." When Mahler repeats the Seventh in Munich a few weeks later, the unsophisticated Cadra observes his rehearsals:

If a passage does not work out, if the orchestra doesn't understand, Mahler nervously scratches his hair and stamps his feet, so that they stop playing. . . . When they finally hush, he folds his hands between his knees, remains immersed in the score, suddenly straightens up, and says what he wants to say. It is impressive how this man controls himself. If the musicians don't understand his intentions, he flies in[to] a rage, jumps up from his chair like a devil, stamps, shouts

"Donnerwetter! [Damnit!]", but immediately calms down, even though in his voice you can trace his anger. He explains—with a whiff of bitterness—how to play it, ends and with spread-out arms "Also meine Herren! [Now, gentlemen!]"

Explaining a steep, strong crescendo with a turbulent high-pitched climax, he pulls his elbows against his waist, fists together and clenches his teeth so that his temples stand out. Then he moves both fists apart, slowly, as if he is pulling a thorn from beneath his fingernail, and with a muffled voice expresses the steady strength and growth of sound, which he illustrates even with his shoulders, before he suddenly shouts—*boom,* stamps with his foot and his fists spread. . . . He does not let them get away with the tiniest nuance between piano and pianissimo. Yet when he asks: "Gentlemen, are you tired?", the reply is "No!" He adds: "I do not want to put a strain on you." This is not said condescendingly but as a sincere expression of concern on seeing fatigue on some faces.[40]

In Vienna he finds Schoenberg in turmoil. His wife, Mathilde, has left him in the summer for the man upstairs, a painter called Richard Gerstl, who hangs himself when Mathilde returns to her husband and children. While Mahler is writing *The Song of the Earth,* Schoenberg tips his Second String Quartet over the precipice into uncharted atonality. Mahler is intrigued to see where this is heading. He persuades his publisher, Emil Hertzka, to print Schoenberg's scores. Schoenberg is more to Mahler than another Otto substitute. He is a leader who includes Mahler in his revolution, promising that his symphonies will still be heard in the newly glimpsed future when diatonic harmony is extinct. It is this endorsement by modernism, as much as his own willpower, that encourages Mahler to override rejection, carry on composing, and bring new music to America.

Expecting a rose-strewn reception in New York, he runs into war on two fronts. Toscanini wants to conduct *Tristan und Isolde* for his Met debut. "Inconceivable," says Mahler. "The form in which this work now appears in New York is my spiritual property."[41] The Italian, incensed, conceives an instant hatred. Down the next half century he tells journalists that Mahler is "crazy" and his music "trivial." His animus is echoed by another totemic conductor, the beaming Walter Damrosch, future music director of the NBC radio network and "Uncle Walter" on its children's hour. "Mahler's moments of real beauty are too rare," writes Damrosch, "and the listener has to wade through pages of dreary emptiness. . . . The feverish restlessness characteristic of the man reflects itself in his music, which is fragmentary in character and lacks continuity of thought and development."[42] Like Toscanini, Damrosch responds like a small boy with a broken toy.

Mahler has arranged to conduct the New York Symphony Orchestra, founded by Damrosch's father, Leopold, and poorly served by Walter's stodgy baton. But before he can start work, Walter hears of a plan to create a new orchestra in New York under Mahler's command, a scheme driven by Mary Sheldon, wife of a Republican kingmaker, with backing from J. P. Morgan, John D. Rockefeller, and the cream of society. Walter Damrosch decides to sabotage Mahler by not advertising his concerts. His first concert is half empty. The second, on December 8, 1908, performs the *Resurrection* Symphony with "completely inadequate forces."[43] The third, a Beethoven concert, is a late sell-out after Mrs. Sheldon writes to the *Times* that she has given up her plan to start a new orchestra. Instead she is taking over the New York Philharmonic and will "procure the best conductor that is available,"[44] meaning Mahler. Damrosch now sees Mahler as a threat to everything his family controls in New York, which is plenty. His brother Frank heads the Oratorio Society and the Institute of Musical Art, forerunner of the Juilliard School. Their sister, Clara Mannes, runs the Mannes School of Music. The family has music in the city sewed up, and they move fast to protect their assets, casting Mahler in an unfavorable light.

Mahler, living with Alma and four-year-old Anna at the Savoy Hotel, spends Christmas with their neighbors Sembrich and Caruso and gets a fright when the tree catches fire. The Mahlers grow closer this winter. Alma becomes pregnant and suffers a miscarriage, or undergoes an abortion, couched by Mahler in euphemisms to the Molls: "Alma is very well. About her *present state* she has doubtless written to you herself. She has been relieved of her *burden*. But this time she actually regrets it."[45] Anna Moll sails out to look after her and gets a checkup from Dr. Fränkel, who finds nothing amiss. (Mother and daughter are prone to malingering; both live to be eighty.)

At the Met, Mahler conducts *Tristan*, an effervescent *Marriage of Figaro* (with Scotti, Eames, Geraldine Farrar, Sembrich), and the U.S. premiere of Smetana's *The Bartered Bride*, which Krehbiel declares an "unalloyed delight."[46] In March 1909 he signs with Mrs. Sheldon as conductor of the New York Philharmonic at $25,000 a season, $10,000 up on his Met deal. (In twenty-first-century values his pay is $300,000 at the Met, $500,000 at the Philharmonic. James Levine and Lorin Maazel, in 2009, are paid $1.9 and $3 million respectively. Mahler is not greedy or greatly overpaid.)

Before he can recruit better players, he is told that the union insists on six months' city residency before a musician is allowed to work. He will have to make do with the men available, whom he test-drives in two Beethoven symphonies, the Seventh and the Ninth. Aldrich notes that Mahler, "like many other *modern* conductors[,] does not hesitate to revise Beethoven's scoring, to reinforce it with a doubling of instruments, to continue the melodic line in certain voices of the bass instruments . . . even to the omission of a few bars in the return of the [scherzo] theme." Krehbiel, sharper than before, attacks Mahler for making "free with the text."

> Obviously his purpose, like those of his predecessors who have done similar things, was to "make more definite and certain" (as the lawyers say) the thoughts of the composer who is supposed, for several reasons, not to have been able to express himself as clearly as he ought or might. . . . Those who think Beethoven wished to have the ears of his auditors assaulted as they were last night by the kettledrum player must have been delighted by the bombardment to which they were subjected; others must have felt outraged. Traditions extending over two generations have not prepared New York's lovers of the symphony for such a reading.[47]

Mahler is empowered by the guarantors to hire a concertmaster in Europe at a salary of six thousand dollars. At the same meeting it is "resolved that Mr. H. E. Krehbiel be engaged to furnish the program annotations for the coming season, terms to be $25 for each concert."[48] Mahler, when he starts work with the Philharmonic, will find a hostile critic on his payroll, a cuckoo in his nest.

SITTING VERY STILL

Paris in the springtime is no place to be indoors, but Mahler is being set in stone. "You cannot imagine how we love this man," Carl Moll tells Auguste Rodin, "and how pleased we are that the only artist who can understand that head now consents in good nature to make his portrait."[49] Rodin cuts his fee from forty thousand francs to ten thousand and sizes Mahler up over lunch with the Clemenceaus. "Mahler is convinced that it is *your* wish to do his bust or he would have refused to pose," Paul Clemenceau warns Rodin, but there is no need for subterfuge. "They didn't speak . . . yet they understood each other perfectly."[50] At Rodin's studio in the Hotel Biron, Alma sees a girl with painted lips. Rodin, sixty-eight, has a wife in the suburbs.

Mahler balks only once in twelve sessions, when Rodin motions him onto his knees so that he can inspect his head from all angles. "He thought it was to humiliate him that I asked him to kneel," grumbles the artist. Two busts emerge, and each is cast in eight copies. Rodin is so pleased with the B set that he has his assistant Aristide Roussaud match it in marble (at the Musée Rodin, this bust is titled *Mozart*). It captures Mahler's forceful determination, the gentleness of his gaze, and the great span of his brow. Copies find their way, over time, into the foyers of the Vienna Opera, Avery Fisher Hall, the Brooklyn Museum, the Bibliothèque Gustav Mahler in Paris, and the University of Western Ontario. At the Ministry of War, Colonel Picquart receives Mahler as royalty, with a guard of honor. Mahler is desperate to get away, back to his composing shack.

The Mahlers part for a month. Alma, her nerves "in a critical state," takes a cure in an Italian resort, Levico, and sits "night after night on my balcony, weeping and looking out at the crowd of gay and happy people whose laughter grated on my ears."[51] Her husband writes daily from Toblach about overdue rent and Goethe's "eternal feminine." They are inhabiting separate planetary systems. In Toblach the weather is wet, and it is too cold at first to occupy his shack. The critic Ernst Decsey takes him for gentle walks in all weathers. "Vita fugax," sighs Mahler, as the sun sets on snowcapped peaks: Life is fleeting. A ninth symphony is taking shape, fearless in his mind.

It is written in six weeks, "in frantic haste."[52] There are four movements, the outer ones slow, the inner pair "in the tempo of a leisurely folk dance, clumsy and very crude" and "rondo, burlesque, very defiant." A "solemn cortège" recalls his First Symphony funeral; instructing the violins to play "like fiddles" is reminiscent of his Fourth. He is back on home turf, as if *The Song of the Earth* had never been written, though a faint continuation of the "Ewig" figure can be heard in the opening cadence.

The symphony begins with a stutter of harp, horn, and lower strings that some identify with Mahler's arrhythmic walk and others attribute, without foundation, to the faltering beat of his heart. Initial diffidence gives way to a summery melody that goes into combat with a D-minor countertheme: The joy of life meets the fact of death. The inner movements edge toward dissonance, dancing with dangerous abandon and leaving the work poised after fifty minutes on a cliff edge of uncertainty. What will he decide: Tonal or atonal? Life or death?

The finale offers no definite solution. The opening chorale, with hints of the Anglican hymn "Abide with Me" (has Mahler heard it through American church doors?) and the Jewish liturgical song, "Adon Olam," is attacked by predatory submotifs, and wasted away into eventual nullity. But at the point where the music breaks down, Mahler, just as in *The Song of the Earth*, finds a harp renewal, an Adagissimo drawn from his fourth death-of-children song and hymned with sweet poignancy on upper strings, slowly fading out, *ersterbend*, dying, until silence is all that remains.

Many see the Ninth as the centerpiece of a triple act of abdication. "He peacefully bids farewell to the world," says Walter,[53] whose intuitions cannot lightly be ignored. But that does not give full account of a symphony that is seeded with long stretches of love and regret, rage and resistance. "With fury" and "with the greatest force" stand out among Mahler's markings. These are not the sighed rustlings of God's waiting room. There is more than one meaning at work, as you would expect in a Mahler symphony.

Try sitting in Mahler's shack, as I have done, and picture the struggle within a vibrant, passionate man who, facing a foreshortened life, tries at one and the same time to confront death and to evade it. Brave and terrified in turn, Mahler in his Ninth Symphony plays hope against despair and settles for a draw. His state of mind is ambiguous. He writes to Carl Moll that he is in "a sort of purgatorio," a gateway to hell. But no sooner does he utter that phrase than he qualifies and reverses it—"or, say, a purging of the mind—*both are right.*"[54] He is in extreme pain, and suddenly pain free. He is able not only to feel extreme sensation but to observe it as an objective, external witness, seeing himself from afar. This is Mahler in excelsis, transcending existential misery—or so the closing music tells us. Yet the page is disfigured with howls of pain. "O Youth! Lost! O Love! Vanished!" and, thirteen pages on, "Leb wol! Leb wol!", farewell.[55] Alma has left him feeling "totally alone."[56] It is not so much death he dreads as a living hell of loneliness.

She rejoins him the week after his birthday, and a flock of visitors follows—Dr. Fränkel from New York, Oskar Fried, the Molls, the Korngolds, Roller, and, unannounced, Richard Strauss, whose wife, Pauline, yells across the lobby of Toblach's Grand Hotel, "Hi, Mahler, how are you? How was America? Filthy, I guess. Hope you saved lots of money."[57] Strauss plays him *Elektra*, showing no reciprocal interest in Mahler's work. "My Ninth is finished!"[58] declares Mahler on September 2, hoping "it will be granted to me to make a fair copy this winter."[59]

Seventy years later Toblach, now Dobbiaco, named its main square after Gustav Mahler, put up a statue by the Slovene Bojan Kunaver, and started a music festival. The Trenker family still owns the farmhouse, and Mahler's composing shack stood unchanged, humbling in its simplicity. I climbed a mountain with Lotte Klemperer, Otto's daughter, lunched with the composer Luciano Berio, who was orchestrating Mahler's early songs, and chatted with a Chinese musicologist who was doing his best to align *Song of the Earth* music with the original Tang poems.

In a new concert hall, named after Mahler, a Philadelphia jazz pianist was recounting Mahler's life in piano improvisations. Uri Caine had been aptly described (by the novelist Chaim Potok's widow, Adena[60]) as musical midrashist, a creator of scriptural subtexts. On record, Caine overlaid Mahler with blues, white noise, world music, and other deconstructions, achieving apotheosis with a *Song of the Earth* finale that segues into a Jewish cantor intoning El Male Rahamim (Lord Full of Mercy), the graveside prayer. The two passages make a perfect musical fit. Caine defined his own experiments as "a commentary and a connection," arguing that "there has always been fusion in music history where people speak more than one language."[61] Like jazz, he reckoned that Mahler was music-plus, that his symphonies were a kind of Internet free space, inviting user contributions as an ongoing conversation. Mahler interactive might help indicate why his music increased its appeal a century beyond his time.

Caine's approach made sense to me. He grasped that Mahler did not belong to any single tradition, least of all exclusively to the Western symphonic. Mahler was a man of several worlds, three times homeless, perpetually searching for connection. Caine, on two revelatory albums,[62] wrested him away from tailcoated conductors and wall-faced orchestras. He revealed another of Mahler's anticipatory modes—Mahler as blogger, as response seeker, the first composer to invite unmoderated feedback, who starts the debate with the howls he scrawled within his working manuscript.

LET'S MAKE AN ORCHESTRA

Strauss's take-the-money attitude toward America is the norm at the time and the very opposite of Mahler's. Given an orchestra of his own, Mahler sets out a plan of mass enlightenment. First he restructures the Carnegie Hall diary into four cycles. There is a Regular Series and a Beethoven cycle "for the education of lovers of classical music, for the education of my orchestra, and for the students." Sunday afternoon is "for all workers and students who are not financially able to pay for seats at the regular concerts." In the Historical Series "I shall try in six evenings to give an outline of the development of classical music from Bach to the modern composer"—in effect, a documentary on the evolution of music. "It will be my aim to educate the public," he tells the press. Education, education, education, is Mahler's watchword. He aims to transform the orchestra from entertainer to think tank. He will conduct forty-six concerts over twenty-four weeks and intends "to let my public and the music critics of the press help me in picking out the musical way we should go."[63] The dialogue of American democracy has entered Mahler's soul, though he remains a tough disciplinarian with the musicians in his orchestra.

"Rehearsals started in New York straight away," reports the new German American concertmaster, Theodore Spiering.

> Mahler worked steadfastly and with enormous concentration of powers. There were no breaks. Hardly ever was a piece played all the way through. The material had to be battled until it was conquered. Unused to such strain, the members of the orchestra were recalcitrant at first but they soon fell into line and admired the man who could simultaneously treat them so roughly and make them soar with him to such unattained heights.[64]

Before the season begins he replaces half the players, firing twenty-five more at the end. A violinist, Hermann Martonne, remembers him picking on weaker, older men. "He had a way of singling out some unfortunate player, rushing over to him, pointing the baton in his face and shouting, 'you, you, play that passage alone.' "[65] He expects everyone to learn German and changes his directions from one session to the next. When a player asks why a pianissimo is now piano, Mahler replies: " 'Well, you know, it all depends on our mood. Mood—it's all mood. Yesterday I thought it was too much, today too little.' " His flexibility, says Martonne, is the very opposite of Toscanini's fixity. "That is one thing that Toscanini never had . . . that inner sensitivity."[66]

The New York Philharmonic Orchestra, founded as a musicians' cooperative in 1842, is relaunched as a corporate benefaction with a concert that conjoins past to present. Beethoven's *Consecration of the House* Overture and *Eroica* Symphony make up the first half, Liszt's *Mazeppa* and *Till Eulenspiegel* by Richard Strauss the second. "Geniuses in the art of conducting must be permitted to have their principles of interpretation . . . before they are condemned unduly," rumbles Krehbiel,[67] unhappy with the heavy program. The Historical Series opens with Bach, Handel, Rameau, Grétry, and Haydn, prefaced by a Bach suite that Mahler has reworked and plays himself from the keyboard of a Steinway piano whose hammers are fitted with tacks to make it sound like a harpsichord.

His next Beethoven night is in Brooklyn, the first time the Philharmonic has stepped off the island of Manhattan to where working people live. "At last, Brooklyn is really in New York," exclaims a borough newspaper.[68] Back at Carnegie Hall the discomfited Krehbiel is sharpening his pencil. A published authority on Beethoven, the future editor of Alexander Wheelock Thayer's monumental biography, he denotes Mahler's changes to the Fifth Symphony more in perplexity at first than in rage.

> The first evidence of erraticism occurred in the famous cadenza in the first movement. This Mr. Mahler phlebotomized by giving it to two oboes and beating time for each note—not in the expressive adagio called for by Beethoven but in a rigid andante. There the rhapsodic utterance contemplated by the composer was turned into a mere connecting link between two parts of the movement. Into the cadence of the second subject of the third movement, Mr. Mahler injected a bit of un-Beethovenian color by changing the horn parts so that listeners familiar with their Wagner were startled by hearing something like Hagen's call.[69]

In a thousand words of pedantic detail, Krehbiel reconducts the symphony move for move, as a football fan might do with instant replay. Had Mahler taken him aside for a coffee, antagonism might have been averted. But Mahler cannot be bothered. He hates the press and does not think they can harm him; he has learned nothing in Vienna. Krehbiel, receiving no response to his salvo, proceeds to savage everything Mahler says and does. He particularly detests his claim to educate the audience, snorting that this foreigner "never discovered that there were Philharmonic subscribers who had inherited not only their seats from their parents and grandparents but also their appreciation of good music. He never knew, or if he knew he was never willing to acknowledge, that the Philharmonic audience would be as quick to resent an outrage on the musical classics as a corruption of the Bible or Shakespeare."[70]

This argument appears in Krehbiel's obituary of Mahler, a morning-after exercise in character assassination that pans his Vienna regime as "expensive and unprofitable" and his American work as "prejudicial to good taste." Citing Mahler's conversion to Christianity as proof of personal insincerity, he rejects his symphonies as falsehoods, adding: "We cannot see how any of his music can long survive him." Just what has made New York's foremost critic so mad? Mahler's refusal to meet the press. Seeing Mahler's First Symphony on the schedule, Krehbiel, the official Philharmonic annotator, asks for help with his notes. Mahler refuses him an explanation. Krehbiel regards this as a rebuff to critics like himself who mediate between composer and listeners. "All writings about music, even those of musicians themselves, he holds injurious to musical enjoyment," he tells concertgoers, apologizing for the lack of further information. "Krehbiel jumped on [Mahler] with both feet"[71] from here on, relates the *Sun* critic, Henry Finck.

Krehbiel should not have been allowed to get away with it. A competent editor would have brought both parties to the table, having warned the critic in private that his writing was unacceptably biased. I have done such things myself as an editor; balance and an open mind are essential to any self-respecting critic. Krehbiel, however, has a weak editor, Ogden Mills Reid, and he is allowed to get away with murder. Mahler ignores the smears and does not try, as others do, to get even. Conductors, in my time, have caused critics to be sacked or demoted in Washington, D.C., Cleveland, and Berlin. Several have threatened critics with legal writs. Once a new music director of the New York Philharmonic took a *Times* staffer to lunch and told him: "In Vienna, every conductor has his critic. I want you to be *my* critic." Mahler stays above such murk.

Critics aside, he is at work. "It was my lifelong desire to have my own concert orchestra," he writes. "Simply making music is still tremendous fun for me—if only my musicians were a bit better." He visits an opium den in Chinatown, meets the designer Louis Comfort Tiffany, who is addicted to hashish, sees President Roosevelt's Oyster Bay house, and goes slumming on the Lower East Side in alleys filled with raucous Jews. "Are these our human brothers?" asks Alma.[72]

Whole weeks are enlivened by interesting soloists. Ferruccio Busoni, a bibliomane in several languages, has composed a *Turandot* suite with Chinese scales that piques Mahler's curiosity. Then Rachmaninoff, popular for a C-sharp-minor Prelude, arrives. His Third Concerto in D minor is premiered by Damrosch at the New Theater ("not a great or a memorable proclamation," writes Henderson). Mahler gives the second performance at Carnegie Hall. "He touched my composer's heart straight away," says Rachmaninoff, "by devoting himself to my concerto until the accompaniment, which is rather complicated, has been practiced to the point of perfection." The session overruns by an hour and, when players prepare to leave, Mahler shouts: "As long as I am sitting, no musician has the right to get up."[73] For Rachmaninoff, in his memoirs, Mahler is the only conductor "worthy of being classed with Nikisch."[74]

That is not how some players remember it. The Philharmonic is split down national lines, those of German origin liking Mahler, the Italians Toscanini, and the Russians neither. Russian players say that Rachmaninoff "was very much disappointed and even offended by the treatment he received at the hands of Mahler."[75] They add a spoonful of bile by telling him (untruthfully) that Mahler hates Tchaikovsky. (These musicians are very old men by the time these stories are recounted.) Rachmaninoff and Mahler have more in common than meets the ear. The tremulous opening phrase of the Russian's recent Second Symphony, unheard by Mahler, is an uncanny pre-echo of the Adagio of Mahler's unwritten Tenth. Both composers have depressive tendencies, and both work against public expectation. It sounds, from Rachmaninoff's account, as if they achieve an intuitive affinity.

Mahler gets through his heavy workload without mishap. "I am getting on famously. . . . I can stand all the strain without being any the worse for it,"[76] he writes. "I am definitely more able to work and happier than I have been in ten years."[77] He conducts twice, sometimes three times a week and tours with the Philharmonic to Philadelphia, New Haven, Springfield (Massachusetts), and Providence (Rhode Island). The climax comes in Boston, where the *Globe* critic is smitten by his performance of the *Symphonie Fantastique*, "luminous with the poetry and the terror of the work."[78] In one season he has fashioned an orchestra to match the Boston Symphony, America's finest, and established the format of multiple subscription series that will govern U.S. concert life ever after.

A little girl climbs out of bed. It is dark outside, but there is a pool of light in the sitting room. Beneath it her father is hunched over a sheet of paper that covers the entire surface of his desk. She shuffles over, clutching a blanket. "What are you doing, Papi?"

He peers down with eyes so weary she feels as if she has been scooped up into his very being. "I am correcting my music," he explains, lifting her onto his lap. Pens and knives are laid out at the paper's margin.

"How do you correct music?" she presses, wanting to extend the moment so that it might never end.

"If I find a bad note I scratch it out, like so," he demonstrates, blade in hand.

"I wouldn't like to be a note." Anna Mahler shudders.

"Why not?" her father murmurs.

"Because you might scratch me out and blow me away."[79]

This was Anna Mahler's fondest memory of her father, at morning before daybreak in a New York hotel when the world slept and they were united in art. She sat quietly as he copied out his Ninth Symphony, careful not to disturb, knowing that "the work" took precedence. There would be other moments together—snowballing in Central Park, away from her governess's eye—but this was the closest she ever felt to her father. Mahler, the child sensed, wanted to imprint something of himself on her. She was all he had left apart from her glamorous mother, of whose affections neither of them could be certain. Her sister's death weighed upon them all.

Over the next eighty years Anna became a sculptor of exceptional force and beauty. "Through truly great art we participate in the secret of creation, the whole of creation," she declared, in a 1962 lecture at the University of Chicago. "The chaos of the so-called reality of everyday life disappears and makes room for a deeper, truer reality, a mysterious ordering, which . . . transmits, in the most sublime cases of perfection, the almost mystical certainty that the universe makes sense."[80] This is Mahler, speaking through the mouth of his child.

I met Anna in 1986, and we became close, talking about anything except Mahler—art, politics, love. We bombarded each other with books and letters. She gave me the Victorian novelist George Henry Borrow. I sent her the travelogues of Graham Greene. We shared many confidences ("I wish I had told you more," she wrote) and waged close combat on onionskin airmail paper. She refused to read George Orwell because he had fought for the wrong group in the Spanish civil war. "Those years," she said, "were the most muddling you could possibly imagine. Everybody had to have an opinion— and everybody was wrong. Looking back, one can peel off one after the other, the lies one was fed from every side."[81] Truth and lies were her moral polarities. Art was truth, the key to life.

Her relations with Alma were always turbulent. At sixteen she ran off and married a family friend. A year later she was in Berlin, living with the composer Ernst Krenek; Alma insisted on marriage ("always a mistake," said Anna). Her third husband was the wealthy Viennese publisher Paul Zsolnay, who lived in a Baroque palace, "where I always felt like a guest."

Across the street from her father's opera house, she had a studio where she sculpted "a kind of museum of famous heads,"[82] including State Chancellor Kurt Schuschnigg and all the leading musicians and writers. "She did not suspect to what extent the museum was a reflection of her mother's life," noted Elias Canetti, the future Nobel laureate, who was briefly Anna's lover. "There were always men," sighed Anna. "That was easy. But if you want a really full life and to work as well, you have to be stronger than a man."[83]

She made a bust of Mahler and destroyed it; the rest of her heads were blown to bits in the war. In 1938 she fled to London where her school friend, Dea Gombrich, sister of Ernst, the art historian, was married to the director of the British Museum, John Forsdyke. After a Sunday roast, Forsdyke would unbuckle a bunch of keys from his waistband and say, "Here you are, dear, have my museum to yourself for the afternoon." One night during the Blitz she met a Russian conductor, Anatole Fistoulari, "and took him in like a stray animal." They had a daughter, Marina. "London is the closest I ever had to a home," said Anna. Alma summoned her to California, where she married the literary scholar Albrecht Joseph and, on her mother's death in 1964, inherited the Mahler legacy just as his music was sweeping the world.

A retrospective of her work was planned for the 1988 Salzburg Festival, and she flew over from California, desperately ill. When I visited her, emaciated, in Marina's London apartment, she greeted me with a point from my last letter and demanded to know, eyes flashing, if my views had changed. Curious to the last, Mahler's daughter died on June 3, 1988, and was buried in Highgate Cemetery, not far from Karl Marx.

12. "To Live for You, To Die for You" (1910–1911)

Mahler docks at Cherbourg, anticipating pleasure. He has concerts in two favorite cities, Paris and Rome, followed by a fiftieth birthday celebration and crowned with the premiere of his Eighth Symphony in Munich, the biggest concert ever staged.

Things go wrong from the start. In Paris his Second Symphony provokes shouts of "À bas la musique allemande [Down with German music]!" Debussy walks out, muttering, "Malheur [Misery]." In Rome the playing is so poor that he cancels the last concert. In Vienna he runs into Lipiner, who has cancer of the tongue. Emil Zuckerkandl is dying. Theobald Pollak is not long for this world. He is reaching an age when ill health dominates dinner-table conversation.

Alma, unwilling to be left out, visits a consultant for her nerves. "I was very ill," she explains. "The wear and tear of being driven by a spirit so intense as his had brought me to complete breakdown."[1] She does not mention that she is drinking heavily, or her resentment at Mahler's Eighth Symphony chorus rehearsals in Vienna, Leipzig, and Munich. Her physician prescribes six weeks of warm baths at Tobelbad, near Graz.

Mahler drives her there on June 1, with Anna and her governess. On the way back to Vienna, he looks at a house for sale where they might live when he finishes in America. Another trip takes him past the castle at Plankenberg where Alma was happiest as a girl. "I live only for you and Gucki [Anna]," he writes to her. "No other living thing could ever come between me and my love for you."[2] These avowals of love reach Alma hours after she takes a lover.

On her third night at the spa, over a meal of lettuce and butter-milk, Alma is joined at her table by a Berlin architect, twenty-six years old. Blue-eyed, terse, and with a trim mustache, Walter Gropius has a military bearing and the stringency of Martin Luther. He aims to reform modern decor, stripping it of ornament and creating a severe white world of functional simplicity. After dinner he asks Alma to dance. Later, she narrates, "we stopped dancing and talked."[3] They take a walk in the night air, sitting by a creek in moonlight. Either that night or the next, her diary records, "Two souls met and the body was forgotten."[4]

Mahler, immersed in rehearsals, receives letters that are "sweeter than ever."[5] He grows suspicious—"Are you concealing something from me?"—and visits her at the end of June. "I found Almschi much fresher and fitter and am convinced the cure is doing her a great deal of good,"[6] he tells her mother, who needs no reassurance. Anna Moll becomes privy to the affair when Alma brings Gropius on a day trip to Vienna. Fifty-three years old and running to fat, Anna Moll volunteers her address as a safe maildrop, reliving her sexual past through her daughter's infidelity. Innately racist, Frau Moll is delighted to dump the Jew Mahler for the Prussian architect. "Hold your head high," she exhorts Gropius, "you have a fine goal ahead of you . . . your devoted Mama."[7]

Mahler is in Toblach for his fiftieth birthday, alone. When Alma joins him a week later, she promises Gropius to be faithful and collects his letters daily at the post office, box AM40. Mahler is composing in his hut. Little Anna has a high fever.

One day at the end of July, the postman knocks at the farmhouse door with a letter addressed to "Herr Direktor Mahler." Sitting at the piano, Mahler slits open the envelope and reads another man's love letter to his wife. "What is this?" Alma, cornered, goes on the offensive. "At last I was able to tell him all. I told him I had longed for his love year after year and that he, in his fanatical concentration on his own life, had simply overlooked me. As I spoke, he felt for the first time that something is owed to the person with whom one's life has once been linked. He suddenly felt a sense of guilt."[8]

Mahler, bludgeoned with his shortcomings as a husband, cries, "it's all my fault." Alma feels her resentment turn to pity, or power, or love. They take weeping walks in the meadow. Tears and fears flood Mahler's symphony. One movement is titled "Purgatorio," a living hell. "Oh, God! Oh, God! Why hast thou forsaken me?" he writes across the five-staved score, commingling music with his sense of failure. At the opening of a Scherzo he writes in an agitated hand:

> The devil dances it with me
> Madness, take me, cursed one!
> Exterminate me *[vernichte mich]*
> So that I forget I exist
> So that I cease to be
>   So that I . . .

Never has a composer's private world been so exposed on music paper. At the end, beneath the New York fire chief's drumstroke, he writes, "You alone know what this means." All his messages are meant for Alma, who will publish them one day:

> Ach! Ach! Ach!
> Farewell *[Leb wol]*, my lyre!
> Farewell
> Farewell
> Farewell
> Ach, w
>   Ach Ach.[9]

The lyre is music and Alma his muse. At the bottom of the last page he writes:

> To live for you *[Für dich leben]*!
> To die for you *[Für dich sterben]*!
>   Almschi!

The symphony opens with an Adagio of defeat, no lurches of rage or resistance, just a stumble into the void. At its coda he piles nine notes one upon the other in a steepling chord, analogous in its agony to Edvard Munch's painting *The Scream*. This nine-note discordance, Mahler's "catastrophe chord," follows no recognized harmonic laws. Like Schoenberg when his wife walked out, Mahler is tipping his music into a chasm of atonality. It is truly the end of his world.

Alma finds him one night standing over her bed, making sure she is still there. She promises never to leave. "When I told him so, his face was transfigured. His love became an ecstasy. He could not be parted from me for a second."[10] Torn, she asks Gropius to stay away—"Don't come here! I beg you!!"—but riding into Toblach she sees him hiding beneath a bridge. When she tells Mahler, he sets out on foot to find his lurking rival. It is night when they return, Mahler leading the way with a lantern. He leaves the pair. Within moments Alma rushes to Mahler, who is sitting in her room, reading the Bible by the light of two candles. "Whatever you do will be right," he assures her. "Make your decision." Next morning she drives Gropius to the station. She has made up her mind. She will stay with Mahler, for now. "I could never have imagined life without him . . . Mahler was the hub of my existence and so he continued to be."[11] The following day her mother arrives.

Told by Alma in her memoirs, the story sounds vaguely familiar, as if it is a Schnitzler melodrama she has seen onstage or read in a magazine. The characters are stock figures: the cuckolded husband, the desirable young wife, the athletic lover, and the meddlesome mother. Her tale is riddled with clichés and selective with truth. She writes what she wants the world to see, appearance over experience, *Schein über Sein*. The reality is more dignified. Gropius is not the heartless stud of Alma's story. He has hung around in Toblach for days hoping to settle matters man-to-man with Mahler. Taken aback by his rival's self-possession, he writes him a letter of apology from the train home to Berlin: "It pains me that I can only cause you pain. Let me at least thank you again for the nobility with which you treated me and shake your hand for one last time."[12] There is a suggestion of complicity in this communication, as if both know the play is not over yet.

Alma's mother has written to Gropius, meanwhile, telling him that Mahler is dying and asking him to be patient: "Gustav has a serious cardiac complaint: it is a miracle the shock hasn't killed him"[13]—

seemingly wishing that it had. Alma follows up with an assurance that they will not be apart for long, picturing a time "when you lie naked next to me at night, when nothing can separate us any more except sleep."[14] Mahler has, it seems, agreed to let her sleep with Gropius in order to save the marriage.

He slips love poems beneath her bedroom door. He will do anything to keep her. Alma, coming in from a walk, hears him playing a song she recognizes as her own. "What have I done?" he cries. "These are good—they are excellent. I insist on your working on them and we'll have them published. I'll never be happy until you start composing again. God, how blind and selfish I was."[15] Unless he is demented, Mahler knows the songs are trivial, lacking a single original phrase. He shows them to Oskar Fried. "Very nice," says Fried politely. Mahler shouts him out of the house. At dawn Alma finds Mahler once more beside her bed. "Would it give you any pleasure if I dedicated the Eighth to you?" he asks. "Don't," she warns. "You might regret it." "Too late," says Mahler. He makes Universal reprint the proofs several times until the dedication, "to my beloved wife, Alma Maria Mahler," appears in the appropriate size.

And so August grinds on, each mealtime and stroll an agony of mistrust; and every day in the woodland hut, the Tenth Symphony grows. The Adagio quotes a shepherd's plaint from *Tristan und Isolde*. The "Purgatorio" recalls the Ninth Symphony's Rondo-Burleske, while a second Scherzo echoes the "Drinking Song" from *The Song of the Earth*. The finale begins in muffled drumbeats and ends in unbearable tenderness, an ache of yearning and regret. This is not Mahler's last word. Given another summer, he would have changed content and texture, maybe the order of movements. But this is how he leaves the Tenth Symphony at the end of August 1910, never touching it again.

THOSE AGONIZED INSCRIPTIONS

Musicians do not as a rule deface a work in progress. The sheets cost good money, and respect is owed to the tools of one's trade. Mahler uses top-quality Johann Eberle (J. E. & Co.) music paper from

Vienna. We can only guess at the torment that drove him to smear words on the pages of a symphony, but unless he was off his head—and his conduct belies it—he must have intended these graffiti to be read by someone.

By Alma, of course: She always saw his work first. Knowing her lack of discretion, he may have expected her to bring his cries to light at some point in time. Apart from Alma, Mahler showed raw scores to Bruno Walter and his editor, Josef Venantius von Wöss. The shrieks on the pages of the Tenth, and the earlier marks on the Ninth, are meant to be seen. He is expressing an existential loneliness, the awful fear that he will die alone. Being abandoned, losing his love, living in dread that his heart will give out—all three miseries leap from the facsimile score in my hands. But why has Mahler chosen to share these agonies? I had a flash of insight one hard day at the office.

Pope John Paul II was nearing the end of his life. Afflicted by Parkinson's disease, his hands trembled and his speech was almost incomprehensible when he appeared each Sunday on his balcony at Saint Peter's to bless the masses below. This pope had changed the world, confronting the Soviet empire and helping to bring it down. He was a figure of historic importance, and with each Sunday blessing he was disintegrating before our eyes. At an editorial meeting one of my colleagues suggested we should comment on his infirmity. Someone took the line that the pope was weakening the church by parading his incapacity, that he should do as past popes had done, withdraw into invisibility, in mute acceptance of God's will. All of a sudden Mahler sprang to mind. "Absolutely not!" I erupted. "What the pope is doing is bringing decline and death out of the closet, showing that it happens to us all, that it is not shameful. He is setting an example. He is telling us not to lock away our popes and grandparents in nursing homes but cherish them in our midst, able or disabled, until the end. He is manifesting the dignity in death, and the value of life."

The news agenda drove us onto other subjects; the pope died in March 2005. But when I left the newspaper that night, the logic of Mahler's inscriptions became clear. This was a composer who shared pain with a purpose. In early symphonies he dealt with his traumas of infant mortality, religious intolerance, and social exclusion. In the last symphonies he dealt with the losses that befall us all. Nothing is held back, nothing redacted. Mahler turned his life inside out so that the rest of us might better understand what happens to us. In the Tenth Symphony as in the first, he is like a three-year-old kid in a pond, splashing water and shouting "I'm getting wet!", reporting life as he experiences it and warning the rest of the world to stand well back.

WHAT FREUD TELLS ME

Little Anna's summer flu spreads to the rest of the household. Alma, waking in a sweat, calls out to Mahler in the next room. Hearing no reply, she runs out. He is on the landing, unconscious and stone cold, a candle burning beside him. With her mother's help she carries him to bed, wrapped in blankets. They soak his hands and feet in hot water and attempt a massage. The doctor, arriving at dawn, finds no risk to life, but Alma tells Gropius she "almost feared the worst,"[16] perhaps wished it.

Illness has a salutary effect on Mahler. "He realised he had lived the life of a neurotic and suddenly decided to consult Sigmund Freud," is how Alma puts it. Mahler knows that Freud tries "to cure everything from one particular standpoint,"[17] placing the sexual origin of neurosis at the root of all problems. His understanding is fairly accurate. Freud writes to his defecting ally Carl Jung: "Promise me never to abandon the sexual theory. That is the most essential thing of all. You see, we must make a dogma of it."[18] Mahler is suspicious of cults and cure-alls, but he also knows that Freud is not as fixated on sex as he is often made out to be. Bruno Walter, consulting him for a nagging arm pain, is sent off for a holiday in Sicily without being asked about his sex life. Mahler also agrees with Freud on the importance of dreams. "We know," he says, "that our second self is active while we sleep, that it grows and becomes and produces what the real self sought and wanted in vain."[19]

Getting an appointment with a psychoanalyst in August is never easy, but Richard Nepallek, Alma's family friend, is a member of the

Vienna Psycho-Analytic Society. He knows where Freud can be reached: at Noordwijk in Holland, taking the sea air with his wife, sister-in-law, and two sons. Freud agrees to break his vacation to treat "a man of Mahler's worth."[20] It is too "lustig" an opportunity, he says, too curious or amusing to be missed. He offers to meet Mahler in the university town of Leiden, north of The Hague. A date is set, then another, then a third. Mahler complains of a stubborn sore throat. Freud interprets his hesitancy as a *"folie de doute* of his obsessional neurosis." He warns that August 27 is his last free day before he leaves with a colleague for Italy. Mahler jumps on a train, traveling thirty hours via Innsbruck and Munich and reaching Leiden late on the twenty-sixth. He checks in at the Golden Lion Hotel, a gabled house on Breestraat, a shopping street. Freud arrives by tram from the coast the following afternoon. They meet at 4:30 at a Breestraat café, the Gilded Turk.

Two Viennese gentlemen sit at a table in a sleepy Dutch town. Both are Jewish and Czech, almost the same age. Both try to save the world by unlocking its unconscious. Both reject their fathers' faith. Neither attends his mother's funeral. They understand each other on sight, "a congruence of cognition,"[21] as a Freud pupil puts it. Freud says he "never met anyone who seemed to understand [psychoanalysis] so swiftly."[22]

Who has the first word in the great conversation? Is it Freud, asking Mahler about his journey, or does Mahler inquire after Freud's family? Freud will have been briefed by Nepallek on Mahler's troubles, while Mahler is plainly anxious, torn between a need for relief and a fear of treatment. "What seems to be the problem?", the standard opener, would be too banal for Freud to offer "a man of Mahler's worth." He has a very short time to effect a cure. He cannot put Mahler on a couch six days a week for months. He needs to perform "a psychoanalytically informed crisis intervention"[23] and he does so by breaking all his own rules. Draining his cup of coffee, he suggests a stroll through the deserted streets of the student-free town. Over the next four hours, until sunset, the two gentlemen perambulate beside the canals, brows furrowed, discussing issues of heart and mind. The talking cure becomes a walking cure. Freud, six feet tall, full bearded and thick at the waistline, smokes a fat cigar. Mahler, barely up to his shoulder, pale faced, clean shaven, and skinny, hops and skips along in his agitated way, interjecting acute incisions, never letting his healer hold forth without objection. They may stop again for coffee, or rest awhile on a bench; these details are unrecorded. They shake hands and part just in time for Freud to catch the last tram.[24]

"Feeling cheerful, interesting discussion," Mahler wires Alma the next morning. He follows up with, "I am living everything as if new."[25] He boards the homeward train and, on the long rattling journey, writes her an explanatory love poem:

> Night shadows are dispelled by a mighty word
> Gone are my agonies of self-immersion
> Flowing together into one single chord:
> My hesitant thoughts, my tempestuous emotion.
> *I love you!* This is my strength, my prize
> Life's own melody that I have gained through pain.
> *Oh, love me!* This is the wisdom by which I abide
> The bass-note to my constant refrain.
>
> *I love you!* That's what I live for
> For that, I'd gladly give up world and thought.
> *Oh, love me!* You, my storm's windfall,
> Greet me—dead to the world—for I have reached port.

In plain terms, Mahler is telling his wife that Freud's "mighty word" has relieved him of *agonies* in his "one single chord" of ninenote dissonance. He knows now what he must do. He will devote himself to Alma, no matter what else he renounces in "world and thought." She is his haven, his harbor, his destiny and destination. He throws in their private codes. "Flowing together" is from the poem he sent her the morning after they met. "Lost to the World" is his most self-depictive song and the emphasized lines of love are from the Rückert song he wrote in their first summer of married life. "World and thought" is a *Traveling Apprentice* line. Mahler is tying up his life in a bundle and laying it at Alma's feet, confident that he has found relief.

Exactly what that relief is—what Freud has said to renew his zest for life—will emerge in partial disclosures. Alma has the first say in her memoirs in 1939. Freud, she reports, scolds Mahler: "How dared a man in your state ask a young woman to be tied to him?" But he reassures Mahler that Alma will never leave him because she "loved her father and can only choose and love a man of his sort."[26] Alma alone can make him happy, says the therapist. "Freud is quite right," agrees Mahler in a letter: "You were always for me the light and the central point! The inner light, I mean, which rose above all; and the blissful consciousness of this—now *unshadowed* and unconfined— raises all my feelings to the infinite. . . . So long as Eros is the ruler of men and gods, so surely will I make a fresh conquest of all, of the heart which once was mine and can only in unison with mine find its way to God and blessedness."[27] From Alma's point of view it appears that Freud has offered elementary marriage guidance embellished with spontaneous flashes of personal empathy.

A second glimpse into the conversation appears in 1953, recounted in a study by Theodor Reik, ex-secretary of the Vienna Psycho-Analytic Society. Reik, working on the psychology of creativity, asks Freud about Mahler. Freud replies:

> The visit appeared necessary to him because his wife at the time rebelled against the fact that he withdrew his libido from her. In highly interesting expeditions through his life history, we discovered his personal conditions for love, especially his Holy Mary complex (mother fixation). I had plenty of opportunity to admire the capacity for psychological understanding of this man of genius. No light fell at the time on the symptomatic façade of his obsessional neurosis. It was as if you would dig a single shaft through a mysterious building.[28]

Mahler's problem, Freud implies in this scenario, is that he stopped having sex with Alma ("withdrew his libido") for fear the exercise might kill him.

In a third report Freud confides that Mahler has become impotent. He tells this to Princess Marie of Greece and Denmark, a Bonaparte descendant with orgasmic inhibitions so severe that she has her clitoris relocated twice[29] (by a surgeon, Josef Halban, who is married to Mahler's singer Selma Kurz[30]). Freud, excited to have a Napoleon on his couch, is lavishly indiscreet. In a lubricious, gossipy exchange, Freud tells the princess that Mahler has "an enormous mother-fixation," and that Alma is attracted to him because his name sounds like *Maler* (painter), her father's craft. Mahler responds with a Freudian intuition. "I now understand something about my music!"[31] he cries, relating how, while his parents were fighting, he heard an organ-grinder playing "Ach, du lieber Augustin," a ditty with the ending "Alles ist hin [everything is doomed]." People, says Mahler, "have often reproached me because my music has sudden changes from the most noble to an ordinary banal melody." Freud brings him back to the physical problem. "This analytic talk evidently produced an effect," Freud tells the princess, "since Mahler recovered his potency and the marriage was a happy one until his death, which unfortunately took place only a year later."[32]*

From Reik and Bonaparte, it seems that Mahler cannot, for one reason or another, make love to his wife. Freud puts it down to his mother fixation. By confusing Alma with Marie, he is making a taboo of sexual relations. Of such men, writes Freud in 1912, "where they love they do not desire, and where they desire they do not love." Mahler "is dangerously close to duplicating the repressed and forbidden oedipal situation of childhood."[33] By separating wife from mother, Freud reboots Mahler's natural urges, and marital relations are resumed. Freud seems to have offered Mahler a full course of psychoanalysis, adding that, had Mahler accepted, he could have been "cured of his neurosis" and "his works would probably have been quite different."[34]

There are two further pieces to the puzzle. On May 23, 1911, in the days after Mahler's funeral, Freud sends an invoice to his executor, Emil Freund, for three hundred crowns "for a consultation of several hours in August 1910 in Leiden, where I had gone at his

* The princess gave a précis to Ernest Jones for his 1957 Freud biography; her original notes appear in volume 4 of La Grange's 2008 Mahler biography.

request from Nordwijk am. Z."[35] The following night the Vienna Psycho-Analytic Society discusses whether the unconscious can accelerate death in a man like Mahler, by weakening his resistance. Freud announces that he can "readily confirm the validity of the assumption expressed . . . for he knows that Mahler was at a turning point in his life at which he had the alternative of either changing, and thereby giving up the basis of his artistic power, or of evading the conflict."[36] He asks for "special discretion" about this remark. Freud confides that he left Mahler with a stark choice: To repair his psyche he will have to give up something of great importance. It is a device that Freud often applies to difficult patients. Princess Marie, during her own psychoanalysis, writes: "Must I give up sex? . . . Absolute chastity frightens me."[37]

So what change, what sacrifice, has Freud demanded of Mahler to help save his mental health and his marriage? Some writers conclude that he is told to give up composing.[38] Mahler, however, does no such thing. During the following winter he plans a summer of "creative work," including a revision of his Fifth Symphony and a completion of the Tenth. If he gives up composing, life is not worth living. If that is what Freud suggests, he cannot agree. More likely the "basis of his artistic power" that he agrees to give up is conducting. Soon after seeing Freud, Mahler asks Josef Hoffmann to build him a house on a plot at Semmering, outside Vienna, where he can retire with Alma on his pension and dollar savings. Freud has assured him that Alma will never leave if she has the freedom to fulfill her creative needs and sleep with whomever she pleases. The confidence enables Mahler to ride home elated and restored.

Freud, too, is affected by the conversation. He admires Mahler's intellect—"the capacity for psychological understanding of this man of genius"—and is fascinated by the "mysterious building" of his personality. He takes away various lessons from the encounter. Never again does Freud attempt a four-hour session or another snap cure. Nor does he accept another patient of Mahler's "worth." A debate is beginning on the effect of psychoanalysis on creative artists. Freud, after Mahler, never attempts another intervention.

As for Alma, she has a will of her own. While the two giants are talking she writes to Gropius and signs herself "dein Weib [your wife]." She cannot wait to see him: "There is not one spot on your body that I would not like to caress with my tongue."[39] They arrange to meet in Munich while Mahler is rehearsing his Eighth Symphony.

AT LAST A REAL FORTISSIMO

Munich in September is a golden vista of wilting leaves and foaming beer jugs. Mahler arrives on a chilly Saturday night, books into the Continental Hotel, and goes to bed shivering. On Sunday morning he has a fever. A doctor finds one side of his throat furred with white sepsis. Mahler elects to sweat it out. He orders all the blankets in the hotel and wraps up for three hours while the impresario Emil Gutmann mops pools of perspiration. Monday morning he is in rehearsal, conducting a children's chorus with a wooden spoon. At the verse "Er wird uns lehren," he asks them to sing so expressively that their parents in the hall will recognize every voice. From the orchestra he demands a sound that will cut "like a knife through butter."

Alma arrives on Tuesday, wearing a Josef Hoffmann diadem that Mahler bought for her birthday. After checking in at the Continental, she walks down to the Regina Palast Hotel, where Gropius awaits her for love. "How could she?" exclaims her daughter, Anna, learning of the tryst by chance seventy-five years later. "Anyone could have seen her. How could she do that to Mahler?"[40]

Eminences gather for Europe's last prewar cultural convocation. Four Viennese writers—Schnitzler, Hofmannsthal, Bahr, and Zweig—are greeted by Thomas Mann, leader of the new German literature. Richard Strauss, Max Reger, and Siegfried Wagner meet the French composers Camille Saint-Saëns and Paul Dukas. Leopold Stokowski squeezes into standing room. A New York reporter wangles himself a seat:

> When Mahler appeared on the podium, the entire audience, as if responding to a secret signal, rose to its feet, initially in silence. The way a king is greeted. Only when Mahler, visibly surprised, gestured

his gratitude, did a cheering erupt of a kind that is seldom heard at such an event. All this before the performance began.[41]

"At this moment," recalls Gutmann, the harried organizer, "there were no singers, no audience, no instruments, no sounding-board—but one single body with many, many veins and nerves, waiting for the blood and breath of art to bring them to life. No other conductor inspires this readiness."[42] Alma is "almost insensible from excitement."[43] Anton Webern finds the beauty "hardly bearable."[44] At the end "the storm broke loose."[45] "I have never seen anything like this," gasps Janko Cadra. "I am not sure how many times [Mahler] had to return, certainly fifteen or twenty, but the applause, banging and calling his name lasted about three-quarters of an hour until they switched off all the lights."[46]

The children's choir "hailed him with shouts of jubilation."[47] "They ran down to meet the helpless victor, seized his hand and rained flowers upon him. Outside the carriages were waiting but when Mahler came, with happiness such as he had hardly ever before experienced written on his features, he could only slowly find his way through the still-excited crowd. . . . It seemed as though Mahler had at last reached the summit of his life and fame."[48]

For Thomas Mann, Mahler is "the first person he'd ever met who gave him the impression of being a great man."[49] Over tea with the Mahlers, Mann observes a "head that seemed a little too large in proportion to his almost delicate stature. His brushed-back hair, thinning at the top, very thick and distinctly gray over the temples, framed a high, deeply-lined, scarred-looking forehead. The bow of a pair of gold spectacles with rimless lenses cuts into the base of his strong, nobly curved nose."[50] This description will soon be imprinted in fiction.

In Vienna, Mahler attends a rehearsal of Schoenberg's quartets and an exhibition of his paintings. He visits Berta Zuckerkandl, in mourning for her husband, Emil. She laments Viennese cynicism, wondering if there is "such a thing as a psychology of cities?" Mahler suggests that "Freud should add a psychology of cities to his list. . . . Unfortunately, you can't uncover the unconscious of a city."[51] Bruno Walter is alarmed at Mahler's air of valediction, evident in his farewell to Guido Adler, fellow Iglauer, his oldest friend:

> He came to me, pale with weary eyes, and spoke the words, incomprehensible to me at the time: "Whatever may happen or put itself between us, we remain old friends in our inmost relations." . . . I obtained his promise; "Gustav, you must never again go to America." He promised, and kept it, as in life every promise was sacred to him.[52]

Alma leaves Vienna separately from Mahler, catches a train with Gropius, and spends three illicit nights with him in Paris. She boards the *Kaiser Wilhelm II* at Boulogne and, on deck in mid-Atlantic, takes photographs of Gustav Mahler, who stares out, defeated, from beneath a peaked cap.

The Philharmonic has a new manager, a moderately corrupt talent agent called Loudon Charlton, who promises to save money by squeezing as many concerts as possible from each rehearsal. That means more tours. In December, Mahler plays Pittsburgh, Cleveland, Buffalo, Rochester, Syracuse, and Utica in six nights. He is "invincible" in Pennsylvania, "herculean" in Ohio.[53] From Buffalo he is taken to Niagara Falls. "Endlich fortissimo!" he tells the orchestra—at last a real fortissimo.

At Christmas his throat is sore. Dr. Fränkel drops by on New Year's Eve. "We three who loved each other joined hands without a word and wept,"[54] writes Alma. At Carnegie Hall he launches a new-music series with a French night of Enescu, Debussy, Bizet, and Chabrier, plus popular arias by Lalo and Massenet. Next in the series is an Anglo-American night—a symphony by the Irishman Charles Villiers Stanford and Elgar's sumptuous *Sea Pictures* (sung by Louise Kirkby-Lunn), with suites by George W. Chadwick, Charles M. Loeffler, Henry K. Hadley, and Edward MacDowell. This is not the music the guarantors ordered, and the box office is below par. Mahler is summoned to Mrs. Sheldon's mansion at 24 East Thirty-eighth Street. He arrives without a translator, or forewarning of confrontation. Mrs. Sheldon is in the chair, and the atmosphere is hostile. There have been complaints from players about a spy in the orchestra, the violinist Theodor Johner, whom Mahler is ordered to dismiss. He is also asked to commit to a hundred concerts next season, a huge undertaking. Mahler, thinking he is being asked for twice as much work for the same fee, refuses. The ladies accuse him of ingratitude. Alma takes up the story:

> At a word from Mrs. Sheldon a curtain was drawn aside and a lawyer who (as came out later) had been taking notes all the time, entered the room. A document was then drawn up in legal form, strictly defining Mahler's powers. He was so taken aback and so furious that he came back to me trembling in every limb.[55]

Fränkel puts him to bed, but there is an all-Italian new-music concert coming up with Busoni. On February 20 he attends a publishers' dinner. "I have found that people in general are kinder than one supposes," says Mahler. "You are an optimist, sir," responds a plump executive's wife. "And more stupid," he snaps.[56] On Tuesday, February 21, bundled in woolens, he is driven from the Savoy to Carnegie Hall for the concert. After conducting an overture by Leone Sinigaglia and Mendelssohn's Italian Symphony, Mahler complains of a headache. He returns to conduct the B-flat-minor Piano Concerto by Giuseppe Martucci, a friend of Toscanini's, followed by the world premiere of Busoni's *Berceuse Elégiaque*. This eight-minute meditation describes a man humming at his mother's funeral a lullaby she sang him in his cradle. Busoni, whose mother died the year before, works the tune over and over to a point of near-abstraction. It sounds as if Wagner's *Siegfried Idyll* has passed through Mahler's Adagietto. On the dedication page Busoni has written:

> The infant cradle rocks,
> The scales of fate are shaken
> The path of life fades out
> Fading into endless distances.

The last words, *die ewigen Fernen*, belong to Mahler's emotional lexicon. Busoni earns two rounds of applause, and Mahler winds up the evening with a Venetian Suite by Marco Enrico Bossi. It is the last piece he will ever perform. Aldrich, in the *Times*, says Italians should stick to writing opera; Krehbiel attacks Busoni's "cacophony."

Mahler awakes in the morning feeling better, but day by day his temperature rises in crazy, ominous zigzags. Fränkel fears Mahler's damaged heart valves are under attack from a mouth infection. He suspects subacute bacterial endocarditis and calls in the man who named the condition. Emanuel Libman, thirty-nine years old, puts a stethoscope to Mahler's chest and hears "a loud systolic-presystolic murmur over the precordium," indicating rheumatic mitral disease, which, with "characteristic petechiae [lesions, or small hemorrhages] on the conjunctivae and skin and slight clubbing of fingers," endorse Fränkel's worst fears. He orders blood tests.[57]

Mahler, shouting that his blood has been "spattered on the walls" during previous tests, is tamed by Libman's assistant, George Baehr, twenty-four years old and a future president of the New York Academy of Medicine. "On arrival," notes Baehr, "I withdrew 20 ccm of blood from an arm vein with syringe and needle, squirting part of it into several bouillon flasks, and mixed the remainder with melted agar media which I then poured into sterile Petri dishes." After four days of incubation "the Petri plates revealed numerous bacterial colonies and all the bouillon flasks were found to show a pure culture of the same organism which was subsequently identified as streptococcus viridans." These results, writes Baehr, "sealed Mahler's doom."[58]

Libman tries treatment with colloidal silver, which can be effective in infections like herpes. Endocarditis is incurable. Penicillin, discovered in 1928, might have killed the streptococcus, but only valve replacement could have saved Mahler's heart, and that is not attempted before 1948 or successful until the 1980s.[59] Mahler's time is up. The only question is whether to tell him. Libman, who treats twenty-seven endocarditis cases that year,[60] generally withholds bad news. It is "extremely unusual," says Baehr, "for Dr. Libman to countenance telling a patient of a fatal diagnosis. It was his rule not to do so in order not to remove a degree of hope. Revealing a fatal diagnosis also made life more difficult for the clinician."[61] Mahler, however, insists on being told. On hearing that he will not recover, he asks to be taken home, to die in Vienna.

Alma's mother arrives. Feeling better, he schedules a rehearsal at Carnegie Hall, but is too weak to leave the hotel. The Philharmonic announces that Mahler has "a light attack of grippe"[62] while opening talks with Felix von Weingartner. Fränkel suggests that he should stop in Paris on the way home to see the great French bacteriologist, André Chantemesse. Alma feeds him broth, spoon by spoon. While he sleeps she writes to Gropius: "I want you. But you? Do you want me also?"[63] On March 30, they are ready to depart:

> Our cabin is booked, the packing was done, and Mahler was dressed. A stretcher was waiting but he waved it aside. He looked as white as a sheet as he walked unsteadily to the lift, leaning on Fränkel's arm. The lift-boy kept out of the way until the last moment, to hide his tears, and then took him down for the last time. The huge hotel lounge was deserted. . . . "We cleared everyone out of the lounge— [said the staff] we knew Mr Mahler wouldn't like to be looked at."[64]

Busoni and Stefan Zweig are also on board the SS *Amerika*. The composer sends Mahler "crazy specimens of counterpoint to amuse him, and bottles of wine."[65] The writer distracts little Anna with fairy tales during disembarkation at Cherbourg. On his first morning in Paris, at the Elysée Palace Hotel, Mahler is dressed, shaved, and ready to go for a drive. By evening he is in a state of collapse. While Alma puts Anna to bed, he gives final orders to Anna Moll. He wants to be buried beside his daughter Maria in the Grinzing cemetery, without fuss, and just "Mahler" on his headstone. "Any who come to look for me will know who I was and the rest don't need to know."[66]

At the clinic in Neuilly his window overlooks the daffodils in the Bois de Boulogne. Professor Chantemesse takes a culture and is delighted with the results. "Madame Mahler, come and look!" he cries, putting her eye to the microscope. "Even I—myself—have never seen streptococci in such a marvelous state of development. Just look at these threads—it's like seaweed."[67] He administers an experimental serum. It appears they may be in Paris for a while, and Alma wonders if Gropius might join her. Bruno Walter arrives, followed by Justi. Twenty-six Viennese celebrities sign a get-well telegram, leaked to the *Neue Freie Presse*, *Schein* triumphant over *Sein*. Vienna, it says, "will never forget its infinite debt of gratitude to you."[68] Arnold Schoenberg writes to Alma, praying for his recovery. "What will happen to Schoenberg?" frets Mahler on one of his last lucid days. "If I go, he will have nobody left."[69]

WHO KILLED GUSTAV MAHLER?

From April 18 the Paris correspondent of the *Neue Freie Presse* files twice-daily bulletins on Mahler's health. "I spoke to Chantemesse after his visit. He found Mahler better than yesterday and in particular he confirmed the satisfactory activity of the heart."[70] Vienna revels in speculative recrimination. "Who Killed Gustav Mahler?" demand the why-oh-why columnists, and Alma gives them instant fuel. In a Paris interview she slams into the New York Philharmonic:

> You cannot imagine what my husband has suffered. In Vienna my husband was all-powerful. Even the Emperor did not dictate to him, but in New York, to his amazement, he had ten ladies ordering him about like a puppet. . . . Then, after an excursion to Springfield, he contracted angina. At his last concert in New York, rather than disappoint the public, he conducted when he was in high fever. Now the angina has been complicated by blood poisoning. My husband cannot read or work. Heaven only knows how it will end.[71]

Busoni endorses her accusation: "It is well known that this woman [Mrs. Sheldon] made life so unpleasant for Mahler that as a result of all the annoyances that he suffered, he was no longer able to withstand his final illness. In a word, she killed him."[72] Loudon Charlton, fired by the Philharmonic a year later, agrees that "too many women" killed Mahler. "Poor Mahler," he recalls. "He used to say every time the doorbell rang: here comes another fat woman. Now for more trouble."[73]

A Berlin newspaper publishes a list of "Victims of the Dollar": "No German artist who has not the reserve and strength of a Schumann-

Heink can hope to survive 'the killing demands of American artistic life.' "[74] Hungarian newspapers accuse America of murdering Mahler. The indictments against America are set in stone, occluding the various other causes—Alma's infidelity, Vienna's anti-Semitism, and his own overexertion. A century later a biographer laments that Mahler's is a "life cut short"[75] when he has, in fact, outlived the average life expectancy of forty-five and is dying of a disease he has carried since boyhood. Nothing Mahler could have done, or the world could have done to Mahler, would have affected its onset or its outcome. Endocarditis is a condition that presents in midlife (the poet Byron dies of it at forty-seven, the actor Rudolph Valentino at thirty-one, the composer Benjamin Britten, after valve replacement, at sixty-three; it may even have killed Mozart[76]). The disease that took his brother Ernst and gave Gustav the urge for self-expression has now called time on his life.

Alma, in a last bid for a cure, summons from Vienna František Chvostek, discoverer of Chvostek anemia. "Now then, Mahler, what's all this about," demands the professor, mustaches bristling. "Working too hard, that's what it is. . . . You've brought it on yourself." Mahler rallies to his bluffness, but late that night Chvostek tells Alma there is no hope—"and may the end come quickly."[77]

On May 10 Mahler has trouble breathing and is given oxygen. He leaves Paris on the *Orient Express*, escorted by Moll, Alma, and Chvostek—"a tragic, heartrending sight," oozes the *Presse*, "to see an artist once filled with artistic passion and the creative urge now lying on a stretcher, helpless and in pain."[78] Journalists surge at every station: "His last journey was like that of a dying king."[79] Thomas Mann, reading the reports, imprints Mahler's name and features on Gustav von Aschenbach, protagonist of his novella *Death in Venice*.

When the *Express* reaches Vienna, police erect screens so that Mahler can be stretchered unseen into an ambulance. He is driven to the Loew sanatorium on Mariannengasse, a fifteen-minute walk from the Opera, and installed in a ground-floor room overlooking a large garden. Chvostek injects morphine. Flowers arrive from the Vienna Philharmonic, "*my* Philharmonic," murmurs Mahler. Alma reads aloud a letter from Richard Strauss, promising to conduct his Third Symphony in Berlin. It gives Mahler, she says, one of his last joys.

The infection reaches his lung, and there is a swelling on his knee. "Be my good girl, my child," he tells little Anna, stroking her head. Alma sees him being washed while the bed linens are changed. "Two attendants lifted his naked, emaciated body. It was a taking down from the cross."[80]

Arthur Schnitzler paces the sanatorium gardens at lunchtime and meets Hermann Bahr, keeping vigil at the street entrance. Alban Berg stalks the corridor. Mahler, half conscious, twitches one finger above the quilt, as if conducting. Alma hears him say "Mozartl," little Mozart. Carl and Anna Moll and Bruno Walter are with him as the final agony begins. Alma, feeling faint, is sent into another room. "I was not allowed in the death chamber. Moll was with him to the last."[81]

Thursday, May 18, 1911, is a stifling day with a forecast of rain. Strauss's *Elektra* is playing at the Opera, the orchestra led by Arnold Rosé in a mounting roar. After dark a storm breaks. Rosé runs to the sanatorium, soaked to the skin. He arrives just in time. At five minutes past eleven the doctors declare Mahler dead, fifty days short of his fifty-first birthday. As the mourners leave the clinic, someone remembers Klimt's comment at a prior leavetaking. "Vorbei," said the artist. "It's over."

13. After Mahler (1911–2010)

H
e left orders for his heart to be pierced with a sharp instrument. Bizarre as this may seem, it was the "modern" way in Vienna, where people feared being buried alive. Schnitzler soon after changed his will, instructing that his heart should be pierced and that, as with Mahler, there should be no religious ceremonies and no mourning.[1]

On the morning of May 19, a district physician, Dr. Stenziger, stabbed the corpse. Carl Moll then covered the face in clay and took a death mask, "sublime and calmly beautiful," said Roller. The body, in a dark suit, was placed in a glass-and-metal coffin under the eyes of Moll, Rosé, Bruno Walter, and Alma's brother-in-law, Wilhelm Legler. Mahler's will (dated April 27, 1904) was published in the Saturday edition of the *Neue Freie Presse*. He had left everything to Alma.

On Monday, May 22, at 4:15 p.m., the coffin was taken from the chapel of the Grinzing cemetery, placed on a four-horse hearse, and escorted beneath lowering skies by men in black and mountains of wreaths. Cultural Vienna turned out in force, along with many earlier acquaintances, among them Moritz Baumgartner of Budapest, who gave Mahler his first summer job. Alma missed the funeral—"on doctor's orders," she said.

Contrary to Mahler's instructions, a short consecration was performed at the parish church by Father Petrus Fourerius Hellebrand. The cortege then wound back under heavy rain, hammering hard on coal black umbrellas, the trees bent double in high winds. As the coffin was lowered into the grave, Moll threw the first clod of earth, Rosé the second. "The crowd, still many hundreds, was scarcely able to speak," recalled Paul Stefan. "The rain ceased, a wonderful rainbow became visible, and a nightingale's voice was heard over the silence."[2] "Somewhere in a tree a bird sang a ragged springtime melody," wrote Josef Bohuslav Foerster. "It reminded me of Mahler's second symphony where . . . a lonely bird, the last in all creation, soars aloft, high as the clouds, free of all terror and sadness."[3] Just then, said Bruno Walter, "the sun burst through the clouds."[4]

Arnold Schoenberg went home and created two works—a painting, *The Burial of Gustav Mahler,* in which a blustery tree provides a canopy for the grave and one bald man stands among crouching mourners; and the last of Six Little Pieces for Piano, op. 19, a muted tolling of bells. "When Mahler is not in Vienna, it is hardly Vienna any more,"[5] he decided. Busoni found him a job in Berlin, and Moll paid his moving expenses. In *Harmonielehre (Theory of Harmony),* dated July 1911, Schoenberg canonized Mahler as "this martyr, this saint," and in a Prague lecture in March 1912 he announced: "Rarely has anyone been so badly treated by the world; nobody, perhaps, worse."[6] A cult of victimhood was created.

Alma mourned at her mother's home for a month before stepping out, saying Mahler had told her not to wear black just to please the neighbors. "Soon I was surrounded by outstanding men, as before."[7] First in line was Joseph Fränkel, the New York doctor who attended Mahler in his final illness. She consorted serially with a zoologist, a composer, and a painter before marrying Gropius and, after him, the mass-market novelist Franz Werfel. At her death in December 1964 the American satirist Tom Lehrer made a ballad, "Alma, Tell Us!", out of her *New York Times* obituary. She is buried in Grinzing, not beside Mahler but in a parallel row.

The Song of the Earth was performed by Walter in Munich November 1911, the Ninth Symphony in Vienna, June 1912. For reasons unknown, it appealed to leading choreographers. Antony Tudor, hearing a 1937 London performance and unable to obtain a score, made *Dark Elegies* out of Mahler's *Songs on the Death of Children.* Kenneth MacMillan, in 1965, showed a lone dancer, parted from vanished friends, whirling in ever-widening circles of blackness, *Ewig . . . Ewig.*

The Ninth Symphony split opinion as to whether it signified resistance or defeat. Alban Berg, writing to his wife, described the ending as "a sort of resignation—always, though, with the thought of 'the other side.' "[8] "Mahler's last marking in the final bar is *ersterbend* (dying away)," noted the British Mahlerian Donald Mitchell. "Words are clumsy, imprecise instruments here. Each listener must make his or her own decision how to interpret—how to 'read'—this infinitely moving coda."[9]

THE TENTH MAN

That left the unfinished Tenth. If the Ninth was Mahler's last word, what could be added by a Tenth? Nobody knew what to do with the leaves from Mahler's last summer. Alma told Specht that Mahler wanted the symphony destroyed. But at the end of the First World War, Richard Strauss was "astonished" to find that the Adagio (I) and Purgatorio (II) were "completely finished, with every instrumental part precisely notated; the sketch could be made into a score without changing a note."[10] Alma commissioned the young composer Ernst Krenek, her son-in-law, to prepare the score for performance, with help from Berg and Franz Schalk. Before the premiere on October 14, 1924, she published a selective facsimile of 116 pages, replete with Mahler's cries of love for her. Walter was enraged. "No composer," he railed at her, "was more averse than Mahler to having an incomplete work made public: you know that as well as I do. I greatly regret that you disregarded this aversion, deeply rooted in his character and works, and are exposing to the public a torso, lacking the corrections and refinements that only the composer could have made."[11] Decsey, reviewing the premiere, noted: "Such was the will of Alma Maria, a fascinating woman, who ruled over Mahler alive as she rules over Mahler dead."[12]

The Tenth Symphony remained dormant until, in 1941, a Canadian airman in London, Jack Diether, decided there was one man who could finish Mahler's Tenth. He wrote, during the Siege of Leningrad, to Dmitry Shostakovich, who declined, saying, "This calls for deep penetration into the spiritual world of the composer."

Diether shared his setback over a beer with Joe Wheeler, a civil servant at the Exchequer and Audit Department, who played in a Sunday-afternoon orchestra on a widow's farm in Essex. Wheeler started tinkering with the sketches that Alma had published in facsimile and tried them out with his amateur ensemble. He was not alone. In Chicago a "socially awkward" insurance clerk, Clinton S. Carpenter, "wanted to be seen as the person who completed the Tenth."[13] Carpenter finished in 1949, Wheeler in 1954. In Hamburg an Adorno student, Hans Wollschläger, started work on the Tenth but wound up translating Joyce's *Ulysses* into German.

Wheeler test-drove four versions with his farmyard band, one of whose members was Deryck Cooke, a BBC employee who wrote classical schedules for the listings magazine, *Radio Times*. Hearing that the classical *Third Programme* was planning a cycle of Mahler symphonies for the 1960 centenary of the composer's birth, Cooke proposed a radio documentary about the unheard Tenth. To conduct the orchestra he booked Berthold Goldschmidt, a German émigré with strong Mahlerian antecedents.

On December 19, 1960, the Cooke-Goldschmidt version of the Tenth went out on the air into British homes and was commented upon abroad. Bruno Walter, in his California dotage, launched another appeal to Alma to ban the work,[14] and she, sloshed on green Benedictines, forbade further performances. In 1963 Goldschmidt arranged for her to be visited by a mutual friend, Harold Byrns, with a tape of the BBC concert. When Byrns asked what she had against attempts to complete the Tenth, she said the symphony was a private letter to her from Gustav and not intended for other ears. Byrns replied, "And I suppose *Tristan* was a private letter from Wagner. . . ." Pouring her another Benedictine, Byrns played her the BBC tape, and Alma was won over.

> Dear Mr. Cooke [she wrote],
>
> I was so moved by this performance that I immediately asked Mr. Byrns to play the work a second time. I then realised that the time had come when I must reconsider my previous decision not to permit the performance of this work.
>
> I have now decided once and for all to give you full permission to

go ahead with performances in any part of the world. I enclose copy of my letter of even date to BBC.

> Yours sincerely
> Alma Maria Mahler[15]

To Cooke's delight, she enclosed another forty pages of the score to be worked into a fuller version. On August 3, 1964, Alma wrote once more:

Dear Mr. Cooke,

I hope you received the pages—I don't know if they are important. This is not really a letter to you—but a message to Goldschmidt. I just heard his performance of the VI symphony and I just wanted him to know how wonderful I think it is.

> Best regards
> Yours sincerely
> Alma Mahler[16]

Goldschmidt proceeded to conduct in the BBC Proms on August 16, 1964, what Cooke called "a performing version of the draft for the tenth symphony"—not a completion, he specified, but "the stage the work had reached when Mahler died."[17] Donald Mitchell, in the *Daily Telegraph*, called it "a completely authentic-sounding structure."[18] In the *Guardian*, Neville Cardus wrote: "Here, unmistakably, is a masterpiece, actual and potential—a masterpiece in and of itself, and also a masterpiece of reconstruction . . . nearly every phrase sounding like the voice of Mahler and of nobody else, a genius of his own period, reaching out to our own, seeing with terrifying prophecy the wrath to come."[19]

And there, in a rational world, the symphony would have been left to find its place. But art seldom advances in a rational line, and objections were heard almost as the final chord faded. In the standing well of the Royal Albert Hall, Joe Wheeler told a diarist[20] that his version was about to be played in America (at the Manhattan School of Music, in November 1966), and Erwin Ratz, chairman of the International Gustav Mahler Society, supported by philosopher

Adorno, declared an international ban on the Cooke Tenth as an act of vandalism.

Conductors, wary of controversy, steered clear. Leonard Bernstein and Rafael Kubelik excluded the Tenth from their premiere recorded cycles. So did Solti, Haitink, Václav Neumann, Maazel, Tennstedt, Inbal, Abravanel, and Abbado. Cooke's score was recorded by Eugene Ormandy, Jean Martinon, Kurt Sanderling, Wyn Morris, and the young Simon Rattle. Cooke died in 1976, Wheeler a year later. In 1983 Carpenter's version was played by Chicago's Civic Orchestra. During rehearsals an assistant, Remo Mazzetti, made his own version, which was recorded in St. Louis, Missouri. The Russian conductor Rudolf Barshai had another go in the 1990s, followed by a pair of Italians, Nicola Samale and Giuseppe Mazzuca. All are recorded. None is conclusive. The differences can be heard in, for instance, the rumble of a bass tuba that Cooke inserts at the start of the finale, where Mazzetti tones down to a solo double bass. Neither seems quite right.

Confused? Well, Cooke—edited by the composers Colin and David Matthews, and published by Faber Music—is by far the most performed score and on the whole the most revealing. Carpenter's is overinfluenced by the Ninth; Barshai suggests how dark the symphony might have been made to sound by Shostakovich. In all versions some textures are disturbingly naive. Yet the opening crash of an ominous side drum and the solo flute melody toward the end are among the most memorable effects in the whole of Mahler. On the last page, where Mahler scrawled to Alma: *Du allein weisst was es bedeutet:* "You alone know what it means," the love is almost unbearable.

It is absurd for any conductor in the twenty-first century to proclaim the Tenth unperformable, and perverse for a biographer to regret "the curiosity—not altogether healthy—which it has aroused."[21] The Tenth exists as Mahler's last word. It reveals Mahler, in his favored metaphor, wrestling with his angel, refusing to let go without a blessing. If the symphony reveals nothing else, it is that Mahler did not surrender to fate, nor to depression at his wife's betrayal, nor to health fears, nor to any other force except his mission to compose. In these final pages he surmounted the fickleness of love and life in a way that only Mahler could, with a never-say-die symphony that offers on its last unfinished page a glimmer of hope. No knowledge of Mahler is complete without the live experience of his Tenth Symphony.

I had heard about Berthold Goldschmidt for years before I dared to approach him. People said, "You must go and see Mr. Goldschmidt, he knows everything about Mahler," but I, with the arrogance of youth, wanted to discover it myself. Truth be told, I was daunted. Mr. Goldschmidt had a reputation for not suffering fools. An abrasive edge to his tongue had gotten him sidelined by the British music establishment to a point where his compositions gathered dust on the mantelpiece of 13 Belsize Crescent, a multitenanted terraced house not far from Hampstead Heath. Nor was I the only one to be daunted. The composer Thomas Adès lived across the street and never once dared to mount the steps and ring the doorbell.

In 1988 an opera of Goldschmidt's, *Beatrice Cenci*, was to have its premiere, and I went around to collect information for a newspaper article. Within minutes we forgot about the article and became friends. Maybe because he was born in the same year as my father, 1903, or because I had grown up among German émigrés, we understood each other. Living nearby, I would drop by at four in the afternoon for coffee, cakes, polemical disputation, and a raid on his infallible memory.

Berthold remembered hearing, at eight years old, the announcement of Mahler's death over the family dinner table in Hamburg. "Gott, war der nervös!" cried an aunt: "God, was that man jittery!" Somehow *nervös* struck the boy as a compliment, and his aunt's comment as a kind of possessiveness, a reflection of the way audiences must have felt about this intense little man. In Berlin, Berthold went to work at the State Opera, coaching singers and playing the celesta at the world premiere of Berg's *Wozzeck* in December 1925. In February 1932 his opera *The Magnificent Cuckold* triumphed at Mannheim, and a critic named him the "white hope" of German music. Three years later he was a penniless refugee in a London cold-water flat.

Half a century passed before a performance of his *Ciaccona Sinfo-*

nica in Berlin by Simon Rattle rekindled interest in his music. We found ourselves sitting one night on the Kurfürstendamm, and I asked him what had changed in Berlin. "Nothing," said Berthold.

"What do you mean, nothing?"

"Berlin"—he smiled—"was always a liberal city, curious and experimental. The Nazis were an aberration. We could not foresee the damage they would do."

"You're saying nothing has changed?"

"Only the audience. It used to be substantially Jewish. Nobody mentions that."

Not just Berlin, he elaborated, but in Hamburg, Munich, Leipzig, and Vienna, the Jewish middle classes formed the core of Mahler's audience. By no means a majority, or an organized entity, they were there wherever his music was performed. Mahler would have known, much as Saul Bellow and Philip Roth did in Chicago and New York, that there were people who lined up for his next work. They might not understand or even like it, but they demanded the installment as of right, as their stake in his story. It was this public that gave Mahler the confidence, in the face of racist opposition, to carry on composing. Goldschmidt knew the audience and its responses—"Gott, war der nervös!"—and he shared with me its role in Mahler's psyche.

At ninety-two he called me over one day to listen, score in hand, to a studio tape of his latest work, a ten-minute Rondeau for Violin and Orchestra, played by Chantal Juillet, and conducted by Charles Dutoit. Captivated by its beauties, I showered him with compliments, and Berthold muttered, "Well, we must show them what a Jew can do."

"What do you mean by that?"

"They killed so many of us. The ones who survive must show that it was worth keeping us alive."

Pacing up and down his carpet we argued out the obligations of survivors, whether being plucked as a brand from the burning entailed a duty to bear witness, and whether being a Jew meant anything more than an accident of genetics. A portrait of Mahler gazed down from the wall, one of the world-weary 1909 set. Was this what he was trying to say in the Tenth Symphony, to show them what a

Jew could do, what a man "with a short arm," "three times homeless," could make of himself? Berthold Goldschmidt, who thought so, died at home a year later, on October 17, 1996.

THE OLD LADY IN THE GARRET

A week after my first Mahler book was published, I moved my desk to a garden apartment around the corner from my home. A laborer on site told me that a lady from the top floor had asked after me. I looked at the doorbell. It said "Rose." Then one of the neighbors said, "Have you met Mrs. Rosé yet?", and the hairs on my nape stood up like a squirrel's on an electricity pylon.

There were three Rosé brothers, born Rosenblum, from Iasi in Romania. Two of them, Arnold and Eduard, married Mahler's sisters. The third, Alexander, was the impresario who took Mahler and the Vienna Philharmonic to Paris and paid for the first performance of *Das Klagende Lied.* I rang the bell and was admitted by Alexander's daughter, Eleanor, born 1894. She extended a hand that had once been held by Brahms. In her nineties, Eleanor lived with two cats and was looked after by the rest of the building. I took to visiting her every few days, sharing a glass of wine and listening to memories of diamantine sharpness.

Eleanor remembered Mahler's wedding and had kept the invitation. "He used to dip his spoon in my dessert, to see if it tasted better than his," she confided. Studying the violin, she observed him in the Munich rehearsals for the Eighth Symphony. She lived in Berlin in the 1920s and Paris in the 1930s, going into hiding during the occupation and reaching England after the war. She showed me, in shabby carpet slippers, how Mahler walked, how he sat down, how he held his glass. She remembered opera productions, ancient gossip, tiny aperçus about Mahler and those around him. Sometimes she would ring up to say: "You can't quote what I told you last night."

"Why not, Eleanor?"

"Because I am no longer sure if I witnessed it or it was reported to me by my mother."

"But surely she didn't lie."

"That's true, but it makes a difference."

"Even with a trivial incident?"

"Of course."

"Why, of course?"

"Because it was to do with Mahler," said Eleanor Rosé. "Everything to do with Mahler had to be correct to the last detail."

After her death, in March 1992, I often wondered how a girl of eight could have assimilated Mahler's concern for accuracy. If ever I pressed her Eleanor would say, "Because that was the truth." There was nothing more to say. Mahler and truth were indivisible in her mind.

Her answer resonated with me more and more as the years passed and we entered a political era of Orwellian spin when any fact could be presented as its opposite, when free nations could be lied into war by elected leaders and image took precedence over substance—when one U.S. president could say, "It depends what the meaning of is, is" and another, "When we talk about war, we're really talking about peace."[22] What Mahler signified for Eleanor, and through her for me, was an adherence to a resolute, non-negotiable truth, a truth that shone a laser of rectitude through our political murk. In that light it seemed worth spending my life searching for Mahler. Mahler was a rock of verity in a sea of illusions, an idealist among pragmatists, a doer as well as a dreamer, a redeemer of truth from lies. His music can mean many things at once, but it cannot equivocate. It comes at you from afar like the light at the end of a tunnel, an irresistible destination. *Why Mahler?* That's why.

It's twenty minutes on the 38 tram from the heart of Vienna to the Heurigen inns in Grinzing, where the wines are drunk young off the vine. The tram passes Schubert's birthplace and skirts Heiligenstadt, where Beethoven went deaf. We are at the northwest edge of the city, the air fragrant, the pace sybaritic. A 1915 song by Ralph Benatzky, "I' Muss Wieder amal in Grinzing Sein [I Wanna Be Back in Grinzing]," sways in a three-four rhythm and vocal swoops. Lotte Lehmann, who recorded the song, remembered sitting "at rough-hewn tables, rich and poor, old and young alike, all held together by the common bonds of music, laughter and wine."[23] The scholar

George Steiner identifies "taking the streetcar to Grinzing" as an amatory colloquialism signifying "a gentle, somewhat respectful anal access."[24] The vices of Grinzing were always suburban and mundane.

Nothing much ever happened in Grinzing, and nobody important lived here. Vienna's giants, from Mozart to Schubert to Arnold Schoenberg, lie in a grove of honor at the Zentralfriedhof, the central cemetery. Mahler resides alone at this periphery.

I get off the 38 at the Grinzinger Allee and walk up the access road, An den langen Lüssen, past the Albanian Embassy and into the cemetery, with its serried rows and preposterous edifices. Minor nobility are entombed in palatial sepulchers, their vanity everlasting. Mahler's headstone is a slab of granite with his name at the top. "Those who seek me will know who I was," he said. And there are always seekers around, pilgrims from Korea, Mexico, or Slovakia who cannot visit Vienna without finding Mahler. Even under snow, one rarely sees the grave free of flower offerings and pebble clusters, the traditional Jewish tribute.

What is Gustav Mahler doing in Grinzing, where he neither lived nor died? He could have rested among equals, if not in Vienna then in Père-Lachaise in Paris, or among the Jews of Iglau. But he chose to be buried in Grinzing because it was close to the house where he wooed Alma, who signified love. He chose Grinzing because it stands in open country. Above all he chose it because he did not belong to Vienna. In death he remains on the outside. Vienna is a nostalgia factory. Mahler refused to be its product.

Why do I visit Mahler's grave? Because he invites us into his life, asks us to share his struggles, his torments, his doubts, as if they were our own, as they often are. And then he withdraws, "Lost to the World," and leaves the rest to us. Life is a fight, says Mahler, and art does not end with death. There are no pat solutions, no magic bullets. Life flows on and art changes, different every day. Seeking Gustav Mahler is a route to the few things that are worth fighting for in the short time that we spend on this good earth. It is the start of a quest for the meaning of life and, sometimes, an end.

PART III

Whose Mahler?

14. A Question of Interpretation

LENNY'S SCOTCH

One Sunday afternoon in 1985 at London's Barbican Hall, after Leonard Bernstein had signed autographs for an hour with a twice-replenished tea glass full of whiskey at his elbow, he dismissed his entourage to sit with me and two friends over the score of Mahler's Ninth that he had just performed. One of my friends was preparing to conduct the symphony for the first time.

We stood around his table, a cigarette curling in an ashtray. Lenny opened the score at the entry point of harp, horn, and cellos. From this tremulous passage, and on almost every page thereafter, the music was peppered with the conductor's colored-pencil marks. He was not, on the whole, one of those maestros who plot performances like military campaigns. Other Mahler scores he had shown us were clean of marks, yet here he could not leave the music alone. On the final page he wrote, "Have the courage to remain in 8!" as if a conductor, drained, might lose traction at the fadeout. "Why so many marks?" we asked. Lenny drew deep on another cigarette. "Mahler," he exhaled expansively, "was a great conductor who premiered most of his own works and showed us how he wanted them to sound. This one he didn't live to conduct. This one he wrote for me."

Staggering as the vanity sounded, it contained a kernel of pure truth. Mahler was one of the most impressive, resourceful conductors of all time. "To hear Mahler conduct feels like you have never heard music played before," wrote an admirer in 1896.[1] His listeners experienced "the pure confession of a great man," and observed "the pain in the smile with which Mahler acknowledged our applause."[2]

He conducted with an awareness of mortal imperfection and made constant changes to his own works, requiring the Fifth Symphony, among others, to be reprinted with extensive changes. "I would like to publish revisions of my scores every five years,"[3] he told Bruno Walter. Every work of his own that he conducted—which is all apart from the Ninth and Tenth Symphonies and *The Song of the Earth*—is annotated to the nth degree.

"When you open a score by Mahler," says the postminimalist composer John Adams, "you can't help but marvel at its immense detail, and especially all the constant verbal imploring that accompanies the notation, cautioning and then prodding ('Don't rush here!' 'Hold back suddenly!' 'Play with a big tone, but not brassy!'). It's almost as if he were standing behind you, whispering, yelling, sobbing, stamping throughout the whole performance. You realise that this man was a conductor. While the music is difficult and challenging, it's never impossible."[4]

The discrepancies between what Mahler wrote, what was printed, and what he actually did in performance are so vast that when a Viennese scholar, Renate Stark-Voit, checked the published edition of the Second Symphony in 2001 against two of Mahler's performing manuscripts, she found no fewer than three hundred material differences in the third movement alone. Mahler was, on the one hand, a precisionist who tried to leave nothing to chance and, on the other, a dreamer in pursuit of an unattainable perfection. Recognizing these limitations, he licensed conductors to use their discretion when performing his works. "If after my death something doesn't sound right," he told Otto Klemperer, "then change it. You have not only the right but the duty to do so."[5] He himself adjusted other men's works, tampering with the holy writ of Beethoven and reorchestrating symphonies by Schumann, who Mahler believed was an amateur at instrumentation. Although the Beethoven changes were done for his own use—"When I conduct, I take responsibility for them"—he wanted to share the Schumann revisions, telling Alma, "They're valuable, have them printed."[6]

Mahler expected conductors to be flexible and intuitive when performing his music. He would have ridiculed the modern conceits that pinpoint accuracy and period style are preferable to impulse and emotion, and he would have roared at the slew of doctoral dissertations arguing as to whether there should be two, three, or five hammerblows in the finale of his Sixth Symphony. It was up to the conductor to decide. Everything Mahler said and did about his music implies that there is more than one way to read the work, and that a conductor should follow fantasy rather than literal fidelity.

Bernstein was, in this respect, very much Mahler's kind of maestro. In the Ninth Symphony I heard him conduct that Sunday afternoon in 1985, he distended tempi and dynamics, stretching the finale almost to the point of inertia and its closing bars to near-inaudibility. The phrasing was lopsided at times, as was the internal balance, yet there was nothing capricious about the performance. Rather, Bernstein was following some inner impetus that persuaded me that there was no other way for this work to be heard on that particular day. The pulse of his performance differed markedly from his recordings in Berlin and New York, themselves strikingly dissimilar. It differed also from the record he made a few weeks later with the same orchestra, the Concertgebouw. It was Mahlerian in impulse, daring, and self-contradiction.

By contrast, so too was an account of *The Song of the Earth* given by Pierre Boulez in the same cycle that season: austere, clinically detailed, emotionally restrained. Boulez told me that the larger the gesture in Mahler, the greater the likelihood of "vulgarity" (he may have meant Bernstein). The two interpretations, his and Lenny's, were antipodal, yet each was an authentic aspect of a composer who once said, "The best music is not to be found in the notes." Mahler also said: "The essence of any interpretation is exactness." Go figure.

The conductor Ernst Lert, who heard Mahler conduct many times, wrote that his was a personality split between the composer who demanded accuracy and the conductor who sought freedom of expression.[7] If we accept this schism theory, the notion of a perfect performance in Mahler becomes impossible, and every account of the music is but one small step in a never-ending evolution. This does not mean that a Mahler conductor has to be a practicing psychoanalyst or a lofty philosopher. Some of the most persuasive performances in my life have come from interpreters of limited knowledge and, sometimes, intellect. A forest of myths has enveloped the act of Mahler interpretation, and this is as good a point as any to clear a pathway of reason through some of the more prevalent popular beliefs.

YOU HAVE TO BE JEWISH TO BE A GREAT MAHLER CONDUCTOR

Walter and Klemperer were born Jewish, as was Bernstein; but not Mengelberg, his greatest contemporary enthusiast, nor Henry Wood and Dimitri Mitropoulos, who pioneered the music in Britain and America, nor Rafael Kubelik, who recorded a premiere cycle, nor Adrian Boult, who championed Mahler at the BBC. Any conductor who claims Jewishness as a qualification in Mahler is a self-convicted fraud.

YOU HAVE TO BE MIDDLE EUROPEAN

It helps to understand all those German exclamations in the score, but the Italians Carlo Maria Giulini, Claudio Abbado, and Riccardo Chailly excelled at Mahler, as have the Finn Esa-Pekka Salonen, the Frenchman Pierre Boulez, the Russian-Caucasian Valery Gergiev, and more.

YOU HAVE TO BE WIDELY READ

Mahler was, but so what? Klaus Tennstedt, one of the most inspirational Mahler conductors, seldom read a book; Georg Solti turned to the financial pages for cerebral stimulus; and Eugene Ormandy was not interested in anything outside the concert hall.

YOU HAVE TO BE VERY OLD

Simon Rattle was twenty-five when he made his name with the Tenth Symphony. Salonen was a similar age when he launched his international career with Mahler's Third, as was the Venezuelan Gustavo Dudamel, with the Fifth.

YOU HAVE TO BE A SYMPHONIC EXPERT

Maurice Abravanel, who conducted an early cycle, was a music-theater man. A New York amateur, Gilbert E. Kaplan, gave credible account of the *Resurrection*.

YOU MUST CONDUCT THE WORKS COMPLETE . . .

Klemperer never touched the Fifth and Sixth Symphonies and positively hated the Third. Walter avoided the Seventh and fell out of love with the Eighth. Mengelberg invented the Mahler cycle as a marketing device in 1920, but no conductor should have to perform music he does not fully believe in.

. . . AND INTACT

Hermann Scherchen, a passionate Mahler conductor, made deep cuts in his landmark recordings of the Fifth Symphony, as did Paul Kletzki in the First. The first truth in Mahler interpretation is that there are no absolutes, no hard-and-fast rules.

MATERIAL EVIDENCE

There is one recording of Mahler playing his own music, but it needs to be treated with caution. On the afternoon of November 9, 1905, returning home from Berlin, where Oskar Fried conducted an overfast performance of the *Resurrection*, Mahler stopped at Leipzig to inspect the Welte-Mignon piano-roll invention. It involved holes being punched by piano keys into a roll of fabric that was connected to electrodes in a bath of mercury. The roll, reproduced on fortified paper, yielded a close resemblance of what the artist played—not just the notes and tempi, but variations of soft and loud. In an age of crackly wind-up gramophones, Welte-Mignon players and rolls were popular both in homes and in the lobbies of grand hotels and oceangoing liners. Gabrilowitsch, Josef Hoffmann, Alfred Grünfeld, Ernst von Dohnányi, and Eugen d'Albert were among many stars who preceded Mahler on Welte-Mignon; soon to follow were Busoni, Edvard Grieg, and Richard Strauss. Camille Saint-Saëns visited the studios two days after Mahler. By 1914 Welte-Mignon had a catalog of 2,500 rolls and a studio on New York's Fifth Avenue. A decade later they were rendered defunct by cheaper and much-improved electrical recordings.

Mahler sat down at the piano that November afternoon and played four rolls before catching the late train to Vienna. Two were songs—"Ging heut' Morgen" (the opening theme of his First Symphony) and "Ich ging mit Lust"; the other two were reductions of the finale of his Fourth Symphony and the opening of his Fifth. At the end of the session he expressed "my astonishment and admiration" in the guest book.

The two songs reveal a forceful presence, a pianist of quick fingers and endearing delicacy. In the Fourth Symphony finale, the tone is restrained, perhaps with awe at the heavenly gathering. Only in the opening of the Fifth Symphony do we obtain a hint of what Mahler might have extracted from an orchestra. The fateful opening notes are struck prosaically, as if a policeman were calling at the door for some minor fine, and the melody takes on a patina of hesitancy, stumbling at times from one note to the next. But the repetition turns impatient, emphatic in rebuttal, and once he reaches the secondary theme, five minutes into the roll, Mahler's playing is propulsive and the music turns maniacal. He cannot wait to get the words out of the way and on with the story. His fingers are no longer fast enough, he is not bothered by wrong notes. He has a symphony to unfold, and nothing may stand in its way. The fact that Mahler approved this roll on playback tells us something about his priorities in a symphonic performance—that the whole is greater than the sum of its parts, and that a spontaneous change of mood is always worth a try.

Mahler conducted the Fifth Symphony three times in the following month. His playing on the piano roll can be taken as a reflection of his podium style, but only in general terms. It is not an imitable model. Any orchestra that attempted these speeds would crash within ten minutes. The piano rolls are a trick, a toy, a wisp of a hint. They have been transferred onto CD at variable speeds, often incorrect. The most reliable transfers are the **Kaplan Foundation**'s on Pickwick Records (1993) and the Wein Museum's made on Mahler's own piano and issued by Preiser (2010).

A second intimation of how Mahler wanted his music to sound comes from conductors who assisted at his performances. **Oskar Fried** was coached by Mahler in the *Resurrection* Symphony and, in 1924, was the first to make a Mahler recording. The Berlin sound is boxy, scratchy, and soupy in the strings, the soloists have an ornithological warble, and the chorus is out of tune. That said, the performance is one of great daring, starting at an unsustainable tempo and building into high drama. Mahler called Fried "a ray of hope," and Anna, his daughter, held his conducting in great esteem.[8] The Berlin State Opera orchestra's account of the Second Symphony, with soloists Gertrud Bindernagel and Emmy Leisner (Polydor, 1924), is, at the very least, a vital professional reference tool.

No one observed Mahler closer than **Bruno Walter**, whose records, starting with *The Song of the Earth* in Vienna. (Columbia, May 1936), are landmarks. Walter differs in almost every aspect from **Otto Klemperer**, who knew Mahler for less than five years but formed a symbiotic affinity with his demonic side. Klemperer's records came mostly late in life, but each of them acts as a counterbalance to Walter's overcivility. "Dr. Walter is a moralist," said Klemperer, with heavy irony, "I am an immoralist." Together they represent the polarities of Mahler's nature. **Willem Mengelberg**, Mahler's Dutch supporter, made one significant recording. **Leopold Stokowski**, who attended the Eighth in Munich and gave its U.S. premiere in 1916, is the only other conductor on record to have heard Mahler in the flesh. **Sarah-Charles Cahier** was the only singer of Mahler's company to record his music, and sadly too late: Her voice is unsteady in "Urlicht" and "I Am Lost to the World" (Ultraphon, Berlin, 1930).

What can be derived from these eyewitness testimonies? Something of the qualities that Mahler sought in performance: intuition, spontaneity, and recklessness, added to high intellect, meticulous preparation, and emotional reflection. It is an irreconcilable set of opposites in which conductors must make some tough personal choices.

Before considering some two thousand published recordings, it is worth pointing out that not all roads lead to Mahler. Conductors who obviate irony commit a travesty. Those who deny emotion— a tendency favored at times by artists as distinguished as Bernard Haitink and Christoph von Dohnányi—miss a crucial ingredient. Those who reinsert the deleted "Blumine" in the First Symphony (Rattle, Ozawa) or make the rough places smooth (Karajan, Muti) contradict the composer's intention. Those who perform Mahler on period instruments, without vibrato (Norrington, Herreweghe), fly in the face of the composer's worldview. There are many no-nos in Mahler: These are just a few of the worst.

No conductor has all the answers in Mahler, and no boxed cycle by a single interpreter will satisfy the questing mind. That said, a consistent path in Mahler can enhance our understanding in ways that an isolated performance cannot. The two earliest complete sets, by Kubelik and Bernstein, adopt opposite extremes. Kubelik, with the orchestra of Bavarian Radio, tends toward refined understatement, sometimes to such a degree that an inattentive listener can miss peak moments, at other times with such beauty as to override underlying miseries. Bernstein, with the vigorous New York Philharmonic, hits the big bangs at the expense of some subtleties in a cycle driven by nervy excitement and apostolic zeal. The two sets complement each other in so many ways that one might be deluded into thinking that they cover the entire Mahler spectrum when each yields only a corner of the music's interpretive possibilities. Georg Solti matches Bernstein's enthusiasm without his symbiotic inspiration, while Giuseppe Sinopoli and Pierre Boulez approach the music from a clinical standpoint that delivers acute insights and limited uplift. The combustible Klaus Tennstedt stuns the ears with empathetic spontaneity. Among later cycles, David Zinman in Zurich and Iván Fischer in Budapest veer toward Kubelik's careful understatement, while Simon Rattle and Riccardo Chailly aim for controlled explosions. Claudio Abbado in Lucerne achieves long spans of meditative elevation. All these sets take a route to Mahler that is personal in both senses of the word: deeply felt and definedly too individual to amount to a final word. As I go to press, news arrives of a Mahler cycle being recorded in 2010–11 by Vladimir Ashkenazy in Sydney, Australia.

A compendium of **Mahler broadcasts by the New York Philharmonic,** issued in 1998, brings together concerts of the highest voltage and variety by, among others, Mitropoulos, Stokowski, Tennstedt, Walter, Barbirolli, and William Steinberg. It may be the only Mahler set that will never exhaust intelligent interest.

THE SYMPHONIES*

SYMPHONY NO. 1 IN D MINOR (FP: BUDAPEST, NOVEMBER 18, 1889)

Of all Mahler's works, none sustains such diversity of interpretation. For Bruno Walter, it is an elegiac work, for Georg Solti a juvenile eruption, for Rafael Kubelik an extension of nineteenth-century folklore, and for Klaus Tennstedt a suppuration of sexual desire. The first take, from **Dimitri Mitropoulos** with the Minneapolis Symphony in November 1940 (Columbia), remains convincing. A lonely, bald Greek on his first job in Middle America, Mitropoulos faced an orchestra that had not recorded in a decade and a board that refused to spend twelve thousand dollars on a symphony nobody would buy. Waiving his own fee, Mitropoulos opened with deceptive languor in the slow introduction, building momentum by subtle degrees and tension by osmosis. He directed the tricky funeral/drunken party just as Mahler ordered, without an excess of finesse, and the finale as an explosive romp. Although the sound is cramped mono, the Mitropoulos interpretation has few equals for incisiveness and energy.

Klaus Tennstedt made the best of his three recordings in Chicago, May 1990 (EMI), a performance released on DVD as well as CD,showing his podium eccentricities to the max. The first move-

---

* Since older recordings are reissued under many labels, I list session dates and orchestras for identification. Key recommendations appear in bold.

ment is five and a half minutes slower than Mitropoulos, but the concentration never slackens and the Chicago Symphony Orchestra is as slick as an Olympic skater, refusing to play rough at the funeral but coming off sleazy instead, an unexpected effect of dazzling aptness.

Georg Solti went wild with the LSO for Decca in 1964, ferocious in the finale. His 1983 retake in Chicago is less successful. Leonard Bernstein, with New York and the Concertgebouw, changes tack without warning or reason. Hermann Scherchen (RPO, 1955) is a tempo extremist.

Bruno Walter, at the opposite end of the spectrum, epitomizes the elegiac tendency. His 1961 Hollywood recording with the Columbia Symphony Orchestra is nostalgic to a fault and preferable in every way to his 1950 New York take. This gentle revisit to lost pastures wears its affection warmly on the sleeve.

Rafael Kubelik (1968, Deutsche Grammophon/DG), whose father played in Vienna the night that Mahler met Alma, evokes Iglau landscapes and woodland sounds with great literalism, at the expense of some mystery. The Bavarian Radio Symphony Orchestra is engagingly flexible, and the village band startlingly rude. More than fellow Czechs Karel Ančerl, Václav Neumann, and Libor Pešek, Kubelik and his Munich players—many of them Czech exiles—achieve an indigenous attitude. A 1954 Kubelik session with the Vienna Philharmonic (Decca) is less secure.

Paul Kletzki, a fugitive from Hitler and Stalin, brings out the Jewish klezmer element in recordings with the Israel Philharmonic (1954) and the Vienna Philharmonic (**EMI, 1961**). In both performances, and for no obvious reason, Kletzki cut twenty-four bars from the finale; the recordings are nonetheless valuable for acute insight and beautiful phrasing. Eliahu Inbal, an Israeli conductor, exaggerates the klezmer tune with the Frankfurt Radio Orchestra (Denon, 1985) in an otherwise neutral rendition.

Many who err in beauty or blandness include Bernard Haitink (Amsterdam, 1972; Berlin, 1987; Chicago, 2009), Riccardo Muti (Philadelphia, 1984), Charles Mackerras (Liverpool, 1991), David Zinman (Zurich, 2006), Jonathan Nott (Bamberg, 2008). The muscularity of John Barbirolli (Manchester, 1957), Zubin Mehta (New

York, 1982), and Lorin Maazel (Vienna, 1985) is much to be preferred. Erich Leinsdorf (Boston, 1962) and Carlo Maria Giulini (Chicago, 1971) achieve both clean lines and emotional challenge. Valery Gergiev (LSO Live, 2008) is impetuous and structurally incoherent.

In October 2009 the Venezuelan **Gustavo Dudamel** performed Mahler's First in his inaugural concert as music director of the Los Angeles Philharmonic. Dudamel was twenty-eight years old, the age Mahler was when he wrote the work. This was the first score he studied with his mentor, José Antonio Abreu, and he had been conducting it since he was seventeen. An international phenomenon, groomed by Abbado, Rattle, and Barenboim, Dudamel was greeted in Los Angeles by tinsel, street banners, and a nickname, "the Dude." It remained to be heard whether he justified the hype. His opening concert (DG, DVD) blew away my doubts. Dudamel's interpretation is both energetic and pinpoint accurate in its rhythms. From the shimmering harmonic A's, he creates an atmosphere more of metropolitan drive than of woodland mystery, but the pace is exhilarating, turning explosive in the finale. The contrary funeral is remarkably true to idiom. All that is missing is the last degree of nuance, which may come with maturity. His account is at all times irresistible without ever suggesting conceptual innovation.

Pierre Boulez (Chicago, DG, 1999) perversely ignores subjective meaning, giving an analytical presentation of great clarity and no penetration, a dehumanized Mahler that is worth hearing nonetheless for its objective detachment. Mahler would not have minded. The freedom he bestowed on interpreters can be measured in the elastic timings for the First Symphony, which extend from Igor Markevich (Turin, RAI, 1954) at a brisk forty-four minutes and thirty-two seconds to Tennstedt at one hour and fifty-three seconds.[9]

SYMPHONY NO. 2 IN C MINOR, *RESURRECTION*
(FP: BERLIN, DECEMBER 13, 1895)

The Second and Eighth Symphonies challenge the limits of recording, both in size and directionality. It is not easy to make the offstage band sound as if it is playing up and above the rest, nor are its exchanges with the main orchestra generally well managed. Four mono, constricted performances are nonetheless precious. **Fried** (Berlin, 1924) is the first Mahler on record. **Ormandy (Minneapolis, 1932)** shivers with excitement and fear. **Walter**, returning to **Vienna** in **1948**, wages a war of sentiment against rage, almost unrecognizable in his laxity in the first and third movements; his soloists, Maria Cebotari and Rosette Anday, are horribly out of tune. In New York in 1958, his smoother self prevails with soloists Emilia Cundari and Maureen Forrester.

There are six recordings by **Otto Klemperer**, most of them live and two irresistible. At the **Holland Festival** in **1951**, with Kathleen Ferrier and Jo Vincent as soloists, the tempi are tightly coiled and the singing is formidable. Klemperer, ignoring his edgy mentor Fried, exerts fluid tempo control and holds back on spiritual uplift. His 1963 EMI release feels, by comparison, too strict, and the singing of Elisabeth Schwarzkopf and Hilde Rössel-Majdan too sterile. A **1968 Munich concert (EMI)**, with Heather Harper and Janet Baker as soloists, is vivid, gripping and numinous, Klemp's best.

Of three **Leopold Stokowskis**, the **1974** RCA recording in Walthamstow Town Hall with the LSO, Brigitte Fassbaender, and Margaret Price is a compelling piece of showmanship. The initial tempo is so deliberate it almost plods, but the man who conducted the music for Walt Disney's *Fantasia* does not lose his grip on our attention, ratcheting up the tension by degrees until it roars for catharsis. The offstage instruments are too loud and close, and there is no letup in momentum. Time is held in a maestro's fist, and no one leaves before the credits roll.

Bernstein's first (of three) recordings, with the **New York Philharmonic** in September **1963**, belongs more to the revivalist's tent than the big screen. Like Stoki, Bernstein takes the opening at a leaden tread and the first *schnell* mark at supersonic pace. Speeds and textures are distended, yoked to a larger message: Hang in there and all will be redeemed. Soloists Lee Venora and Jennie Tourel are pallid, and the chorus is stiff, but the climax cracks open the heavens. Neither of Bernstein's subsequent takes, with the LSO in 1973 and New

York in 1987, achieves the same blast; maybe he fiddles too much with small details.

Georg Solti (LSO, 1966, Chicago, 1980) does sonic spectaculars of immediate impact and little lasting interest. **Claudio Abbado (DG, 1992)**, in his third attempt, draws voluptuous playing from the **Vienna Philharmonic** at a tempo very close to the composer's. The *Resurrection* has been a door opener in Abbado's career, and nothing he does in it is ill-considered. His soloists are Cheryl Studer and Waltraud Meier, with the Arnold Schoenberg Chorus. A fourth take, with low-key soloists in Lucerne, 2003 (DG, DVD), follows his recovery from stomach cancer and suggests a memoirist undercurrent that, moving on first hearing, turns mundane on repetition.

Gilbert E. Kaplan's 1987 Cardiff recording with the LSO was epochal for being the work of an amateur. The top-selling Mahler record of all time, sold with a full score and other accessories, it conveys sense of occasion, intricacy of detail, and some inelasticity in transitions from fast to slow. Kaplan's repetition with the **Vienna Philharmonic** in **2003** (DG) incorporates Mahler's final revisions. Setting aside low-key soloists, it achieves accuracy, enthusiasm, and beauty. It comes as close as any record has gotten to absolute notational accuracy—I know because I was at the sessions.

Kubelik understates the *Resurrection*. Mariss Jansons (Oslo, 1990) is too polite, Maazel (Vienna, 1983) dull, and Rattle (Watford, 1986) bumptious. Václav Neumann's Czech Philharmonic validates a brisk speed with two superb soloists, Eva Randová and Gabriela Beňačková. The Naxos Polish cycle of Antoni Wit (Katowice, 1993) is haphazardly phrased and played. Zubin Mehta's 1989 performance on top of Mount Masada is a sorry piece of political showboating.

Among twenty-first-century sets, Gergiev (LSO Live, 2008) has wobbly soloists and no clear line, while Christoph Eschenbach in Philadelphia (Ondine, 2008) is lumpen. Riccardo Chailly's 2002 Amsterdam account is confident and convincing. **Adam Fischer** in **Budapest, 2006**, is highly energized and delicately detailed, with Brigitte Rennert and Lisa Milne. Boulez is dramatic but dry with the Vienna Philharmonic (DG, 2006).

Giuseppe Sinopoli (DG, 1985), with the Philharmonia, refused to let the *Resurrection* rise. An opera maestro with a psychology degree, Sinopoli overanalyzed symphonic music. His Mahler cycle is full of unjustified oddities. At the "Urlicht," where the spirit starts to soar, Sinopoli depresses expectations and discourages faith. The finale feels like Los Alamos, a lot of displaced scientists seeking nuclear fusion. Mahler survives the distortion, but it takes me awhile to recover from Sinopoli's anticlimax.

A concert recording by **Klaus Tennstedt**, brought to light in 2010 (LPO Live) and longer at ninety-four minutes than almost any other, imposes a seat-gripping tension and a rising sense of terror. By stretching the textures, Tennstedt brings out inner details like finger-prints in a crime investigation, underpinned by a growling bass line of suspicion. By the end of the first movement, the evidence is over-powering yet the mystery remains unsolved, perhaps insoluble. Slow as the unfolding may be, concentration and conviction never slacken. Soloists Yvonne Kenny and Jard Van Nes and the London Philharmonic Choir enter at a whisper. The climax is nothing short of revelation.

SYMPHONY NO. 3 IN D MINOR (FP: KREFELD, JUNE 9, 1902)

Almost the last Mahler work to get on disc, the Third Symphony is sparsely recorded. Neither Walter nor Klemperer performed a work they deemed immature, and others stumble at the first downbeat. Miss the irony of the false Brahms theme and the first movement fails. Conductors as adept as Haitink, Solti, Bernstein, Tennstedt, James Levine, and Kent Nagano take a tumble. Kubelik (DG, 1967) survives behind a facade of rustic naïveté. Rattle (EMI, 1997) is underpowered; Bernstein (1967, 1988) is a city boy at heart.

With a half-hour adagio as its finale, a conductor needs to sustain a line of steel and beauty. **Jascha Horenstein** (Croydon, 1970) got it right. A Russian refugee who lived in Berlin between the wars and recorded Mahler songs as early as 1927, his volatile temperament maimed his career, but his 1960s Mahler concerts in London won a cult following and his recording of the Third is a milestone, despite anemic playing from the LSO and singing from an unkempt boys' choir; Norma Procter is the urbane contralto soloist. Throughout the ninety minutes the ear is beguiled by sounds and ideas, as if it were hearing Socrates give a lecture beside a country lake.

A BBC relay by **Sir John Barbirolli** and the Halle Orchestra (**Manchester, 1969**), ebullient at the opening, sheds mystery in the Nietzsche song (soloist: Kerstin Meyer) and warms the hands like a log-cabin fire in a wondrous adagio. Its chief competition is a resplendent **1966 RCA Boston** reading by **Erich Leinsdorf**, the irony biting, the mystery shrouded (soloist: Shirley Verrett), and the finale melting.

Neeme Järvi (Glasgow, 1992) has some idyllic stretches marred by uneven phrasing. Hermann Scherchen (Leipzig, 1960) makes little tweaks and cuts. Gary Bertini (Cologne, 1985) manages a lovely finale after a long way getting there. Esa-Pekka Salonen (Los Angeles, 1988) launched his career with Mahler's Third but avoids ironic inflection and is generally too bright and breezy. The modern account to have is **Abbado**'s summer serenity from the **2007** Lucerne Festival, issued on DVD (sample viewable on YouTube). An unreleased BBC tape of Berthold Goldschmidt's 1960 performance with the LSO, the symphony's UK broadcast premiere, contains in the fourth movement a reverse glissando on the oboe, marked *wie ein Naturlaut* (like a natural sound), which makes instant sense of a tricky passage. Abbado, along with Rattle and Benjamin Zander (Telarc, 2004) is among the very few who observe this singular, significant detail.

The very first Mahler Third on record is still among the most effective, led by a London-born banker's son, **F. Charles Adler,** who assisted Mahler in the Eighth Symphony. Alma Mahler wrote a befuddled program note to the 1952 release, but after three years in the shops, the disc vanished. Adler grasps both texture and architecture. The irony is caustic, the innocence endearing, and the "rapturous Love-Adagio" just as Alma describes it. Adler, who died in Vienna in 1959, aged seventy, was a born Mahlerian. The Vienna Symphony Orchestra plays with pinpoint alertness. Hilde Rössel-Majdan is the contralto, and the Vienna Boys' Choir and opera chorus can hardly be bettered. The recording was reissued as a Conifer CD in 1997.

SYMPHONY NO. 4 IN G MAJOR (FP: MUNICH, NOVEMBER 25, 1901)

The first problem is the sleigh bells. Are the opening bells meant to set a rhythm for the symphony, or is Christmas just around the corner? **Mengelberg (November 1939)**, with the Concertgebouw and soloist Jo Vincent, sets the bells off quite fast, clippety-clop, then slows the strings to a squeaky standstill before galloping off once more. Each time he repeats the passage, he quickens a notch, challenging players to keep up with his runaway coach. The third-movement adagio is emotionally gaunt, but the finale has a picture-book playfulness and is beautifully sung.

The soloist can make or wreck the work. The earliest recording, capably conducted by **Viscount Hidemaro Konoye** at Kawasaki in May 1930 (Denon CD, 1988), is derailed by soprano Eiko Kitazawa's soupy warble. **David Oistrakh** leads an exemplary Moscow concert in 1967, only to run into a Galina Vishnevskaya squall. Bernstein, in his 1986 Amsterdam take, opts for no good reason to employ a boy treble—innocent, perhaps, but wrong in timbre. Renée Fleming is too full-voiced to be credible in Abbado's 2005 Berlin release. Elisabeth Schwarzkopf, for Klemperer (EMI, 1962), is a matter of taste: Many find her delivery brittle and calculated, the opposite of naive.

Bruno Walter, with the New York Philharmonic in May 1945 at Carnegie Hall, employed an amateur soprano, Desi Halban; but Desi was the daughter of Mahler's singer-sweetheart Selma Kurz, and, though fighting to override the orchestra, she sang with confidence and serenity in what Walter felt would be "a point of reference for the next generation of young conductors."[10] Other Walter takes are with Irmgard Seefried, Elisabeth Schwarzkopf, Maria Stader, and, sweetest of all, **Hilde Güden** and the Vienna Philharmonic in a 1955 concert, issued by DG in 1991.

Lisa Della Casa is the making of **Fritz Reiner**'s repressed Chicago recording of 1958, a songbird if ever there was one, and Lucia Popp is perfect for Tennstedt in 1982. Dawn Upshaw shines for Dohnányi (Cleveland, 1992), as does Felicity Lott for Franz Welser-Möst (London, 1988) in a reading of youthful exuberance that is undermined by an overslow adagio.

Less apt choices were Reri Grist (Bernstein), Kathleen Battle (Maazel), and Sylvia Stahlman and Kiri Te Kanawa (both Solti). Horenstein, with London roadworks going on outside, is overwhelmed by the richness of Margaret Price. George Szell's 1965 Cleveland record with Judith Raskin is neutered of emotion, Herbert von Karajan's (Berlin, 1979, with Edith Mathis) of conceptual penetration.

Among later interpreters, Chailly (Amsterdam, 1999, Barbara Bonney) and Zinman (Zurich, 2006, Luba Orgonasova) give exemplary readings in lucid sound. **Daniele Gatti,** with the Royal Philharmonic Orchestra and Ruth Ziesak in 1999 (RCA), sets a light and witty tone, full of incidental surprise. Boulez, in Cleveland (DG, 2000, Juliane Banse), tolerates no jokes, and his adagio reflects more angst than pleasure.

Benjamin Britten's 1961 Aldeburgh concert of the Fourth with the LSO (recently exhumed on BBC Legends) is more daring at the bends than anyone bar Mengelberg, and full of little composer intuitions. Much of the revelation is in the first movement; in the middle, Britten settles for rural calm. The soloist, Joan Carlyle, is an Ellen Orford schoolmarm straight out of *Peter Grimes*, but the performance as a whole is absorbing and the disc includes Britten directing half a dozen Mahler songs, with Anna Reynolds and Elly Ameling.

SYMPHONY NO. 5 IN C-SHARP MINOR
(FP: COLOGNE, OCTOBER 18, 1904)

The Fifth Symphony is a litmus test for many weaknesses. The opening statement separates good orchestras from the best, and experience from aspiration. Kirill Kondrashin's 1974 USSR Symphony Orchestra release cracks on the opening trumpet note. Maurice Abravanel's Utah Symphony Orchestra gets caught short at the pass, while Wyn Morris's halting half phrases (IMP, 1973) expose a perpetual flaw in his cultish, intermittently arresting enterprise. Morris, admiring Wilhelm Furtwängler, tried to express more than his players could follow. Benjamin Zander gets a terrific sound from the Philharmonia (Telarc, 2001) but sacrifices narrative line for acute contrast. Charles Mackerras came unstuck (Liverpool, 1990) with a trumpet that sounds like a traffic horn and speeds that are strictly pedestrian.

This symphony separates Mahler specialists from all-arounders. Herbert von Karajan and Daniel Barenboim use the Fifth to show off their shining brass sections in Berlin and Chicago. Karajan, an unrepentant Nazi, shunned Mahler's music until it became popular. Barenboim hated Mahler as a young man and, later, sought to "purify" the music of "vulgarity" and "non-musical preconceptions."[11] Both recordings contain barefaced banalities. Christoph von Dohnányi (Cleveland, 1989) developed an irrelevant Brahmsian meditation in the second movement.

Bruno Walter (New York, February 1947, CBS) was the first on record. He is also the fastest, at two minutes over an hour. Walter does not stint on warmth, even in a seven-minute forty-three-second Adagietto, and his entry to the finale sounds almost like a Beethoven transition. His take, in the absence of a Klemperer counterthrust, counts as a benchmark. A 1928 Mengelberg Adagietto (EMI) matches Mahler's speed estimate of seven minutes but could have been rushed to squeeze the piece onto two record sides.

Hermann Scherchen, with the Vienna Opera orchestra in 1952 (Westminster/DG), is tentative at the outset, building by degree a world of fears and fantasies, evocative of Mahler's night terrors and romantic fevers. A self-taught modernist, Scherchen gave the first performance of works by Schoenberg, Berg, Webern, and Karl Amadeus Hartmann. His futurism reveals another face of the Fifth, complementary to Walter's retro-perspective, and is a foundation stone of interpretive thought (do not confuse this release with 1962 and 1965 concerts from Milan and Paris, where Scherchen made drastic cuts to the third and fifth movements). Scherchen's chief disciple is Pierre Boulez, whose 1997 DG Vienna reading is notable for its restraint.

Rudolf Schwartz, an Auschwitz survivor and Simon Rattle's teacher, led a 1959 LSO reading of immense character and variable playing, superfast in the Adagietto (7'26") and adroit at drawing disparate strands into meaningful themes. **Rattle** (EMI, 2002) programmed the symphony for his opening night as boss of the Berlin

Philharmonic in September 2002, drawing exquisite instrumental effects, from harp to horn, and striking a leaner timbre than Karajan (1973), Haitink (1989), and Abbado (DG, 1993).

Kubelik is agreeably bucolic. Bernstein (DG, 1989) drives the Vienna Philharmonic hard and slow, in sensuous contrast to his bustling New York account (CBS, 1963). **Georg Solti,** a pressure cooker in Chicago (Decca, 1970), is sunny, relaxed, and often hushed in the final concert of his life, **Zurich,** July 13, 1997 (Decca).

John Barbirolli's New Philharmonia release (EMI) was an overnight sensation, notwithstanding some broken notes that had to be replaced on reissue. Of Italian descent and Cockney accent, JB relied on gut instinct for interpretation. He made this recording over three days in July 1969 at Watford Town Hall, near London, while fighting depression and alcohol addiction; a year later he was dead. The performance is joyous, energized, lyrical, sweet toned, and conversational. Entering the finale, the orchestra sound as if they are off on a Sunday stroll. The disc was reissued as a GROC—Great Recording of the Century. It is.

Klaus Tennstedt, with the London Philharmonic on **December 13, 1988** (EMI), held nothing back. Recovering from cancer treatment, he led with wild abandon, breaking hearts and bursting lungs. The event defies analysis; emotion is all. What appears on record is an edit of two concerts, the first a roof raiser, the second more sedate. As a compromise it is less satisfactory than either of the live experiences, which I attended, but the dance rhythms are organic and the heat could burn a hole in a bank wall. Tennstedt live—also in the New York Philharmonic Mahler set—is indelible.

Chailly (1998), Abbado (Lucerne, 2004), and Zinman (2007) are links in the chain of interpretation. Gustavo Dudamel and his Simón Bolívar Youth Orchestra of Venezuela (DG, 2007) achieve visceral excitement through exaggerated contrasts. **Markus Stenz** (Oehms, 2009) with Cologne's Gurzenich Orchestra, which gave the premiere under Mahler, manages an intriguing fusion of modern character and rustic tradition.

In September 1999 online Mahler chat reported a "remarkable performance" by a youth orchestra in Cologne, the Junge Deutsche Philharmonie. Issued on a private label, Laurel Records, it sold out on word of mouth and a Dutch label, Brilliant, gave it mass distribution. The conductor was **Rudolf Barshai**, viola player and cofounder of the Borodin Quartet. After leaving Russia in 1976, Barshai worked as an international guest conductor. In his seventies he added vast experience to the unblushing energies of the youth orchestra, whose players had not learned to fear risk or hold anything in reserve. Their fortissimi are louder than Solti's Chicago, and the bowing in the strings longer and sleeker than Vienna's. The Adagietto, lacking poignancy, wears its love on a sleeve. The Fifth Symphony is the work of a man in midlife, infatuated with a young girl. This performance perfectly captures that elixir of elusive youth.

SYMPHONY NO. 6 IN A MINOR (FP: ESSEN, MAY 27, 1906)

The first thing to sort out is the order of movements. Mahler published the symphony as Allegro–Scherzo–Andante–Finale. But during rehearsals for the 1906 premiere he reversed the middle pair to Andante–Scherzo. The score was republished and Mahler gave two more performances in that A–S order, his final word. In 1919 Willem Mengelberg had doubts and asked Alma, who replied "First Scherzo, then Andante." Capricious and unconcerned with musical niceties, she gave no source for her decision. Mengelberg, however, treated her word as writ and performed the work S–A at his 1920 Mahler Festival.[12] Fried and Walter stuck with A–S and Alma, in her memoirs, referred to the Scherzo as the third movement. Consistency was never her forte.

In 1963 a self-important musicologist, Erwin Ratz, cofounder of the International Gustav Mahler Society (IGMG), published a critical edition of the score in S–A order, claiming Alma, Walter, Mengelberg, and Adorno by way of authority. The new edition, coming just as the music world was reawakening to Mahler, became the standard text. Conductors, few of whom investigate beyond the printed page, took up S–A as standard practice, Simon Rattle honorably excepted.

At the turn of the next century a new IGMG editor, Reinhold Kubik, delved into the files and found that Ratz had committed fraud, presenting the aged Alma with false information, and suppressing a letter from Walter, affirming A–S as the correct order. In 2004 Jerry Bruck, a New York Mahler specialist, found that "no record exists of any written or verbal instruction by Mahler himself to friends, associates, other conductors or his publishers to indicate that he ever intended to revert to his earlier [S–A] ordering of these movements." Kubik added that Ratz had engaged in a "semiconscious maneuvering into self-deception." The publication of these findings[13] and an article by Gilbert Kaplan in the *New York Times*[14] persuaded most maestros to accept Andante–Scherzo, A–S, as the composer's final intention. The composer David Matthews[15] and biographer Henry-Louis de La Grange continued to argue that S–A made more musical sense. A new critical edition of the Sixth Symphony that follows Mahler's final wishes—Andante–Scherzo—is being published by C. F. Peters in 2010.

On record, all performances before 1963 are A–S—significantly Mitropoulos, who gave the 1947 U.S. premiere in Alma's presence, F. Charles Adler, and the admirable **Eduard Flipse**, with the Rotterdam Philharmonic (Philips, 1955). From 1963 most recordings are S–A—scandalously so in one instance when Barbirolli's A–S order was reversed by EMI editors under pressure from Ratz. **Mitropoulos** (NYPO Special Edition) is utterly terrifying at the first theme's reappearance in the Scherzo, after the Andante interlude—a clinching argument for the A–S order. Rattle, live in Berlin in 1987 (BPO Special Edition) and in 1989 with his City of Birmingham Symphony Orchestra (EMI), is energized but not harsh enough—too much Mr. Nice Guy to bring out the threat in Mahler's irredeemably grim finale, a movement that Furtwängler called "nihilist" and Karajan (Berlin, 1977) "the bleakest in all symphonic music."

George Szell (Cleveland, 1967) was not one to flinch from delivering bad news. Live from Severance Hall, he pounds away at the marching rhythms for fully half an hour, affording a hiatus of andante relief before reimmersing us in the unrelieved finale gloom. The only drawback is a hint of anthropomorphism, a suggestion that Szell is positively enjoying the horror. The same orchestra under Christoph von Dohnányi plays with more warmth and less terror (Decca, 1992).

Jascha Horenstein gave a very fine account of the Sixth in 1966 with a very poor Stockholm orchestra (Unicorn, 1989) and a better played though less incisive 1968 reading in Bournemouth (BBC Legends). Bernstein, who understood the work well, got closer to its heart of darkness in New York, 1967, than in Vienna, 1988. Kubelik is quick, Haitink ponderous. Michael Gielen does sententiousness rather too well with the Southwest German Radio Orchestra (Hänssler, 2002), while Michael Tilson Thomas injects an unavoidable aura of breaking news, recording the symphony in San Francisco days after the 9/11 attacks on New York (Avie, 2002). Zinman (Zurich, 2008) builds from an overdeliberate base to an overbeautiful finale. **Mariss Jansons**, often inhibited in the studio, gave a thrilling and majestic **LSO Live** performance in 2002, full of dash and daring. A Concertgebouw Live concert in 2004 sounds a tad overrehearsed.

With Pierre Boulez (Vienna, 1995), the analysis is pathological, every sound strung out like entrails on a mortician's table. Boulez can show emotion but he cannot show fury. Valery Gergiev (LSO Live, 2008) shows rage and little else. **Klaus Tennstedt,** on instinct, gets almost everything right. The tramping rhythms draw in from afar until they threaten our personal space. The Andante becomes an extension of the Fifth Symphony's Adagietto, its tenderness softening us up for the terrible blows of the finale, deadly thwacks of the drum which none can survive. EMI's Royal Festival Hall concert of **November 1991** is the one to have; the studio take is less shattering. A live BBC Prom from 1983 (Medici Arts) is atmospherically taut though less well recorded.

THE INSTINCT CONDUCTOR

I have seen many lives changed by Mahler but none so decisively as Klaus Tennstedt's. The son of an orchestral player in the Saxon town of Halle—"Handel's birthplace," he would remind you—Tennstedt grew up in Nazi Germany, resenting its prohibitions and focusing on his music. After pulling bodies out of the Dresden firestorm, he became concertmaster in Halle and was getting good solo opportunities when a freak growth between two knuckles on his left hand ended his playing. Kurt Masur, conducting in Halle in 1948, "with Klaus leading the first violins and his father the seconds," was smitten by his awkwardness, his romanticism, and his magnetic helplessness. Masur, future chief of the New York Philharmonic, had one foot on the fast track while Tennstedt meandered aimless and depressed. "His mother used to say: 'Klaus, why can't you be more like Kurt?'"[16] said Masur. At twenty-one, Klaus had a failed marriage, a child to feed, and a career in ruins. He wore self-doubt as a badge of pride.

Staggering from one podium to the next in a haze of drink, love, and self-doubt, slipping from Dresden's second opera house to the seaside town of Schwerin, he lost his only daughter to suicide and his mind to grief. He hated Communism and did not care who knew it. He was a loose cannon, a danger to himself and others. In March 1971 Masur persuaded the East German government to let him out with his second wife, Inge—"I told them he was not doing himself or us any good."

Friendless and forty-five, Tennstedt defected to Sweden and on to West Germany, where he found a job in Kiel, on the northern seaboard. "I thought maybe I might get asked one day to Mannheim or Wiesbaden," he said, "but never to Hamburg or Munich."[17]

Chance brought a talent scout his way. The Toronto Symphony was looking for guest conductors in 1973 after Karel Ancerl's sudden death. Landing in Hamburg on a concert-free night, the Toronto manager, Walter Homburger, barreled two hours up the Autobahn to catch a Bruckner Seventh in Kiel. Impressed, he booked Tennstedt for Toronto and invited Seiji Ozawa's agent to his debut. Ozawa called the next day to offer a date. "What would you like to conduct?" he said. "You mean I get to choose?" Tennstedt choked out.

"I was so scared," he said, recalling his Boston rehearsal. "I was never sure I could convince them." He called Inge in Germany to say he was coming home. "Get in there," she replied, slamming down the phone. The concert was explosive. "Bruckner—Tennstedt—BSO—Once in a Lifetime," read the *Globe* headline. Before the week was out Tennstedt was on every orchestra's hot list. With each concert he grew more nervous. "The man often resembles a stoned stork," noted *Time*.[18] "A croucher and dancer, a stabber and jabber," was Harold Schonberg's depiction in the *New York Times*.[19] In front of the Philadelphia Orchestra, he burst into tears. Who am I, a provincial musician, he asked himself, to direct these fine performers, players who work only with the very greatest? At the Berlin Philharmonic he was swaying drunk. Having a nervous breakdown, he crept home to his Kiel high-rise to watch the Baltic ferries shuttle in and out of the bay.

"It was then that my love for Gustav Mahler began," he recounted. Reading Mahler's biography, he wept at the composer's response to his daughter's death, thinking, I, too, had led a complicated life. "He talked about the black hole that was life without his daughter," said a close friend. "He woke every morning with one wish: that he could see her again. Through Mahler he found meaning to his existence."[20]

After a Mahler debut with the London Philharmonic Orchestra, he was appointed music director in place of Georg Solti. The audience response was electrifying. Tennstedt would enter the Royal Festival Hall to a roaring ovation. At the end there would be yells of joy and relief. "I see his hands and lips turn blue in a concert,"[21] said the principal cellist, Bob Truman. "To my inexperienced eyes," said chorus member Janice Morley, "his baton technique was somewhat wayward (appearing to involve no beat whatsoever) and he didn't have the more obvious charisma of some of our flashier conductors. Nonetheless, I (and a large number of my fellow sopranos) completely adored him. It was partly that he seemed so vulnerable. . . . Remarkably for a great orchestral conductor, he also appeared to have no ego whatsoever."[22]

When he talked about Mahler, Tennstedt's big, clumsy hands would tug at ears, twist locks of hair, and, without warning, be flung out wide on either side to the peril of household ornaments. "Not every man can conduct Mahler," he would mutter. Off the rostrum he lit a fresh cigarette every six minutes. "I remember sitting with Klaus in a Chinese restaurant in Leicester Square," said Masur. "We were very happy and he was smoking and smoking. I told him: 'Klaus, you have been given a talent, you have a duty. Try to stay healthy.' He said: 'You sound like my mother.' "[23]

Cancer was diagnosed on a 1985 U.S. tour, a tickle in the throat during a Philadelphia concert. He underwent surgery, then radiation. The prognosis was good, but his confidence was shot. He quit as music director in 1987, broke his arm in rehearsal at Carnegie Hall, and raised his last baton with a student orchestra in Oxford in the spring of 1995. Klaus Tennstedt died at Kiel in January 1998, aged seventy-one.

His late performances were acts of human sacrifice, a surrender of the self. His cycle of the symphonies, recorded in Abbey Road, is impressive; a second set, taken from live concerts, overwhelms. The opening of the Sixth Symphony proclaims Tennstedt's idea that Mahler foretold two world wars and the Holocaust. "He would march around the dinner table, demonstrating the jackboots rhythm," said a friend. The risks he took in concert were uninsurable. After a static, fourteen-minute Adagietto, he zipped into the helter-skelter finale while wiping his spectacles calmly on a handkerchief, leading the orchestra with blurred eyes and the rhythm of his trousered right knee.

The least intellectual of men—his apartment revealed nothing more nourishing than *Reader's Digest* condensed books—he would say that Mahler was a matter of instinct. He ridiculed the "öffentliche Wichserei [public masturbation]" of how-and-why lectures by Leonard Bernstein.[24] I once wondered whether he had been preconditioned to love Mahler by growing up under Hitler, when the music was racially verboten, and under Communism, which restricted expressive exuberance. "Quatsch! [Rubbish!]" cried Klaus, resisting analysis.

Anguish was ever close at hand. The East Germans limited him to two visits a year to his aged mother and his daughter's grave. He wore his emotions on flapping half-length, fashion-free sleeves. His sweating, flailing, gawky presence left German audiences unmoved, but Germany's foremost conductor, the sleek Herbert von Karajan, treated him with respect until Tennstedt imprudently pointed out Karajan's errors in a Strauss recording, after which the line went dead. He could never place his own career interest above musical truth.

Klaus Tennstedt was a wild card, a soul imprinted with Mahlerian suffering, relived before my incredulous eyes. He conducted as if Mahler were alive, as relevant as the nightly news. Mahler, he said, "was writing not for his time but for ours." Mahler, he often repeated, "is a matter of life or death."

SYMPHONY NO. 7 IN E MINOR (FP: PRAGUE, SEPTEMBER 19, 1908)

Arnold Schoenberg grasped the Seventh on first hearing, and so did **Hermann Scherchen (Vienna State Opera Orchestra, 1953)**. Hearing Oskar Fried conduct it in Berlin in the year of Mahler's death, Scherchen was smitten by "the powerfully confessional music of the opening movement, the two strangely absorbed Night Music sections, the wildest of Scherzos and the 'brash' American finale with its suppressed Viennese tenderness. The vast spaciousness of Mahler's symphonic vision was effortlessly opened up to me—nothing was too long, nothing too insignificant, nothing too over-weighty in this eighty-minute symphony."[25] Scherchen never heard the work again until he recorded it forty years later, an interpretation of irresistible linear clarity. There are five Scherchen recordings—**Vienna 1950, 1953**, 1955, 1960, and Toronto 1965. The first two (Orfeo and Westminster) are seminal.

Bernstein sets off with the New York Philharmonic in **1967** in a ghostly, cobwebbed search for vanished worlds. Mahler's Seventh contains some of Lenny's most creative insights, a paranormal adventure that deepens in the "Night Musics" and darkens in a gritty Rondo-Finale. His repeat (DG, New York, 1986) is wayward. His apostle Michael Tilson Thomas is stuck too much in his tracks (RCA, 1997).

Hans Rosbaud (Berlin, 1953), Scherchen's immediate rival, offers a modernist interpretation, its strengths structured and subtle. Michael Gielen follows rather stiffly along the same line (Southwest German Radio, 1993). **Kubelik**'s is a heartwarming account (Bavarian Radio, 1968), love and loss intertwined. **Haitink**'s steady hand at the Berlin Philharmonic (Philips, 1995) is both free in fantasy and explicit in detail, among the most useful recordings for following the work score in hand.

Horenstein (1969, BBC Legends) cannot find the loneliness of night in the vastness of the Royal Albert Hall. Barbirolli's (1960, BBC Legends) Halle Orchestra does not sound well nourished.

Klemperer (EMI, 1968) takes one hundred minutes for a symphony that averages eighty—or in Scherchen's case seventy. Tennstedt (EMI, 1993) is irresistible for long stretches without quite filling the picture. Abbado (DG, Chicago, 1984) creates a loving ambience, bypassing the work's shadows, while Chailly's somber Amsterdam opening does not entice the ear (Decca, 1995). Michael Halasz, a staff conductor at the Vienna Opera, gets an idiomatic response from the Polish Radio Orchestra (Naxos, 1994) and a superfine second "Night Music," though textures elsewhere are variable. Rattle and the Birmingham (EMI, 1991) are good at the odder sonorities, but the dance rhythms stick to the floor. The Seventh is the least commercial of the symphonies.

SYMPHONY NO. 8 IN E-FLAT MAJOR

(FP: MUNICH, SEPTEMBER 12, 1910)

Almost unachievable in concert, the *Symphony of a Thousand* is seldom credible on record. Leopold Stokowski, whose 1916 U.S. premiere pushed the Battle of Verdun off Philadelphia's front pages, recorded a 1950 Carnegie Hall concert with the New York Philharmonic in an acoustic too boxy to convey monumentalism. **Horenstein** (BBC Legends), equally historic, appears in a March 1959 concert that launched the BBC's centennial Mahler cycle. None of the performers, conductor included, had tackled this symphony before, and the energies released are palpable. The drama builds episode by episode, and the final choral entry of "Alles vergängliche" has the angelic quality that Mahler sought. The orchestra is the LSO, the choruses are amateur, and the soloists include Kerstin Meyer and Helen Watts.

Mitropoulos (Orfeo) closed the 1960 Salzburg Festival with the Vienna Philharmonic, fully professional choirs, and Hilde Zadek and Hermann Prey among the soloists. The choral singing is devotional, but the sound is credible, thanks to careful microphone placements by Austrian Radio. The giant Greek's passion is irreducible. He died two months later, during a La Scala rehearsal of Mahler's Third.

Bernstein opened Avery Fisher Hall with the Eighth in September

1962, a livelier concert than his ragged, dim-lit 1966 London sessions (both Columbia), or his 1975 Salzburg assault (DG). **Tennstedt** was leaden in studio (EMI, 1986) but like a small boy with three birthday parties when let loose in the concert hall. At his orchestra-only rehearsals, I heard the symphony's skeleton laid bare. His **1991 EMI DVD** is epic. Soloists include Julia Varady, Jane Eaglen, Susan Bullock, and Hans Sotin.

An exuberant **Boulez** is out of character in his Berlin 2007 DG sessions. He lets the choruses rampage off the leash and, though stricter with soloists, treats the work as Wagnerian myth and nonsense, in which a fastidious person can ignore the text while admiring the music.

Robert Shaw, an excellent chorus conductor, faced the armies of Atlanta Symphony Orchestra, two Ohio university chorales, and a third from Florida, with soloists led by Deborah Voigt (Telarc, 1991). No one died in the assault, nor was much gained. Robert Olson's 1995 Colorado Mahler Festival celebration rallied mostly amateur performers in a thrilling one-off experience. Valery Gergiev (LSO Live, 2009) drowned in the vastness of Saint Paul's Cathedral. Michael Tilson Thomas (Avie, 2009) lost his inner pilot in the noise.

Solti, with the best sound of his era and the best forces in Vienna (Decca, 1972), kept clean textures at the loudest tutti, but did not scale down well for soft passages. Sinopoli (DG, 1992) understood dramaturgy and handled his resources to operatic effect. Rattle (EMI, 2004) captured Brittenite anticipations in the plangent orchestral interlude; Abbado (Berlin, 1998) attained a chamber-music meditation. Chailly (Amsterdam, 2000) employed such restraint you wonder why he needed an army.

THE SONG OF THE EARTH (DAS LIED VON DER ERDE)
(FP: MUNICH, NOVEMBER 20, 1911)

Everything hinges on the singing pair. The tenor needs to surmount a large orchestra at forte, and the contralto to hold a low "Ewig" steady through a long fadeout. Mahler, when he asked Bruno Walter "Is this performable?", must have had its technical difficulty in mind as well as its spiritual challenge. Balancing timbres is tough when the singers never meet in duet. Making the match is no easy matter. Tennstedt tried out a dozen tenors in studio before he found a partner for Agnes Baltsa, and still he got it wrong (EMI, 1992). Plácido Domingo rehearsed in his bathroom for many years before going three rounds with Esa-Pekka Salonen in Los Angeles (Sony, 2000), too florid and full of artifice. Jessye Norman and Jon Vickers, with conductor Colin Davis (Philips, 1982), are a casting disaster.

Walter left three recordings, Klemperer two. Seldom was their dichotomy more acute. Walter took a redemptive view, Klemperer a resolute march to oblivion. In 1936 Walter had the expressionless Charles Kullman and the shimmering Kerstin Thorborg. A quarter of a century later he cast overexpressive Ernst Haefliger with fridge-cool Mildred Miller. In between he struck a model partnership of Kathleen Ferrier and Julius Patzak (Decca, 1952). Ferrier, who had risen from switchboard operator to concert star, was in awe of Walter, who was more than half in love with her honest chastity. Old-fashioned in style and intonation, reminiscent of Victorian drawing rooms, she emoted in Mahler with just the right reticence. Patzak, a light-toned Mozartian, took the swell of the Vienna Philharmonic full-on and crested it with a pronounced retro tinge. Ferrier died a year later of breast cancer, aged forty-one.

Klemperer's 1957 Vienna Symphony take had Anton Dermota and Elsa Cavelti as soloists, the tenor elucidating every precious syllable, the contralto dropping every other consonant. In 1967 he found a dream team. Christa Ludwig, a young, strong mezzo, revered the old conductor but, as the daughter and wife of professional singers, held her corner and took her own beat against the oboe solos. Fritz Wunderlich, who sang his part months later, was a roisterer with a career that took off like a rocket. His attack on the "Drinking Song of Earth's Sorrow" was voracious yet vulnerable. An exponent of male frailty, Wunderlich died in a mysterious hunting-lodge accident, aged thirty-six, before the record was released.

All other recordings must be measured beside Walter's and Klemperer's. Karajan (Berlin, 1975), with the heroic-Wagner tenor René Kollo, smoothed the piece out to a point so anodyne that even Christa Ludwig could not redeem it. Eugen Jochum (Amsterdam, 1963), with Haefliger and the elegant Nan Merriman, played down most contrasts. **Fritz Reiner** (Chicago, 1959) employed the Canadian Maureen Forrester, trained by Walter, and the British tenor Richard Lewis, coached by Berthold Goldschmidt, using the voices as instruments to steer him to a sunlit outcome. Szell, with the same soloists (Berlin, 1967), was stiff. Eugene Ormandy, with Lewis and Lili Chookasian (Philadelphia, 1966), was tentative and far too tolerant of the mezzo's blancmange-like vibrato.

Bernstein, being Bernstein, had to be different. He took Mahler's alternative menu of a tenor-baritone pairing, James King and Dietrich Fischer-Dieskau (Vienna, 1966). Mahler thought it might work; it doesn't. The colors are too similar, whether for Bernstein's pair or for Paul Kletzki's of Fischer-Dieskau and Murray Dickie (EMI, 1960) or for Simon Rattle's of Peter Seiffert and Thomas Hampson (EMI, 1995). Fischer-Dieskau himself conducted Yvi Jänicke and Christian Elsner on Stuttgart Radio (Orfeo, 1996) with discreet, light tempi and a lack of burdensome philosophy. Michael Halasz (Naxos, 1994) had a breezy Irish orchestra and brittle soloists. Pierre Boulez (Vienna, 2001), with Michael Schade, Violeta Urmana, and exquisite Vienna Philharmonic sound, played the Wagner defense of to-hell-with-the-meaning. Daniel Barenboim (Warner, 1992) wavered with the Chicago Symphony Orchestra and two ill-suited soloists, Waltraud Meier and Siegfried Jerusalem. A live 1972 Horenstein date from Manchester, with John Mitchinson and Alfreda Hodgson (BBC Legends), deftly shaped and nicely sung, lost the BBC Northern Symphony Orchestra in the background. Solti with Kollo and Yvonne Minton, Haitink with James King and Janet Baker are less convincing.

The one release to challenge the Walter-Klemperer hegemony is **Carlo Maria Giulini**'s with Francisco Araiza, Brigitte Fassbaender, and the Berlin Philharmonic (DG, 1984). Giulini, the humblest of men, made no claim for himself as a Mahlerian beyond suggesting that he knew the South Tyrol mountains well and understood the influence of landscape on music. Discretion is his watchword in *Das Lied*. At no point does he force a line, fostering instead an organic evolution of tone and volume, an even balance of soloists and orchestra. Araiza, a Mexican tenor adept in Mozart, has a lightness that verges on effervescence, while Fassbaender's tone is tart and singular, her diction crystal-clear, and her intelligence arresting. Her opening to the "Farewell" is an object lesson in the art of singing. The same team can be found live on Orfeo, and there is a further Fassbaender sing-through of *Das Lied* with Thomas Moser in Mahler's piano version, played by Cyprien Katsaris (Warner, 2008). A conversion of *Das Lied* to Chinese text was recorded by the Singapore Symphony Orchestra under Lan Shui, with soloists Warren Mok and Ning Liang. At the concluding "Ewig," no Chinese word suffices and German is used.

SYMPHONY NO. 9 IN D MAJOR (FP: VIENNA, JUNE 26, 1912)

The finale of the Sixth and the opening of the Ninth are Mahler's least typical movements, concealing his authorship in a bewilderment of emptiness. The absence of fingerprints encouraged some conductors to approach the Ninth as non-Mahler. **Karajan** (Berlin, 1984), in a release that won sackloads of awards, locates the symphony somewhere between Brahms and Bartók, all rolling hillsides and biting insects. In this two-dimensional country walk, lone instruments pipe up a Concerto for Orchestra. The beauties are sumptuous, but an important human document becomes a picture postcard. What does this symphony mean? Beauty, said Karajan, that's all.

According to the producer Peter Andry, Karajan may have been reacting to a 1964 Mahler Ninth when the Berlin Philharmonic played the symphony for the first time in three decades under **John Barbirolli (EMI)**. JB went for every emotion in Freud's casebook, flickering the changes in a troubled personality. Although rough at the edges, the Barbirolli Ninth was a beacon of evolutionary interpretation.

Bernstein flubbed it, three times. In New York in 1968, Berlin in 1979, and Amsterdam in 1986, he led a madcap country dance and a dangerous Rondo-Burleske, but the opening rhythms never jell and the compassion in the finale sounds like self-pity. **Kubelik** (DG, 1967) stuck close to country lore, lots of cowbells and lowing noises, jaunty dances, and a mood that flicks like the weather from sunny to overcast. The finale sounds like the end of day—and there's another one tomorrow. Walter and Klemperer are at their usual polarities. **Walter's 1938 Vienna concert** (EMI) is hypertense, his 1961 Hollywood performance (Columbia) idyllic and affectionate. Klemperer's 1967 New Philharmonia recording (EMI) is indomitable, muscular in the Rondo-Burleske and unflinching in the closing pages. Klemperer does not go gently into that good night, and his pessimism is gravely unsettling.

There are four recordings of **Jascha Horenstein**, all but the first (Vienna Symphony Orchestra, Vox, 1952) live. His **1964** BBC Prom with the LSO is marred by audience catarrh, but the reading, especially of the finale, is not easily forgotten. Horenstein's gradation of orchestral dynamics is a constant surprise; he somehow finds just the right level of noise for each emotion, darkening as he goes.

Karel Ančerl with the Czech Philharmonic (Supraphon, 1966) was introspective and lyrical, manifesting a Schweik-like contempt for fate, a performance that engages entirely on its own terms. **Kurt Sanderling**, aged eighty (Warner, 1992), balanced warmth and clarity to a remarkable degree. **Carlo Maria Giulini** (DG, 1977) evokes the Toblach landscape to fond effect, just as he did in *Das Lied*. Haitink's 1970 Amsterdam performance (Philips), lauded by Deryck Cooke, is fastidiously literal, as Klaus Tennstedt's (EMI, 1979) is overheatedly not.

Among the foothills Inbal (Frankfurt, 1987) gets his balances wrong in the opening pages and never recovers. Libor Pešek's honest quest (Liverpool, 1990) takes too long to feel its way into the work. Barenboim (Berlin Staatskapelle, 2008) oversprings his second movement rhythms and overbeautifies the finale. Maazel (Vienna, 1984) and Boulez (Chicago, 1998) draw emotional blanks. Solti (London, 1967, Chicago, 1982) overemotes. Kletzki (Israel, 1954) cuts 115 measures out of the second movement. Haitink, with the Concertgebouw in 1970 and subsequently, achieves revelations of detail while flatlining dynamic contrast.

Rattle has two live EMI releases, with the Vienna Philharmonic in 1993 and Berlin in 2008. Both are skewed by deliberateness in dance rhythms at the start of the second movement and by an overbright sound in the finale. Despite these flaws, the Vienna performance is characterized by a steely emotional intensity. Riccardo Chailly

(Amsterdam, 2003) fusses too much with detail. Alan Gilbert (Stockholm, 2009) is duller than a hundred metronomes. An off-the-air recording exists of **Mitropoulos** in Vienna in the last weeks of his life (Andante, 2001). The sound is appalling, but the spirit transcends all material qualms.

SYMPHONY NO. 10 IN F-SHARP MINOR
(FP: LONDON, AUGUST 13, 1964)

The Deryck Cooke performing version was taken up by Ormandy (Philadelphia, 1965), Wyn Morris (London, 1974), James Levine (Philadelphia, 1978), and Kurt Sanderling (Berlin, 1979). Sanderling and Simon Rattle put in many hours with Berthold Goldschmidt to amplify details. **Rattle's 1980 Bournemouth Symphony Orchestra (EMI)** recording established the score as integral to the Mahler canon. Although the playing is English provincial, the performance is a formidable act of advocacy. Rattle, at twenty-five years old, lets the Adagio breathe without fear of transparency and takes the scherzos at a busy clip. The fireman's drum blows set the finale on a death march, but the ambience is never morbid, and the music is not without hope. Rattle's second take, live with the Berlin Philharmonic (EMI, 1999), is finely played but overdeliberate at the outset and jittery in the scherzos. The "Purgatorio" is friendlier than it ought to be, and the drum blows altogether too stagy.

Riccardo Chailly involved many Mahler scholars in his contemplations (Decca, 1986), keeping the agitation in middle movements under cool control and enhancing the finale with sharp contrast. Mark Wigglesworth (BBC, 1993), Gianandrea Noseda (Chandos, 2007), and Daniel Harding with the Vienna Philharmonic (DG, 2008) have little to add to the Cooke work-in-progress.

Of the alternative completions, Leonard Slatkin conducts Remo Mazzetti's first effort in St. Louis (RCA, 1994) and Jesús López-Cobos his second in Cincinnati (Telarc, 2000). Andrew Litton directs the Dallas Symphony Orchestra in the Carpenter version (Delos, 2001), and Martin Sieghart the Arnhem Philharmonic in the Samale/Mazzuca edition (Exton, 2008). Robert Olson has two goes at Joe Wheeler, with the Colorado Mahler Festival (1997) and the

Polish Radio Orchestra (Naxos, 2000). The least assertive of all real-izations, this comes closest to how Mahler left the score at his death, but not to how he would have developed it.

The most ambitious version, and the best played, is **Rudolf Bar-shai** with the Junge Deutsche Philharmonie (Brilliant, 2001) in the conductor's own extrapolation, replete with such exotica as man-dolins and other effects borrowed from Mahler's middle sym-phonies. There is no way of knowing whether Mahler would have gone down this route, but Barshai's approach is imaginative and the performance arresting.

THE MAHLER EFFECT

In July 2004, two weeks after the birth of his daughter, the flutist Gareth Davies visited his doctor and was given terrible news: He had testicular cancer. He went "from the highest of highs to depths of despair in a short space of time." After surgery and chemotherapy he returned to work at the end of summer as principal flute of the London Symphony Orchestra. In physical discomfort and woozy from the drugs, he struggled to find his way back into high perfor-mance mode. Playing Beethoven's Ninth Symphony in Saint Paul's Cathedral was a dispiriting experience. There was a black hole where the thrill ought to be when you play great music—the moments, he put it, "when the music surges forward and you feel excitement . . . a shiver goes up your spine." For the rest of the year he missed that vital feeling, at once motivating and fulfilling. It reached the point where he discussed giving up the job. The princi-pal flute in an international orchestra has no place to hide; it's an all-or-nothing position. And while a London orchestra can be a wonderfully supportive family when someone is seriously ill and off work, it has little tolerance for anyone who gives less than the max in performance.

Shortly before Christmas, after two rehearsals, the orchestra played Mahler's Tenth Symphony with conductor Daniel Harding. Knowing little about the piece except that it represents a struggle with death, Gareth played four movements without incident. At the start of the finale, he heard the leaden thuds of the bass drum, the fire chief's funeral. Five years later, on an orchestra blog, he described what followed:

> Another dull thud.
> And silence.
> This continues until we reach a strange chordal procession and then a simple flute solo. In the score it is marked piano semplice— quietly and simply, that's it. It is a beautiful tune that winds its way around a quiet string section who change to chords which never quite go exactly where you expect them to. It is a deeply unsettling and eerily beautiful and heartbreaking moment at the same time. I've written about the loneliness of playing stuff like this, but this solo is possibly one of the most stunning pieces of music for the orchestral flautist in the repertoire. Anyway, in the concert, we worked our way through the piece until that first funereal thud and my heartbeat increased as the solo grew closer, but this time it felt different. . . . As the tuba plodded away and the drum became more insistent, I could sense something in the music which exactly mirrored my state of mind. . . . Daniel looked across the orchestra, cued me in, I closed my eyes and played. I can't describe how it felt, but time seemed to stop, a wave swept across me, something I had not felt in a concert for months, and suddenly something about that night and that piece changed something in me. I opened my eyes again towards the end to make sure we were all in the same place and it was over. . . . The music of Mahler flicked a switch somewhere in my brain. I have spoken to Dan about it over a year later and explained to him how I had felt . . . ; he just smiled and we both knew what each other was thinking.[26]

What Gareth Davies experienced is Mahler's capacity to pierce human defenses. The components of sound can be enumerated— the strings do this and the flute plays that—but the effect defies explanation. Mahler lasers through body walls and goes straight to the soul. In the Tenth Symphony, on the cusp of love and loss, life and death, that penetration overwhelms the shields that surround us in the recovery period after severe trauma. Musicians have an extra-strong professional firewall. They cannot do their job if personal feelings intrude. Mahler, alone among composers, allows them to emote and still to perform. In Gareth's case it restored feeling. I asked if he could amplify how it worked. He replied that the music took him back to the chilling moment in the doctor's office when the word "cancer" was first mentioned:

> Two bars before the flute solo, where the horns almost pre-echo the opening phrase, I felt completely isolated, almost as if on a thin mountain ridge with a drop either side—perhaps even with life on one side and death on the other. The music searches for peace and finally as it drops down, for me I felt a sense of acceptance of what will be.
>
> I don't know whether resisting emotional surrender is always required as a musician, but on this occasion above all others I felt that I understood exactly what Mahler felt and wanted. Ironically, unlike most of his orchestral music, there is very little instruction as to how he wants it played. I think it is just marked, semplice. A very good instruction for life and music.[27]

That is one of the best expositions available of the Mahler effect on musicians. He exposes the emotion, then allows the player to find a personal resolution. It is one of the reasons why orchestral musicians get so excited about playing Mahler, more than they might be about Strauss or Sibelius. Mahler restores the capacity to feel and liberates us to act on that feeling. Why Mahler? Just ask the players.

THE SONGS

Mahler used his songs as raw material for symphonies. His self-quotation, like Handel's, drains some works of freshness. Few stand out as jewels, nor do the cycles match Schubert and Schumann for innovation. The exceptions are the two Rückert sets, which are the very essence of Mahler.

EARLY SONGS (FRÜHE LIEDER/LIEDER UND GESÄNGE
AUS DER JUGENDZEIT, 1876–90, PUB. 1892)

Of the fourteen songs in this set, **Desi Halban** sang eight with Bruno
Walter at his Hollywood piano in December 1947 (Columbia). Her
voice strains for top notes, and she runs out of breath before the end
of a line, but her amateurism is excusable in a drawing-room entertainment. **Dietrich Fischer-Dieskau**, with Bernstein at the piano in
eleven songs (Columbia, 1968), makes a case for masculine interpretation. His concert-hall manner is declamatory, but the conviction
never falters. He sang the set complete with Barenboim at the piano
(EMI, 1980).

   Thomas Hampson, with pianist David Lutz (Warner, 1994), captures both the desperation and the anticipation in Mahler's songs for
Josefine Poisl, placing them in the yodeling countryside and at the
foundations of his symphonic enterprise. Hampson also sings eleven
early songs sensitively orchestrated and conducted by the Italian
composer **Luciano Berio**, in a style that havers between Schumann
and early Schoenberg. Other voice-piano selections come from
Janet Baker (with Geoffrey Parsons, Hyperion, 1983), Brigitte Fassbaender (with Irwin Gage, DG, 1980), and Anne-Sofie von Otter
(with Ralf Gothóni, DG, 1988). Six Berio transcriptions are sung by
Bernd Weikl, conducted by Giuseppe Sinopoli (DG, 1985).

THE BOY'S MAGIC HORN (DES KNABEN WUNDERHORN, 1892–1901

Naïveté triumphs. The highly praised Fischer-Dieskau and Elisabeth
Schwarzkopf, with George Szell and the LSO (EMI, 1968), are
faultlessly sophisticated. To hear a donkey's "ee-aw" from such
pearly lips runs close to travesty, though the beauty is above
reproach. **Geraint Evans with Janet Baker**, conducted by Wyn Morris (EMI, 1966), find more of the magic. Lucia Popp has her
moments with Klaus Tennstedt (EMI, 1987) but her baritone, Bernd
Weikl, is not up to scratch. Bernstein's first pair, Walter Berry and
Christa Ludwig (Columbia, 1968), are his best. Jessye Norman dominates Haitink and John Shirley-Quirk (Philips, 1976).

Thomas Quasthoff strikes the happiest and saddest of moods in a plush, sun-kissed production with an occasionally shrill **Anne-Sofie von Otter** and the Berlin Philharmonic under Claudio Abbado (DG, 1999). Matthias Goerne and Barbara Bonney are overcooked in Chailly's cycle (Decca, 2003). With the period-instrument Orchestre des Champs-Élysées, Philippe Herreweghe directs Dietrich Henschel and Sarah Connolly (Harmonia Mundi, 2006) in a performance that sounds, for all their bid for rustic simplicity, academically contrived.

THE SONG OF LAMENT (DAS KLAGENDE LIED, 1880, 1893, FINAL REVISION 1899)

Snatches of the Second Symphony grip the ear at the opening and return often through the forty-minute tableau. Fritz Mahler, a cousin, recorded a set on Vanguard at Hartford, Connecticut, in April 1959, with soloists Margaret Hoswell, Lili Chookasian, and Rudolf Petrak. **Wyn Morris** (EMI, 1967) is beguiling with Teresa Żylis-Gara, Anna Reynolds, and Andor Kaposy, though there is not much for a conductor to do other than make an occasional left turn. Haitink (Philips, 1973), Rattle (EMI, 1983), Richard Hickox (Chandos, 1993), and **Tilson Thomas** (Avie, 2007) are fine. A restoration of the 1880 version was premiered in Manchester by **Kent Nagano** and the Halle (Erato, 1997) to no obvious benefit.

SONGS OF A TRAVELING APPRENTICE
(LIEDER EINES FAHRENDEN GESELLEN, 1884–85, ORCHESTRATED 1896)

The only Mahler record by **Wilhelm Furtwängler**, who conducted some of the symphonies in his early career but never after 1933, features a robust Fischer-Dieskau with the Philharmonia Orchestra (EMI, 1952) in a sound that is more Brahmsian than Mahlerian. "Ging heut' Morgen" is taken at a somnambulist plod.

Kirsten Flagstad, a mighty Brünnhilde, applies epic resonance to these agonies of young love. The tragedy is real and the regret carried across to the *Songs on the Death of Children* which she sang at the same Vienna session, under Adrian Boult (Decca, 1957). No Mahlerian should miss this disc.

Janet Baker's virtue in Mahler was a lack of pretension. Like Flagstad, she finds connections between these songs and the *Death of Children* and, while lighter toned, is no less chilling; the Halle Orchestra and Barbirolli accompany (EMI, 1967). Christa Ludwig, with Boult and the Philharmonia (EMI, 1958), is a mite too careful. Mildred Miller is effective, if restricted, with Bruno Walter (Hollywood, 1960), and Fischer-Dieskau is at his peak for Kubelik (Munich, 1968). Others who impress are Yvonne Minton with Solti (Chicago, 1970), Marilyn Horne with Zubin Mehta (Los Angeles, 1978), Brigitte Fassbaender with Sinopoli (London, 1985). In the piano version Thomas Hampson, with David Lutz, is outstanding (Warner, 1994).

FIVE SONGS AFTER RÜCKERT (FÜNF RÜCKERTLIEDER, 1901–2)

Four of the songs were recorded by **Sarah-Charles Cahier** in January 1930 in Berlin, with an orchestra conducted by Selmar Meyrowitz and a voice well past its use-by date; but one can still hear the devotion of singer to composer. Maureen Forrester was first to record the set intact, with the Berlin Radio Orchestra and Ferenc Fricsay (DG, 1959). **Janet Baker**, with Barbirolli (EMI, 1968), calibrated the moods cleverly from the lighthearted "Don't Look for Me in My Songs" through the darkness of "At Midnight" to the quintessence of "I Am Lost to the World." Christa Ludwig, with Klemperer (EMI, 1964), opened with a forlorn "Lost to the World" and sang only four songs, closing with a *Magic Horn* number. **Thomas Hampson's** (DG, 1991) collaboration with Leonard Bernstein makes up in opulence for what it lacks in introspection. A 2008 BBC Scottish set by the Dutch mezzo-soprano **Christianne Stotijn** is floated over the orchestra, and "At Midnight" is thoughtfully understated. No one quite masters "I Am Lost to the World."

SONGS ON THE DEATH OF CHILDREN

(*KINDERTOTENLIEDER*, FP: VIENNA, JANUARY 29, 1905)

Mahler designated the cycle for a male singer, underlining its auto-biographical content. Most of its exponents have been women. **Ferrier** (with Walter, Vienna Philharmonic, 1949) and **Flagstad** (with Boult, Vienna Philharmonic, 1957) are natural antipodes, one a plum-textured contralto, the other a massive instrument at the end of its strength. Tenderness is Ferrier's strength. Her low first note in each of the middle songs enfolds the listener in a security blanket. With Klemperer at the Holland Festival, 1951 (Decca), she invokes in the closing song an intimation of the *Song of the Earth*. Flagstad is forceful, monolithic, and unyielding, riding a full orchestra with nonchalance. In the final song she is Wagnerian, coloring a river of gold and holding grief in the check of an impermeable dignity.

Two recordings exist of the heroic **Marian Anderson**—with Pierre Monteux in 1950 and Horenstein in 1956—her voice too florid for these songs but her empathy perfect. Janet Baker, live with Horenstein (BBC Legends, 1967), is regal; with Barbirolli in studio (EMI, 1968), emotional; with Bernstein in Israel (Columbia, 1974), unsettled.

Christa Ludwig (with André Vandernoot, EMI, 1958) applies a light voice to limitless varieties of pain, achieving gaunt agony in the middle song, "When Your Little Mother." Her Berlin retake with Karajan (DG, 1974) is analgesic. **Brigitte Fassbaender** is bold and incisive in live concerts with Tennstedt in London (unreleased, 1987) and Chailly in Berlin (Decca, 1988). **Lorraine Hunt Lieberson**'s recital with piano (Wigmore Hall, 1998) is poignancy itself.

Baritone Heinrich Rehkemper, conducted by the young Jascha Horenstein (DG, 1928), has serene gravity, steady tempi, and a surprisingly realistic orchestral sound for the date of production. **Fischer-Dieskau**, in his 1955 EMI Berlin performance under Rudolf Kempe, adopts a tremulous sorrow; he is fiercer, and less likable, in a 1963 DG session with Karl Böhm.

The clinching argument for male interpretation is made by the well-poised Hampson (Bernstein, Vienna, DG, 1988) and by the Welsh baritone **Bryn Terfel** in a reading of Schubertian subtlety

(Sinopoli, Philharmonia, DG, 1992). Toward the end of the first song, Terfel emits a musical sigh that is dredged from the deepest sorrow, a point where art and life, for once, converge.

FRACTIONS, FRAGMENTS, AND ADAPTATIONS

Mahler's student Piano Quartet in A minor, in one extant movement, is well played by members of the Georges Enescu Bucharest Philharmonic Orchestra (Arte Nova, 2000). Alfred Schnittke's two-movement extension is done by Ludmilla Berlinsky with the Borodin Quartet (Virgin Classics, 1990). Schnittke reuses the work at the end of the second movement of his Fifth Symphony, also titled Concerto Grosso no. 4.

The torso sections of "Blumine" from the First Symphony and "Totenfeier" from the Second are widely recorded. Paavo Järvi groups them with the Adagio from the Tenth Symphony and Benjamin Britten's chamber-orchestra version of a movement from the Third Symphony in a single release (Virgin, 2009).

Mahler's completion of the Weber opera *Die Drei Pintos* is recorded under Gary Bertini in Munich (RCA, 1995) and Paolo Arrivabeni in Wexford (Naxos, 2003). His arrangements of Schumann symphonies were conducted in Leipzig by Chailly (Decca, 2007). Dohnányi in Cleveland performed Mahler's string-orchestra expansion of Beethoven's F-minor Quartet, op. 95 (Decca, 1996). Jeffrey Tate (EMI, 1996) led the enlargement of Schubert's *Death and the Maiden* Quartet.

In 1919 Arnold Schoenberg formed a Society for Private Musical Performances, whose subscribers could hear brand-new music and recent adaptations. Schoenberg reworked the *Traveling Apprentice* songs for flute, clarinet, harmonium, piano, percussion, and string quintet (recorded by Camerata de Versailles on the Auvidis label, 1986) and *The Song of the Earth* (by Sinfonia Lahti, with Monica Groop, download available). Erwin Stein made small-orchestra versions of four symphonies; the Fourth is on record (Capriccio, 2001).

All the Mahler symphonies exist in two- and four-hand piano versions by such allies as Walter (Second), Zemlinsky (Sixth), Alfredo

Casella (Seventh), and Josef von Wöss, his publishing editor. In the early 1990s, planning Sweden's first Mahler cycle, the Royal Stockholm Philharmonic Orchestra asked me for suggestions for a Mahler weekend. I suggested playing all the four-hand symphonies in a day, and thought students might be roped in to do them. But once the idea got out, all the top pianists in Sweden lined up, and two of them shuttled in rehearsal for three weeks from Göteborg to Stockholm and back. Their curiosity was all-consuming.

Starting at nine in the morning and ending just before ten at night, the piano scores offered a CT scan of Mahler's mind, revealing connective lines from the first symphony to the last in a way that could never be obtained through an orchestral series. More than five hundred people bought all-day tickets, and fifteen of them never left their seats, except for designated bathroom breaks. A four-hand cycle is recorded by two German pianists, Silvia Zenker and Evelinde Trenkner (MDG, 1991).

The Fifth Symphony is played on the organ of Gloucester Cathedral by David Briggs (Priory, 1991). Inauthentically, the Arcangelos Chamber Ensemble plays a therapeutic version of Mahler's Fourth Symphony as "music to de-stress, 30–60 beats a minute," for ABT Media's SoundHealth program (www.abtmedia.com).

A QUICK WORD ABOUT EDITIONS

Mahler always believed the latest edition of his music was the best. That remains true. The International Gustav Mahler Society aims to eliminate past errors from its new editions. "The first symphony, for instance, which I have conducted many times," said Claudio Abbado in 2009: "I bought a new edition and found a lot of new things."[28]

DERIVATIONS, IMITATIONS, INTIMATIONS

Zemlinsky and Shostakovich copied the form of *The Song of the Earth*. Zemlinsky's *Lyric* Symphony (1924), to seven poems by the Bengali philosopher Rabindranath Tagore, alternating baritone and soprano, imitates structure and ambience. The Fourteenth Symphony of **Shostakovich** (1969)—setting eleven poems for soprano, bass, percussion, and string ensemble—is dedicated to the mortally ill Benjamin Britten and anticipates death with Russian requiem quotes. **Britten,** in his **Sinfonia da Requiem** (1940), floated a Mahlerian line in the first and third sections. The "Sea Music" in his opera *Peter Grimes* (1945) echoes the orchestral interlude of Mahler's Eighth Symphony.

Luciano Berio based the Scherzo of his **Sinfonia** (1968) on quotations from the same movement in Mahler's Second Symphony. **Wolfgang Rihm** wrote a prelude, *Abkehr* (1986), to Mahler's Ninth Symphony and a requiem, *Mein Tod* (1989), which followed Mahler's line of lamentation. **Peter Ruzicka**'s Viola Concerto (1981) regurgitates a passage from Mahler's Ninth.

Kurt Weill, a Busoni student, refers repeatedly to Mahler in the text and music of his *New Orpheus* cantata (1925). **Busoni's** *Berceuse élégiaque* (1909), the penultimate score on Mahler's conducting stand, echoes the Fifth Symphony Adagietto; it is recorded in two versions: the composer's orchestration and a haunting Schoenberg reduction for flute, clarinet, harmonium, and string quintet. **Schoenberg** quotes Mahler's Seventh Symphony in his Second Chamber Symphony (1938). **Alban Berg** quotes Zemlinsky's *Lyric* Symphony in his tributary **Lyric Suite** (1927), and applies Mahler's method of ironic quotation throughout his works.

America's signature concert work, **Samuel Barber's** *Adagio for Strings*, contains temperamental affinities with Mahler's Adagietto; Barber liked to disparage Mahler and Strauss, perhaps to conceal a stylistic debt. **Aaron Copland's Clarinet Concerto** (1950) opens with the dying cadence of Mahler's Ninth Symphony, a figure also quoted near the end of **Bernstein's** score for Elia Kazan's movie *On the Waterfront* (1954). The cadence of the Ninth Symphony appears unexpectedly in the middle of **Henryk Górecki's Third** (1976), the first million-selling symphony on record. The Russian Nikolai Korndorf wrote a 1990 *Hymn in Honour of Gustav Mahler* for soprano and orchestra, a celebration of natural beauty and scriptural faith.

Mahler's influence extends a century beyond his death, not univer-sally or pervasively but at many of the critical junctions of musical development.

Among Mahler's close associates, **Josef Bohuslav Foerster** wrote naive suites, symphonies, and operas in the national style of Dvořák. **Bruno Walter** wrote a D-minor Symphony with early Mahler ges-tures. Mahler is heard in many works of **Erich Wolfgang Korngold** (1897–1957), typically mingled with Strauss and Puccini. **Karl Weigl** (1881–1949), employed by Mahler at the Vienna Opera, wrote six late-romantic symphonies; the Fifth (1945), titled *Apocalypse* and dedicated to "the Memory of Franklin Delano Roosevelt," employs Mahlerian motifs in its "Dance Around the Golden Calf." The ele-giac **Joseph Marx** (1882–1964), whom Furtwängler called "the lead-ing force in Austrian music," developed a style from Mahler's pastoral music. **Egon Wellesz** (1885–1974) wrote eight symphonies, of which the first has a finale modeled upon Mahler's last adagio. **Alfredo Casella** (1883–1947) composed a 1909 C-minor Symphony inspired by Mahler; in 1918 he switched allegiance to Mussolini. The songs of **Alma Mahler-Werfel**, fourteen in all, are extensively recorded. Of the rest of Mahler's family, 1928 recordings survive of **Arnold Rosé** playing the Bach Double Concerto with his daughter, Alma.

STAGE AND SCREEN

Thomas Mann did not expect anyone to recognize Mahler as Aschenbach in *Death in Venice* and was taken aback when his illustra-tor, Wolfgang Born, drew a lifelike sketch from his fictional descrip-tion. That likeness carried over into Dirk Bogarde's portrayal of Aschenbach in Luchino Visconti's film of the novella.

Plays by Joshua Sobol and Ronald Harwood address Mahler's Jewishness. Sobol's "polydrama" *Alma*, created for the 1996 Vienna Festival, is a multimedia history with a live Web site (www.alma-mahler.com). Harwood's *Mahler's Conversion*, staged in London in the month of the 9/11 attacks, drew on Bernstein's ethnopsychological speculations. The play closed in weeks; the script was published by Faber & Faber (London, 2001).

Ken Russell's film *Mahler* (1974) was a feature-length extension of one of his BBC biodocs. Shot over six weeks in the English Lake District and a flat in London's Portobello Road,[29] it relied on Alma's memoir and committed anachronisms of style, conduct, and speech. However, many, conductors included, found it inspiring. When Mahler is asked, "What religion are you?" he replies: "I am a composer." The exchange is fictive, but it rings true. Mahler is played by Robert Powell, later to appear as Jesus in Franco Zeffirelli's TV miniseries and as a nurse in the weekly BBC hospital soap opera *Holby City.*

In Bruce Beresford's *Bride of the Wind* (2001), Mahler is played by Jonathan Pryce in a script that screeches clichés. Its nadir is an orgy scene with live cardinals.[30]

BROUGHT TO BOOK

Mahler's first biographers, **Paul Stefan** and **Richard Specht**, struck a querulous tone of polemical hagiolatry. "Calmness," said Stefan (1879–1943) on his opening page, "is not my concern."[31] Specht (1879–1932) took his information from Alma and tilted his portrait in her favor. His 1913 biography was reprinted twenty-four times.

So powerful was this partisan approach that it pervades Mahler biographies a century later. **Henry-Louis de La Grange** (born 1924) spent his life researching and writing Mahler's biography, stuffing four huge volumes with rants against Mahler's detractors, real and imagined, past and present. The son of a French aviation pioneer and an American furniture heiress, Emily Sloane, La Grange discovered Mahler in 1945 at a Carnegie Hall concert of the Fourth Symphony, conducted by Bruno Walter. Getting to know Alma Mahler, he set about accumulating raw materials, among them the uncut manuscripts of Natalie Bauer-Lechner, and William Ritter's diaries. His Médiathèque Musicale Mahler contains one of France's largest collections of musical manuscripts, including the legacies of Saint-

Saëns, Alfred Cortot, Selma Kurz, and the Hungarian-born song-writer Joseph Kosma. The collection can be accessed online at www.bgm.org. La Grange's discoveries are crucial, and his day-by-day coverage of Mahler's life is indispensable for Mahler-geeks like me. After a while, though, the repetition of mundane events becomes tedious, and the analysis of character and music is often superficial. His biography is more for reference than for reading.

Donald Mitchell (1925), as a young critic, served Benjamin Britten as Paul Stefan did Mahler, shooting flak at doubters and detractors. Groundbreaking on the relation of song to symphony, Mitchell's Mahler studies are a delicatessen of revealed delights—to be sampled in small tastings for prolonged cogitation.

Constantin Floros (born 1930), a Greek-born, German musicologist, applies scriptural exegesis to Mahler, examining words and notes in the context of works and life. Brilliant at thematic links, Floros sounds prescriptive at times, but his ideas are fresh and his verdicts ice clear; the 1993 translation is excellent.

Kurt Blaukopf (1914–99), in the postlude to his 1969 Mahler biography, admitted that "my love for Mahler was not constant; there were years when I turned away from his music."[32] A law student who fled Vienna in 1938 for Paris and spent the war in Palestine, Blaukopf and his second wife, Herta (1924–2005), gave freely of their findings to Mahler seekers, this writer included. His biography is dated but the *Documentary Study* (1976) is a rewarding read for the Mahler newbie. Other useful modern biographies are by Michael Kennedy, Jonathan Carr, Peter Franklin, and Wolfgang Schreiber.

These are the main portals to Mahler knowledge. Intrinsic, often blinkered, they are not concerned with Mahler in the modern world. That story needed to be told from a twenty-first-century perspective. That is what this book has set out to do.

WHAT MAHLER TELLS ME

The walls around my desk are stacked with books, scores, and manuscripts, all about Mahler. Six shelves of CDs groan to my left, winnowed from hundreds I have tried and tested. If fire broke out I would save my children first, then my Mahler objects.

Too much Mahler? Not from where I sit. You can accuse me of having too many designer shirts and far too many malt whiskeys for one man to consume in recommended moderation, but Mahler furnishes my life. Thirty-five years of quest surround me. Everyone needs a personal benchmark. Mahler is mine.

So what have I learned? From the life, a sheaf of truths and ideals:

that every child stands a chance;

that love can wait;

that the difference between ordinary and excellent is the last degree of effort;

that the best is never good enough;

that striving is all;

that dignity survives defeat;

and above all, that no is not an answer; it's not even a barrier. The impossible takes just that little bit longer.

Mahler's resilience is a source of courage in my times of adversity and hope in my depressions. He is not so much a moral exemplar as a practical guide to living a creative life, knowing when to dig in the heels and when to yield, when to force the pace and when to let the world catch up. Working beyond the expectations of his own time, he was confident of his durability. In art there is no other way.

From his music other principles arise, no less applicable to present times. The modern world is a blizzard of information without an igloo for shelter. How we receive and make sense of it all becomes tenuous as new media are invented that make news instantaneous and every transient acquaintance a Facebook friend. Mahler's music is a fast track to deep-core emotion, a way of connection with true self and, through that connection, with cherished others.

It is not a narrow channel but a complex web of messages, not all of them interesting or fit for purpose. Mahler anticipates the information blizzard by way of random intrusions and offstage bands. He teaches us that no message can be taken literally or in isolation. Every statement has subtext, commentary, and inbuilt contradiction;

every declaration needs to be treated with more skepticism than our forebears might have applied to speeches by Churchill, Gandhi, or Abraham Lincoln.

When we listen to leaders in the third millennium, we need to hear what they are saying beneath the message if we are to avoid disaster. When we trawl the information superhighway, each discovery must be treated with kid gloves, put on hold, and worked into a larger perspective if the human mind is not to be atrophied to that of a firefly. Mahler offers breadth and depth to the thought process. In a speeded-up, homogenized society, he allows us to think that the individual mind can survive. He urges us to see the bigger picture, to listen to the unsaid. He continues the conversation. He makes critics of us all.

PART IV

How to Mahler

15. Finding the Key to a Private Space

The symphonies are dauntingly long, and the songs are in German. For those who lack patience and languages, Mahler can seem impossibly forbidding, a fortress with no entry point. "How do I get in?" is a question commonly asked by new listeners and music professionals alike. Tell me, demands a classical broadcasting producer, where I should begin and why I should bother.

If this were Beethoven, what would you say? Fifth Symphony, maybe, finale of the Ninth, "Für Elise," *Kreutzer* Sonata, *Moonlight* . . . there are temptations for every age, intellectual level, and individual taste within a defined range of cultural appetites. Mahler, however, offers no menu. It's symphonies or songs, take it or leave it. The choice depends on who you are and what is troubling you at any particular moment. In my occasional role as the Record Doctor on WNYC's *Soundcheck* show, I have prescribed the finale of the Ninth Symphony and the Adagietto of the Fifth for callers in situations of grief and loss. Those passages of music can ease pain and assist recovery in some, in others not. The trick is to find a piece of Mahler that suits your particular character and stage in life and then to work your way outward.

So how to begin? Buy, beg, or borrow a ticket to the next upcoming concert of the *Resurrection* Symphony. Do not sit in the best seats with the corporate types but go for the upper reaches of the hall; the music is highly dimensional and best appreciated from afar. Go without preconceptions or religious bias. Don't read the program notes. Go alone. See if anything happens. Talk to the people around you. Suspend judgment until the next morning (unless you are a newspaper critic on an overnight deadline). If nothing happens, it could be that Mahler's not for you. Don't give up yet.

Wait until a momentous happening. If a child is born, treat the parents to the Fourth Symphony—its hectic opening and generous adagio throw open windows to a world of innocent joy. If you've landed the job of your dreams, play the "Night Musics" of the Seventh Symphony for courage and perspective. A medical intern facing a vertical learning curve might find encouragement in the brutal rhythms of the Sixth Symphony. If it's bad news, go to the Ninth Symphony. For the worst news of all, the finale of the Tenth.

These are general remedies, and Mahler is not an over-the-counter medicine. What works for one person may leave another cold. Much depends on the interpretation you choose and the mood in which you receive it. A senior Hungarian artist, averse to anything German, was won over by my gift to her of Bruno Walter's account of the First Symphony. A skeptical opera singer was blown away by the naive serenity of Kathleen Ferrier in *The Song of the Earth*. An orchestral administrator was captivated while wrestling at the piano with Zemlinsky's reduction of the Sixth Symphony. Throughout this book you will find epiphanic moments of how one Mahler symphony or another changed someone—how a confused French student found a mission in the Fourth, a conductor got over his breakdown with the Sixth, a composer found personal messages in the Ninth. You never know when and how Mahler is going to strike.

If you are taking a new listener to a Mahler concert, talk to them first about one trademark moment—the child's funeral in the First Symphony, the offstage ensemble in the Second, the introductory ironics in the Third, and so on. A small piece of concentrated information is worth more than a general description of the work. It also gives the neophyte a focal clue to the uniqueness of Mahler's method. If they don't respond to the music, blame the conductor. There will always be another chance.

For someone who has never listened to classical music in any form, I would start with Uri Caine's reworkings on the album *Primal Light*, drawn from the fusions of postmodern art. For a disco addict, I would try the pounding opening of the Sixth at full blast on a top-end stereo. To my broadcast colleague with a Mahler block, I think I'll play Kirsten Flagstad in the *Songs on the Death of Children*, or perhaps Lorraine Hunt Lieberson with piano accompaniment. Neither has a typical Mahler voice, and both come at the songs from a tangential angle. Not every civilized person is susceptible to Mahler, but within the monumental edifice of his works there are chinks that allow a listener to be at one with him- or herself. And those are the points when the Mahler fortress becomes a private refuge.

ACKNOWLEDGMENTS

My greatest debt in this book is to an unsung hero of Mahler scholarship. For more than forty years, Knud Martner has been a source of meticulous exactitude about the chronology of Mahler's life and works. He has assisted as editor and fact-checker on many books, starting with the English publication of *Mahler's Letters* in 1979, but he seldom received full credit and his corrections were often ignored by hasty authors. Based in Copenhagen, Knud has an attentiveness to detail that almost equals Mahler's. When he agreed to read my manuscript, I was filled with confidence to have such rigor at my side. When Knud, chapter by e-mailed chapter, told me that I was giving him fresh information and food for thought, I knew that the book was worth writing.

In addition to fact-checking, Knud has offered me valued insights, such as a clue to the origin of the Fifth Symphony's opening. I have enjoyed our correspondence so much that I won't let it end with this acknowledgment. But I want to state with unequivocal emphasis that this book could not have been written without the enthusiastic participation of Knud Martner, whom I thank in deep humility.

My Mahler dialogue with Gilbert E. Kaplan goes back a quarter of a century. Hardly a month has gone by in that time when we have not called each other to discuss some point of contention. Gil's story is told in this book. I owe him and Lena a debt of friendship, laughter, and collaboration. It was through Gil that I met Jonathan Carr, head of *The Economist*'s bureau in Germany and the world's greatest expert on *Die Meistersinger*, which he saw more than sixty times. Jonathan and his wife, Dorothea, became friends. I am sorrier than I can put into words that he did not live to see this book in print. I gave Jonathan the title for his book, *The Real Mahler*, and I expected him to repay the compliment.

Donald Mitchell commissioned my first book on Mahler in 1985, and Henry-Louis de La Grange gave me the run of his Paris library at the start of my researches. The late Kurt and Herta Blaukopf were ever courteous and welcoming in Vienna. I have thanked them all before and am glad to do so again.

Anna Mahler was a close friend, our correspondence bulging from a drawer behind me as I write. The late Lotte Klemperer, whom I met in Toblach, was an early stimulant. The late Berthold Goldschmidt was a warm and wise friend. Klaus Tennstedt was an inspiration in all he said and did. Georg Solti was a joy.

Jiří Rychetský was my first point of contact in Mahler's land. Others who helped me there are Milan Palak (Ostrava), Michael Srba (Bratislava), Lida Jirásova, Berenika Ovčákova, Libor Pešek, Zdena Pošvicová, Dr. Jitka Sláviková, and Ivana Stehliková (Prague).

In Vienna, Peter Poltun introduced me to the music archives of the State Opera and the Philharmonic Orchestra. Wolfgang Herles and Susanne Obermayer were inestimable sources of local knowledge and ever-welcoming friends. Oscar Hinteregger, Ines Feuerstein, and Nicole Bachmann facilitated research trips.

Attila Csampai invited me to lecture at his festival at Toblach. Felix and Annina Mikl were our hosts at Maiernigg. I enjoyed the hospitality of the Föttinger family at Steinbach am Attersee, just as Mahler did. Ulla Kalchmair helped me in Salzburg, as did Franz Willnauer in a conversation he will long since have forgotten.

In Hamburg I walked beside the waterways with Sonia Simmenauer and crossed lances with György Ligeti. In Holland the late Anneke Daalder and her husband, Hans, were empathetic partners, Dr. H. J. Nieman helped clarify points of detail. In Finland, the late Seppo Heikinheimo was ever challenging. In New York, J. Rigbie Turner gave me access to the Mahler scores at the Pierpont Morgan Library, Stephen E. Hefling helped with a quotation, and Mahler Society stalwarts, Gerald S. Fox and Guy Fairstein, gave encouragement. Elsewhere in the United States, I benefited from the wisdom of the late Jack Diether, William Malloch, and Edward R. Reilly. More recent Mahler exchanges were with Stephen Rubin, Allan Kozinn, Lorin Maazel, Karen Painter, John Rockwell, Leonard Slatkin, and Benjamin Zander. The late Betty Freeman, antiromantic, was a useful corrective to Mahlerian excess.

Zoltan Roman, in Canada, taught me much about Mahler's terms in Budapest and New York. Alexandra Samur captured the mysterious Mahler wall daubings that appeared overnight in Toronto.

My China researches were aided by Dr. Shen Yung of Shanghai, along with Dr. Jane V. Portal and Dr. Yang Yang of the British Museum, whose director, Neil MacGregor, and director of public engagement, Joanna Mackle, persuaded me to accompany them to China. Joanna, twenty years earlier, was the publicist for my book *Mahler Remembered*.

Mahler's health in this book has been checked by Dr. Michael P. Schachter (Imperial College, London), Dr. Jeffrey M. Graham (U.K. Department of Health), and Dr. Sylvia Lacquer (Hampstead). His psychological history has been read by therapists Dr. Emmanuel M. Garcia (New Zealand) and Esther Klag and Marlene Bensimon (London), and his child psychology has been discussed with Claire Meljac and Aviva Cohen (Paris).

Nobody who researches events that took place 100–150 years before can hope to find enlightenment without the assistance of antiquarian booksellers. I was lucky to know the late Hermann Baron, Albi Rosenthal, and Valerie Travis, and to maintain contact with Christel Wallbaum.

My editors in newspapers and broadcasting have put up with a lot of Mahler from me over the years and allowed me more space than I perhaps deserved. On the former *Evening Standard* I thank Veronica Wadley, Ian Macgregor, Fiona Hughes, David Sexton, and Katie Law. At the *Daily Telegraph*, Sarah Crompton and Paul Gent. At BBC Radio 3, Roger Wright, Tony Cheevers, Abigail Appleton, and Jeremy Evans. At Bloomberg Muse, Manuela Hoelterhoff, Jim Ruane, and Mark Beech. At the *Sunday Times*, far back, Don Berry, Harry Coen, Hannah Charlton, and Steve Boyd.

Others who lent support at times of particular stress are the late Ewen Balfour, David Drew, and Ruth Jordan; Aythen Elkind, Judy Grahame, Daniella and Rafi Grunfeld, Ronald Harwood, Gavin Henderson, Douglas Kennedy, the late Aharon Lizra, Fiona Maddocks, Belinda Matthews, Colin Matthews, Maria Muller, Felix Pirani, Zsuzsi Roboz, and John Tusa (London); Shirley Apthorp, Dietrich Fischer-Dieskau (Berlin); Mariss and Irina Jansons, Marie-Christine Mikl (Zurich); Mona Levin (Oslo); Lin Bender, John Manger (Melbourne); Nuria Schoenberg-Nono (Venice); Tatiana Hoffmann (Jerusalem), Noam Sherriff (Tel Aviv). At a very late stage in the book, a blog by the LSO principal flute Gareth Davies set off a conversation about Mahler's impact on professional musicians.

No writer could wish for more intuitive agents than Jonny Geller and Jane Gelfman. My Random House editors, Marty Asher and Lexy Bloom, have kept me awake at night for all the right reasons; Lisa Weinert was chamomile to their coffee; my thanks to Sue Llewellyn for her copyediting; without them this book would not exist.

Finally I owe a huge hug of thanks to my family for putting up with Mahler and me. Elbie, Naama, Abigail, and Gabriella were in the front line; Simon, Bernard, and Jayjay received secondary burns. They know, in Mahler's phrase, what love tells me. At least, I hope they do.

NOTES

A NOTE ON TEXTS AND SOURCES

Much Mahler literature is available in English. Where the translation is inadequate or inaccurate, especially of Mahler's poetic texts, I substitute my own.

Preface to the Anchor Edition • After Mahler, Another Deluge?

1. For more information, visit: http://www.mahler-penzion.cz/en/.
2. The original German lyrics and music are available at: http://www.volksmusik.cc/lieder/wanniamalstirb.htm.

Chapter 1 • Some Frequently Asked Questions

1. Mikhail S. Gorbachev, "My Final Hours," *Time*, May 1992.
2. Borchardt, *Mahler: Meine Zeit wird kommen; Aspekte der Mahler-Rezeption*, 61.
3. David Schiff, *The Nation*, July 13, 2009.
4. Mervyn Cooke, *A History of Film Music*, 457.
5. *High Fidelity*, September 1967.
6. Walter, *Theme and Variations*, 93.
7. Gustav Mahler, *Selected Letters*, 300.
8. Dukas and Hoffmann, *Albert Einstein*, 37.
9. Gay, *A Godless Jew*, 137.
10. Karl Ekman, *Jean Sibelius: The Life and Personality of an Artist*, translated by Edward Birse (Helsinki: Holger Schildts Forlag, 1935), 190–91.
11. Bauer-Lechner, *Recollections of Gustav Mahler*, 38.
12. Oskar Fried, quoted in Lebrecht, *Mahler Remembered*, 174–76.
13. Lebrecht, *Mahler Remembered*, 50.
14. Eric Davis to Mahler-List: http://listserv.uh.edu/cgi-bin/wa?A2= ind9612&L=mahler-list&d=0&I=-3&P=17132.
15. Ian Parsons to Mahler-List: http://listserv.uh.edu/cgi-bin/wa?A2= ind9612&L=mahler-list&d=0&i=-3&P=16758.

16. Christopher Abbott to Mahler-List: http://listserv.uh.edu/cgi-bin/wa?A2=ind0109b&L=mahler-list&T=0&P=16211.

17. David Alderman, leader of the London Symphony Orchestra second violins, on *Lebrecht.live*, BBC Radio 3, June 27, 2004.

18. "91 Years After Dying, Mahler Hits His Stride," *New York Times*, January 17, 2002.

19. Oliver Sacks, *Musicophilia* (London: Picador, 2007), 280.

20. Martha C. Nussbaum, *Upheavals of Thought: The Intelligence of Emotions* (Cambridge: Cambridge University Press, 2001), 642–44.

21. Gustav Mahler, *Selected Letters*, 55.

22. Bauer-Lechner, *Recollections of Gustav Mahler*, 186.

23. Lebrecht, *Mahler Remembered*, 155.

24. Stefan, *Gustav Mahler: Eine Studie über Persönlichkeit und Werk*; Specht, *Gustav Mahler*.

25. Lebrecht, *Mahler Remembered*, 264–65.

26. James Boswell, *Life of Johnson*, advertisement to the Second Edition, London, 1793.

27. Judy Gahagan, *Did Gustav Mahler Ski?* (New York: New Directions, 1991).

28. Lebrecht, *Mahler Remembered*, 157, 152.

29. Ibid., 317.

30. Ibid., 169.

31. Bauer-Lechner, *Recollections of Gustav Mahler*, 19–21.

32. Walter, *Gustav Mahler*, 4.

33. Charles Burney, *An Account of the Musical Performances in Westminster Abbey and the Pantheon, 1784, in Commemoration of Handel* (London, 1785), n.p.

34. Bauer-Lechner, *Recollections of Gustav Mahler*, 82.

35. Alma Mahler, *Gustav Mahler: Memories and Letters*, 116.

36. Bauer-Lechner, *Recollections of Gustav Mahler*, 81.

37. de La Grange, *Mahler*, vol. 4, *A New Life Cut Short*, 931.

38. Gustav Mahler, *Briefe, 1870–1911*, 5–9 (italics in original).

39. Gustav Mahler, *Selected Letters*, 57.

40. Ibid., 456.

41. Ibid., 56–57.

42. See Barham, *Perspectives on Gustav Mahler*, 214.

43. See de La Grange, *Mahler*, vol. 4, *A New Life Cut Short*, 1660–62.

44. *Time*, February 7, 1938.

45. A. L. Bacharach, *The Musical Companion* (London: Cassell, 1934), 456, 237.

46. Ludwig Wittgenstein, *Culture and Value* (Oxford: Blackwell, 1948), 67e (italics in original).

47. Stephen Walsh, *The Observer*, newspaper clipping, n.d.

48. See www.imdb.com.

49. Alexandra Samur, in *The Torontoist*, October 11, 2007.

Chapter 2 · Living in a Nowhere Land (1860–1875)

1. Walter, *Gustav Mahler*, 25.

2. Bauer-Lechner, *Erinnerungen an Gustav Mahler*, 147.

3. Cf. John Murray, *Handbook for Travellers in Southern Germany* (London: John Murray, 1858), 471; Sverak et al., *Počátek cesty: Gustav Mahler a Jihlava*, 17. Gives seventeen thousand in 1860.

4. Entry *Jewish Encyclopedia* s.v. "Iglau" (New York: Funk & Wagnalls, 1901–5).

5. Alma Mahler, *Gustav Mahler: Memories and Letters*, 109.

6. Bauer-Lechner, *Recollections of Gustav Mahler*, 69.

7. Sverak et al., *Počátek cesty*, 17.

8. Gustav Mahler, *Selected Letters*, 377.

9. Bauer-Lechner, *Erinnerungen an Gustav Mahler*, 60.

10. Lebrecht, *Mahler Remembered*, 224.

11. Bauer-Lechner, *Erinnerungen an Gustav Mahler*, 60.

12. Lebrecht, *Mahler Remembered*, 92.

13. Kurt Blaukopf, *Mahler: A Documentary Study*, 148.

14. Alma Mahler, *Gustav Mahler: Memories and Letters*, 5.

15. Sverak et al., *Počátek cesty*, 17.

16. Bauer-Lechner, *Recollections of Gustav Mahler*, 28.

17. McClatchie, *The Mahler Family Letters*, 25.

18. Szeps-Zuckerkandl, *My Life and History*, 38–43.

19. Lebrecht, *Mahler Remembered*, 11–12.

20. Bauer-Lechner, *Recollections of Gustav Mahler*, 85.

21. Ibid., 152.

22. Lebrecht, *Mahler Remembered*, 9–10.

23. Document from Professor Jiří Rychetský, published in *Hlas Revoluce* (Prague), December 5, 1991.

24. de La Grange, *Mahler*, vol. 1, 23.

25. Alma Mahler, *Gustav Mahler: Memories and Letters*, 7.

26. Grünfeld, *In Dur und Moll*, 19.

27. Information from Knud Martner, e-mail, January 30, 2009.

28. McClatchie, *The Mahler Family Letters*, 74.

29. Ibid., 27, 263.

30. Bauer-Lechner, *Recollections of Gustav Mahler*, 94.

31. McClatchie, *The Mahler Family Letters*, 301.

32. de La Grange, *Mahler*, vol. 2, *Vienna: The Years of Challenge*, 173.

33. Alma Mahler, *Gustav Mahler: Memories and Letters*, 7.

34. Bauer-Lechner, *Recollections of Gustav Mahler*, 164–65.

35. de La Grange, *Mahler*, vol. 1, 28.

36. Sverak et al., *Počátek cesty*, 125.

37. Bauer-Lechner, *Erinnerungen an Gustav Mahler*, 52.

38. www.mcdonalds.com.

39. Reed, *Britten and Mahler: Essays in Honour of Donald Mitchell on his 70th Birthday*, 91.

40. *News About Mahler Research* 23 (March 1990).

Chapter 3 · City of Dreams (1875–1887)

1. Statistiches Amt, 40.

2. George E. Berkeley, *Vienna and Its Jews* (Cambridge, Mass.: Abt Books, 1988), 35.

3. Köhler, *Richard Wagner*, 480.

4. Wolf, *Eine Persönlichkeit in Briefe, Familienbriefe*, 10–14.

5. Bauer-Lechner, *Erinnerungen an Gustav Mahler*, 17.

6. Adler, quoted in Stefan, *Gustav Mahler: Eine Studie über Persönlichkeit und Werk*, 27.

7. Hamann, *Hitler's Vienna*, 78.

8. Schnitzler, *My Youth in Vienna*, 128.

9. Gustav Mahler, *Selected Letters*, 200.

10. See Herta Blaukopf, in Aspertsberger, *Mahler-Gespräche*, 96–116.

11. Specht, *Gustav Mahler*, 17.

12. Gustav Mahler, *Selected Letters*, 58.

13. Emma Adler, quoted in Blaukopf, *Mahler: A Documentary Study*, 156.

14. Gustav Mahler, *Selected Letters*, 243.

15. Ibid., 329.

16. de La Grange, *Mahler*, vol. 1, 65–66.

17. Emanuel E. Garcia, e-mail to NL, May 5, 2009.

18. Blaukopf, *Mahler: A Documentary Study*, 162.

19. Bauer-Lechner, *Erinnerungen an Gustav Mahler*, 104.

20. Lebrecht, *Mahler Remembered*, 30.

21. Gustav Mahler, *Selected Letters*, 68–69.
22. Lebrecht, *Mahler Remembered*, 31.
23. Gustav Mahler, *Selected Letters*, 33–34.
24. de La Grange, *Mahler*, vol. 1, 113.
25. Lebrecht, *Mahler Remembered*, 38.
26. Blaukopf, *Mahler: A Documentary Study*, 177.
27. Bela Diosy, quoted in Roman, *Gustav Mahler and Hungary*, 149–50.
28. Bauer-Lechner, *Erinnerungen an Gustav Mahler*, 169–70.
29. Gustav Mahler, *Selected Letters*, 101.
30. Bauer-Lechner, *Erinnerungen an Gustav Mahler*, 150.
31. Ibid.
32. Lebrecht, *Mahler Remembered*, 43–44.
33. Gustav Mahler, *Selected Letters*, 109.
34. McClatchie, *The Mahler Family Letters*, 51.
35. Ibid., 54.

Chapter 4 · A Symphony Like the World (1887–1891)

1. Roman, *Gustav Mahler and Hungary*, 26–27.
2. Ibid., 55.
3. Quoted in ibid., 57; Blaukopf, *Mahler: A Documentary Study*, 184, and elsewhere.
4. See McClatchie, *The Mahler Family Letters*, 87.
5. Ibid., 65.
6. Ibid., 70.
7. Gustav Mahler, *Selected Letters*, 121.
8. de La Grange, *Mahler*, vol. 1, 203.
9. Mervyn Cooke, *A History of Film Music*, 35.
10. Blaukopf, *Mahler: A Documentary Study*, 66.
11. Bauer-Lechner, *Erinnerungen an Gustav Mahler*, 152.
12. Ibid., 148.
13. Gustav Mahler, *Selected Letters*, 180.
14. Ibid., 178.
15. Fritz Wittels, *Freud and the Child Woman: The Memoirs of Fritz Wittels*, ed. Edward Timms (New Haven, Conn. and London: Yale University Press, 1995), 24–25.
16. Bauer-Lechner, *Recollections of Gustav Mahler*, 240.
17. Ibid., 240.
18. See Wullschlager, *Chagall: Life and Exile*, 74–75.

19. Bauer-Lechner, *Erinnerungen an Gustav Mahler*, 25.
20. Blaukopf, *Mahler: A Documentary Study*, 187; Roman, *Gustav Mahler and Hungary*, 88.
21. Blaukopf, *Mahler: A Documentary Study*, 190.
22. Gustav Mahler, *Selected Letters*, 130.
23. Bauer-Lechner, *Erinnerungen an Gustav Mahler*, 1.
24. Roman, *Gustav Mahler and Hungary*, 219.
25. Lebrecht, *Mahler Remembered*, 63.
26. Constantin Floros, "Diener am Werk," *Das Orchester*, February 2009, 34–37.

Chapter 5 · Rise Again (1891–1894)

1. Information from Berthold Goldschmidt, who lived there 1903–19.
2. Evans, *Death in Hamburg*, 102.
3. McClatchie, *The Mahler Family Letters*, 111–12.
4. Ibid.
5. McClatchie, *The Mahler Family Letters*, 146.
6. Lebrecht, *Mahler Remembered*, 77–78.
7. Gustav Mahler and Richard Strauss, *Gustav Mahler—Richard Strauss: Correspondence, 1888–1911*, 21.
8. Gustav Mahler, *Selected Letters*, 139.
9. de La Grange, *Mahler*, vol. 1, 249.
10. McClatchie, *The Mahler Family Letters*, 166.
11. Ibid., 176.
12. Lebrecht, *Mahler Remembered*, 66.
13. George Bernard Shaw, *Music in London, 1890–94* (London: Constable, 1931), 118–19.
14. See Evans, *Death in Hamburg*, 289ff.
15. de La Grange, *Mahler*, vol. 1, 268.
16. McClatchie, *The Mahler Family Letters*, 196.
17. Ibid., 215.
18. Ibid., 237.
19. Research by Knud Martner; e-mail to NL, February 2, 2009.
20. Data at the Newberry Library, collated by Henry Mahler; e-mail to NL, April 25, 2008.
21. McClatchie, *The Mahler Family Letters*, 217.
22. Bauer-Lechner, *Erinnerungen an Gustav Mahler*, 16.
23. Zakrewska, "Alienation and Powerlessness," n.p.

24. Bauer-Lechner, *Erinnerungen an Gustav Mahler*, 10.
25. Ibid., 8.
26. Ibid., 11–12.
27. Lebrecht, *Mahler Remembered*, 71–72.
28. Statistic from Knud Martner; e-mail to NL, February 5, 2009.
29. Blaukopf, *Mahler: A Documentary Study*, 198.
30. Cf. collection of composer Theodor Kirchner, Brahms Collection, University of Lübeck Library.
31. Mitchell, *Gustav Mahler: The Wunderhorn Years*, 169.
32. Ibid., 169.
33. McClatchie, *The Mahler Family Letters*, 281; see also Gustav Mahler, *Selected Letters*, 154–55.
34. Gustav Mahler, *Selected Letters*, 212.
35. See Mitchell, *Gustav Mahler: The Wunderhorn Years*, 416–18.
36. Mahler's program note for Dresden performance, December 20, 1901.
37. Brod, *Israel's Music*, 31.
38. Adorno, *Mahler, eine musikalische Physiognomik*, 29.
39. Reik, *The Haunting Melody*, 269.
40. Writing in *The Times Book Section* (London), March 22, 2008, 5.
41. de La Grange, *Mahler*, vol. 1, 22.
42. Bauer-Lechner, *Erinnerungen an Gustav Mahler*, 23.
43. See Kaplan, *Introduction to Facsimile*, 53.
44. www.vatican.va/holy_father/john_paul_ii//speeches/2004/january/documents/hf_jp-ii_spe_20040117_concerto-riconciliazione_en.html.
45. Walter, *Gustav Mahler*, 77.
46. Walter, *Briefe, 1894–1962*, 11.
47. Walter, *Gustav Mahler*, 5.
48. Ibid., 4.
49. Ibid., 6.
50. Walter, *Theme and Variations*, 85–86.
51. Ryding, *Bruno Walter: A World Elsewhere*, 15, 424n43.
52. McClatchie, *The Mahler Family Letters*, 285–86.
53. Ibid.
54. McClatchie, *The Mahler Family Letters*, 7.
55. Gustav Mahler, *Briefe, 1870–1911*, 153.
56. See Grass, *Peeling the Onion*, 331–32.

Chapter 6 · What Love Tells Me (1895–1897)

1. Bauer-Lechner, *Erinnerungen an Gustav Mahler*, 19.
2. Gustav Mahler to Oskar Fried, *Mahler's Unknown Letters*, 55.
3. Alma Mahler, *Gustav Mahler: Memories and Letters*, 19.
4. Bauer-Lechner, *Erinnerungen an Gustav Mahler*, 44.
5. Gustav Mahler, *Selected Letters*, 198.
6. Eric Blom, *Stepchildren of Music* (London: Foulis, 1924), 136–37.
7. Floros, *Gustav Mahler: The Symphonies*, 95.
8. Bauer-Lechner, *Erinnerungen an Gustav Mahler*, 45.
9. Ernst Decsey, quoted in Lebrecht, *Mahler Remembered*, 263.
10. Gustav Mahler, *Mein lieber Trotzkopf, meine süsse Mohnblume*, 12–13.
11. Ibid., 41.
12. Ibid., 43.
13. Ibid., 72.
14. Ibid., 43.
15. Ibid., 39.
16. de La Grange, *Mahler*, vol. 1, 341.
17. Gustav Mahler, *Mein lieber Trotzkopf, meine süsse Mohnblume*, 77.
18. Ibid., 76–77.
19. Stuart Feder article in Hefling, *Mahler Studies*, 94n38.
20. Ibid., 39.
21. Letter to Natalie, in de La Grange, *Mahler*, vol. 1, 354.
22. Gustav Mahler, *Mein lieber Trotzkopf, meine süsse Mohnblume*, 47–48.
23. Walter, *Gustav Mahler*, 21.
24. de La Grange, *Mahler*, vol. 1, 345–47; Kaplan, *Introduction to Facsimile*, 51–55.
25. Gustav Mahler, letter to Arnold Berliner in *Selected Letters*, 127.
26. Article by Susan Gould, www.leonardbernstein.com.
27. Kenyon, *Simon Rattle: From Birmingham to Berlin*, 58, 71.
28. Gilbert E. Kaplan, interview with NL for BBC TV *Saturday Review*, Cardiff, July 27–29, 1987: GEK/NL, all quotes from this source, unless otherwise indicated.
29. Interview with Marc Bridle, www.musicweb-international.com/sandh/2003/Oct03/kaplan_interview.htm.
30. Norman Lebrecht, "The Conduct of Obsession," *Sunday Times Magazine* (London), December 9, 1984, 36–41.
31. Steve Smith, "A Centennial Moment for a Mahler Epic," *New York Times*, December 10, 2008.

32. http://davidfinlayson.typepad.com/fin_notes/.
33. www.nytimes.com/2008/12/18/arts/music/18kapl.html.
34. www.artsjournal.com/slippeddisc/2008/12/alls_quiet_at_the_ny_ philharmo.html.
35. Karpath, *Begegnung mit dem Genius*, 35.
36. de La Grange, *Mahler*, vol. 1, 390.
37. Walter, quoted in Lebrecht, *Mahler Remembered*, 104.
38. de La Grange, *Mahler*, vol. 1, 390.
39. Gustav Mahler, *Selected Letters*, 208 (retranslated by NL).
40. Ibid., 210.
41. Karpath, *Begegnung mit dem Genius*, 105.
42. Pfohl, *Gustav Mahler: Eindrücke und Erinnerungen aus den Hamburger Jahren*, 58.
43. Graf, *Legends of a Musical City*, 56.
44. Alma Mahler, *Gustav Mahler: Memories and Letters*, 101.
45. de La Grange, *Mahler*, vol. 1, 394.
46. Information from Knud Martner, e-mail to NL, February 12, 2009.
47. Alma Mahler, *Gustav Mahler: Memories and Letters*, 12.
48. Stuart Feder article in Hefling, *Mahler Studies*, 98n50.
49. Blaukopf, *Mahler: A Documentary Study*, 213.
50. de La Grange, *Mahler*, vol. 1, 424–25.

Chapter 7 · A Taste of Power (1897–1900)

1. Zweig, *The World of Yesterday*, 1–4.
2. Robert Musil, *The Man Without Qualities*, vol. 1, trans. Eithne Wilkins and Ernst Kaiser (London: Secker and Warburg, 1954), 32–33.
3. Zweig, *The World of Yesterday*, 26.
4. Karpath, *Begegnung mit dem Genius*, 126; see also de La Grange, *Mahler*, vol. 3, *Vienna: Triumph and Disillusion*, 4.
5. Hamann, *Hitler's Vienna*, 279.
6. Marie Beskiba, in ibid., 284.
7. April 9, 1897; McColl, *Music Criticism in Vienna, 1896–97*, 101.
8. Blaukopf, *Mahler: A Documentary Study*, 210.
9. Karpath, *Begegnung mit dem Genius*, 66.
10. Ibid., 67.
11. See Willnauer, *Gustav Mahler und die Wiener Oper*, 273–78.
12. Bauer-Lechner, *Erinnerungen an Gustav Mahler*, 84.
13. Ibid., 85.

14. Blaukopf, *Mahler: A Documentary Study*, 215.

15. Gustav Mahler, *Selected Letters*, 233 (retranslated by NL).

16. Blaukopf, *Mahler: A Documentary Study*, 210.

17. Theodor Reichmann, quoted in Korngold, *Memoirs*, 101.

18. Franz Schmidt, in Lebrecht, *Mahler Remembered*, 108.

19. Lebrecht, *Mahler Remembered*, 305.

20. de La Grange, *Mahler*, vol. 2, *Vienna: The Years of Challenge*, 59.

21. Bauer-Lechner, *Erinnerungen an Gustav Mahler*, 94.

22. Stefan, *Gustav Mahler: Eine Studie über Persönlichkeit und Werk*, 46.

23. Blaukopf, *Mahler: A Documentary Study*, 215.

24. Lebrecht, *Mahler Remembered*, 108–9.

25. de La Grange, *Mahler*, vol. 2, *Vienna: The Years of Challenge*, 546.

26. Lebrecht, *Mahler Remembered*, 115–17.

27. Ibid., 144.

28. Ibid., 118–19.

29. Ibid., 119–20.

30. Ibid., 110–11.

31. Statistics courtesy of Knud Martner, e-mail to NL, February 12, 2009.

32. Graf, *Legends of a Musical City*, 204.

33. Gustav Mahler, *Selected Letters*, 235 (retranslated by NL).

34. Gustav Mahler, *Selected Letters*, 239.

35. "Die Judenherrschaft in der Wiener Hofoper," November 4, 1898.

36. Willnauer, *Gustav Mahler und die Wiener Oper*, 145.

37. de La Grange, *Mahler*, vol. 2, *Vienna: The Years of Challenge*, 151.

38. Information from AR's daughter, Eleanor Rosé, ca. 1988.

39. See Whyte, *The Accused: The Dreyfus Trilogy*, 165.

40. Jacques Chirac, transcript of Bastille Day speech, July 13, 2006, on the centenary of Dreyfus's acquittal.

41. de La Grange, *Mahler*, vol. 2, *Vienna: The Years of Challenge*, 263.

42. Information from Eleanor Rosé, ca. 1988.

43. Information from Desi Halban-Kurz, ca. 1986.

44. Bauer-Lechner, *Erinnerungen an Gustav Mahler*, 119–20.

45. Ibid., 145.

46. Bauer-Lechner, *Gustav Mahler in den Erinnerungen*, 179.

47. Adorno, *Mahler: A Musical Physiognomy*, 55.

48. Bauer-Lechner, *Erinnerungen an Gustav Mahler*, 145.

49. Cardus, *Gustav Mahler: His Mind and His Music*, 119.

50. Bauer-Lechner, *Gustav Mahler in den Erinnerungen*, 179.
51. Floros, *Gustav Mahler: The Symphonies*, 122, 112.
52. Walter to Ludwig Schiedemair, Walter, *Briefe: 1894–1962*, 50.
53. de La Grange, *Mahler*, vol. 2, *Vienna: The Years of Challenge*, 400–401.
54. *Die Musik*, December 1901, 548–49.
55. de La Grange, *Mahler*, vol. 2, *Vienna: The Years of Challenge*, 474–75.
56. McColl, *Music Criticism in Vienna*, 16; and information from Knud Martner, e-mail dated February 11, 2009.
57. Graf, *Composer and Critic*, 18.
58. See de La Grange, *Mahler*, vol. 2, *Vienna: The Years of Challenge*, 235.
59. Gustav Mahler, *Selected Letters*, 231.
60. Karpath, *Begegnung mit dem Genius*, 104–5.

Chapter 8 · *The Most Beautiful Girl in Vienna* (1901)

1. Alma Mahler, *Gustav Mahler: Memories and Letters*, 14.
2. Ibid., translated by NL.
3. Gustav Mahler and Richard Strauss, *Gustav Mahler—Richard Strauss: Correspondence 1888–1911*, 51.
4. Natalie ms. quoted in de La Grange, *Mahler*, vol. 2, *Vienna: The Years of Challenge*, 334–35.
5. Bauer-Lechner, *Erinnerungen an Gustav Mahler*, 157.
6. Natalie ms. quoted in de La Grange, *Mahler*, vol. 2, *Vienna: The Years of Challenge*, 340.
7. Bauer-Lechner, *Erinnerungen an Gustav Mahler*, 159.
8. Translation by NL (emphasis added).
9. Gustav Mahler, *Sieben Lieder aus letzter Zeit* (Vienna: Universal Edition, 1905).
10. Gustav Mahler, *Sieben letzter Lieder* (Vienna: Philharmonia Edition, 1926).
11. With Johannes Maesschart, in Berlin, February 14, 1907.
12. Bauer-Lechner, *Erinnerungen an Gustav Mahler*, 166.
13. *Das gläserne Herz*, [Au: Full cite].
14. Zuckerkandl, *Österreich intim. Erinnerungen*, 42–43.
15. Alma Mahler, *Gustav Mahler: Memories and Letters*, 5.
16. Alma Mahler, *Diaries 1898–1902*, 442–43.
17. Ibid., 444.
18. Alma Mahler, *Gustav Mahler: Memories and Letters*, 15.

19. Chronology by Knud Martner, e-mail to NL, February 12, 2009.

20. See Kristan, "Josef Hoffmann und die Villenkolonie," 2007.

21. Alma Mahler, *Diaries 1898–1902*, 447.

22. Ibid., 448.

23. Ibid., 450–51.

24. Gustav Mahler, *Letters to His Wife*, 54.

25. Alma Mahler, *Diaries 1898–1902*, 455.

26. Beaumont, *Zemlinsky*, 98.

27. Alma Mahler, *Diaries 1898–1902*, 457.

28. Gustav Mahler, *Letters to His Wife*, 59–60.

29. Alma Mahler, *Diaries 1898–1902*, 459–60.

30. Ibid., 461.

31. Anna Mahler, quoted in Carr, *The Real Mahler*, 105.

32. Franz Werfel, quoted in Carr, *The Real Mahler*, 106.

33. Gustav Mahler, *Letters to His Wife*, 78–84.

34. Ibid., 81.

35. Martner, "Verwelkte Blütenträume," 3–41.

36. Alma Mahler, *Diaries 1898–1902*, 462.

37. Ibid., 462–63.

38. Ibid., 466.

39. Ibid., 467.

40. http://burgenkunde.at/niederoesterreich/noe_schloss_plankenberg/noe_schloss_plankenberg.htm.

41. Hilmes, *Witwe im Wahn: Das Leben der Alma Mahler-Werfel*, 36.

42. Ibid., 35; Alma Mahler, *Mein Leben*, 14–15.

43. Alma Mahler, *Diaries 1898–1902*, 5.

44. Ibid., 468.

45. Gustav Mahler, *Letters to His Wife*, 96.

46. Alma Mahler, *Diaries 1898–1902*, 467.

47. Alma ms., quoted in de La Grange, *Mahler*, vol. 2, *Vienna: The Years of Challenge*, 463.

48. Alma Mahler, *Gustav Mahler: Memories and Letters*, 28.

49. Ibid., 221 (retranslated by NL).

50. Letter to Strauss, February 17, 1897, in Gustav Mahler and Richard Strauss, *Gustav Mahler—Richard Strauss: Correspondence, 1888–1911*.

51. Alma Mahler, *Gustav Mahler: Memories and Letters*, 33.

52. Conversation with NL, 1987.

53. Alma Mahler, *Gustav Mahler: Memories and Letters*, 34.

54. Gustav Mahler, *Briefe, 1870–1911.*
55. Alma Mahler, *Gustav Mahler: Memories and Letters,*
56. Alma Mahler, *Mein Leben.*
57. Carr, *The Real Mahler,* 107.
58. Alma Mahler, *Diaries 1898–1902,* 377.
59. Alma Mahler, *Mein Leben,* 23.
60. Gustav Mahler, *Letters to His Wife,* 99.
61. E-mail, Martner to NL, January 30, 2009.

Chapter 9 · Small Interludes of Happiness (1902–1906)

1. See Carnegy, *Wagner and the Art of the Theatre,* 163.
2. See it here: http://tizian.at/system2E.html?/staticE/page3167.html.
3. de La Grange, *Mahler,* vol. 2, *Vienna: The Years of Challenge,* 536–37.
4. Gustav Mahler, *Selected Letters,* 372.
5. Walter, *Gustav Mahler,* 122.
6. Ibid., 121–22.
7. First identified by Knud Martner, e-mail to NL, April 12, 2009.
8. Foerster, *Der Pilger,* 408.
9. Gustav Mahler, *Adagietto. Facsimile, Documentation, Recording,* 21;
   Mitchell, *Gustav Mahler: Songs and Symphonies of Life and Death,* 131.
10. Gustav Mahler, *Adagietto. Facsimile, Documentation, Recording,* 19.
11. Heyworth, *Conversations with Klemperer,* 34.
12. Alma Mahler, *Gustav Mahler: Memories and Letters,* 47–48.
13. Gustav Mahler and Richard Strauss, *Gustav Mahler—Richard Strauss: Correspondence, 1888–1911,* 75.
14. de La Grange, *Mahler,* vol. 2, *Vienna: The Years of Challenge,* 541.
15. McClatchie, *The Mahler Family Letters,* 376.
16. To be seen in the Austrian National Library's theater collection in Vienna.
17. Lebrecht, *Mahler Remembered,* 266.
18. Stefan, *Gustav Mahler: Eine Studie über Persönlichkeit und Werk,* 58–59.
19. Alma Mahler, *Gustav Mahler: Memories and Letters,* 55–56.
20. *Wiener Allgemeine Zeitung,* February 25, 1903.
21. Korngold, *Memoirs,* manuscript copy in NL's possession, 94.
22. de La Grange, *Mahler,* vol. 2, *Vienna: The Years of Challenge,* 583.
23. Gustav Mahler, *Selected Letters,* 267–68.
24. Lebrecht, *Mahler Remembered,* 159.
25. Hamann, *Hitler's Vienna,* 61.

26. Mahler to Natalie Bauer-Lechner, July 25, 1900, Bauer-Lechner, *Erinnerungen an Gustav Mahler*, 141.

27. Lebrecht, *Mahler Remembered*, 157.

28. Walter, *Gustav Mahler*, 122–23.

29. Specht, quoted in Floros, *Gustav Mahler: The Symphonies*, 163.

30. Alma Mahler, *Gustav Mahler: Memories and Letters*, 100.

31. Blaukopf, *Mahler: A Documentary Study*, 236.

32. Gustav Mahler, *Letters to His Wife*, 167.

33. de La Grange, *Mahler*, vol. 2, *Vienna: The Years of Challenge*, 619.

34. Alma Mahler, *Gustav Mahler: Memories and Letters*, 70.

35. Diary entry by Alma Mahler, translated by Jonathan Carr, letter to G. E. Kaplan, November 28, 1995.

36. Mitchell, *Gustav Mahler: The World Listens*, 18.

37. de La Grange, *Mahler*, vol. 2, *Vienna: The Years of Challenge*, 682.

38. Gustav Mahler, *Selected Letters*, 342.

39. Auner, *A Schoenberg Reader*, 46.

40. See Floros, *Gustav Mahler: The Symphonies*, 188.

41. Reilly, Adler, and Gustav Mahler, *Records of a Friendship*, 103.

42. Alma Mahler, *Gustav Mahler: Memories and Letters*, 326.

43. Zychowicz, *The Seventh Symphony of Gustav Mahler: A Symposium*, 97.

44. Schoenberg, *Schoenberg Letters*, 260–61.

45. Alma's diary, quoted in Hilmes, *Witwe im Wahn*, 85.

46. Information from Anna Mahler.

47. Alma's diary, entry for July 6, 1905; e-mail, Knud Martner to NL, April 12, 2009.

48. Lebrecht, *Mahler Remembered*, 174–75.

49. Letter of October 11, 1905, in Gustav Mahler and Richard Strauss, *Gustav Mahler—Richard Strauss: Correspondence, 1888–1911*, 88.

50. Ibid.

51. Blaukopf, *Mahler: A Documentary Study*, 243.

52. Ross, *The Rest Is Noise*, 11.

53. Klaus Pringsheim, quoted in Lebrecht, *Mahler Remembered*, 193.

54. Lebrecht, ibid., 209–10.

55. Gustav Mahler, *Letters to His Wife*, 356–57.

56. Specht, quoted in Floros, *Gustav Mahler: The Symphonies*, 214.

57. Decsey in Lebrecht, *Mahler Remembered*, 253–54.

58. Gustav Mahler, *Selected Letters*, 291–92.

59. Specht, quoted in Floros, *Gustav Mahler: The Symphonies*, 214.

60. Korngold, *Memoirs*.

61. Zuckerkandl, *Österreich intim. Erinnerungen*, 151.
62. Alma Mahler, *Gustav Mahler: Memories and Letters*, 105.
63. All quotes (unless otherwise cited) from Norman Lebrecht, "Mahler Goes Home," *Daily Telegraph*, May 17, 1997.
64. *The Guardian*, February 6, 2002.

Chapter 10 · Three Hammerblows (1907)

1. Gustav Mahler, *Letters to His Wife*, 263–64.
2. Alma Mahler, *Gustav Mahler: Memories and Letters*, 112.
3. Lebrecht, *Mahler Remembered*, 213–14.
4. Korngold, *Memoirs*, 101.
5. Walter, *Gustav Mahler*, 53.
6. Ibid., 52–53 (retranslated by NL).
7. Lehmann, quoted in Lebrecht, *Mahler Remembered*, 214–15.
8. Karpath, *Begegnung mit dem Genius*, 184–85.
9. Korngold, *Memoirs*, 103–4.
10. Roman, *Gustav Mahler's American Years, 1907–1911*, 32–33.
11. Alma Mahler, *Gustav Mahler: Memories and Letters*, 121.
12. Ibid., 121.
13. Gustav Mahler, *Letters to His Wife*, 271.
14. Quoted in Lebrecht, *Mahler Remembered*, 274–75, and conversations with NL, 1986.
15. Gustav Mahler, *Letters to His Wife*, 254.
16. Alma Mahler, *Gustav Mahler: Memories and Letters*, 122.
17. Ibid.
18. July 6, 1905, discovered by Knud Martner, e-mail to NL, April 12, 2009.
19. Gustav Mahler, *Letters to His Wife*, 279.
20. Ibid., 290–91.
21. Lebrecht, *Mahler Remembered*, 218.
22. Grun, *Alban Berg: Letters to His Wife*, 32.
23. Lebrecht, *Mahler Remembered*, 212; de La Grange, *Mahler*, vol. 3, *Vienna: Triumph and Disillusion*, 788.
24. *Sunday Times* (London), January 9, 1983.
25. Lebrecht, *The Maestro Myth*, 204.

Chapter 11 · Discovering America (1907–1910)

1. *New York Times*, November 30, 1907, C1.
2. Roman, *Gustav Mahler's American Years, 1907–1911*, 44–45.
3. Davenport, *Too Strong for Fantasy*, 52–53.
4. Bosworth, "The Ellis Island U.S. Arrival Records for Gustav Mahler," 2–3.
5. *New York Mail*, quoted in de La Grange, *Mahler*, vol. 4, *A New Life Cut Short*, 44.
6. *New York Times*, December 22, 1907, 9.
7. Ibid., December 24, 1907, 7.
8. Alma Mahler, *Gustav Mahler: Memories and Letters*, 129–30.
9. Samuel Chotzinoff, quoted in Lebrecht, *Mahler Remembered*, 232.
10. Graf, *Composer and Critic*, 312.
11. Gustav Mahler, *Selected Letters*, 309–11.
12. Fiedler, *Molto Agitato: The Mayhem Behind the Music at the Metropolitan Opera*, 12–13.
13. Gustav Mahler, *Selected Letters*, 316.
14. Roman, *Gustav Mahler's American Years, 1907–1911*, 76.
15. Gustav Mahler, *Selected Letters*, 319.
16. Alma Mahler, *Gustav Mahler: Memories and Letters*, 136.
17. Lebrecht, *Mahler Remembered*, 247.
18. "THOUSANDS MOURN DEAD FIRE CHIEF, Great Tribute to [Charles W.] Kruger, Who Sacrificed His Life in the Service," *New York Times*, February 17, 1908, 1.
19. Alma Mahler, *Gustav Mahler: Memories and Letters*, 135.
20. Gustav Mahler, *Letters to His Wife*, 303.
21. Lebrecht, *Mahler Remembered*, 248–49.
22. Walter, *Gustav Mahler*, 62.
23. Gustav Mahler, *Selected Letters*, 321–22.
24. Ibid., 324.
25. See Floros, *Gustav Mahler: The Symphonies*, 340n5.
26. Walter, *Gustav Mahler*, 59.
27. Gustav Mahler, *Selected Letters*, 326.
28. Full Chinese, German, and English texts can be read at: www .mahlerarchives.net/DLvDE/DLvDE.htm.
29. Bethge, *Die Chinesische Flöte*, 101.
30. Information from Dr. Yan Yang and Dr. Jane V. Portal, e-mail, March 24, 2009.

31. Dr. Sheng Yun, Shanghai; e-mail, March 19, 2009.
32. Three bars after 68; see Floros, *Gustav Mahler: The Symphonies*, 248.
33. Walter, *Gustav Mahler*, 60.
34. Heyworth, *Conversations with Klemperer*, 33–34.
35. Kaplan, *The Mahler Album*, 97–101.
36. Klemperer, *Klemperer on Music*, 137–38.
37. Gustav Mahler, *Letters to His Wife*, 254.
38. de La Grange, *Mahler*, vol. 4, *A New Life Cut Short*, 231.
39. Klemperer, *Klemperer on Music*, 138.
40. Cadra, *Diaries*, entry for October 31, 1908.
41. Alma Mahler, *Gustav Mahler: Memories and Letters*, 317.
42. Damrosch, *My Musical Life*, 334.
43. Roman, *Gustav Mahler's American Years, 1907–1911*, 179.
44. *New York Times*, December 13, 1908, 12.
45. To Carl Moll, in Gustav Mahler, *Selected Letters*, 333.
46. Roman, *Gustav Mahler's American Years, 1907–1911*, 222.
47. Ibid., 233–34.
48. Ibid., 235.
49. de La Grange, *Mahler*, vol. 4, *A New Life Cut Short*, 399; from letter in Musée Rodin, Paris.
50. Grunfeld, *Rodin*, 534–35.
51. Alma Mahler, *Gustav Mahler: Memories and Letters*, 151.
52. Gustav Mahler, *Selected Letters*, 341.
53. Walter, *Gustav Mahler*, 127.
54. Gustav Mahler, *Selected Letters*, 340.
55. Gustav Mahler, *Gustav Mahler IX. Symphonie, Facsimile nach der Handschrift*, 29 and 52.
56. Gustav Mahler, *Briefe, 1870–1911*, 368.
57. Alma Mahler, *Gustav Mahler: Memories and Letters*, 152; de La Grange, *Mahler*, vol. 4, *A New Life Cut Short*, 500.
58. Gustav Mahler, *Mahler's Unknown Letters*, 57.
59. Gustav Mahler, *Selected Letters*, 341.
60. http://www.pjvoice.com/v19/19700judaism.aspx.
61. Interview with NL, *Daily Telegraph*, February 6, 2002.
62. Issue nos. 910 004-2, 910 095-2, (p) & (c) 1997, 1999, Winter & Winter, Munich, Germany.
63. Roman, *Gustav Mahler's American Years, 1907–1911*, 285–86.
64. Theodore Spiering, unpublished manuscript in NL's possession.
65. Ibid.

66. William Malloch interviews for KPFK, "I Remember Mahler," 1962.

67. Roman, *Gustav Mahler's American Years, 1907–1911*, 292.

68. Ibid., 305–7.

69. de La Grange, *Mahler*, vol. 4, *A New Life Cut Short*, 580.

70. *New York Tribune*, May 21, 1911.

71. Henry T. Finck, *My Adventures in the Golden Age of Music* (New York and London: Funk & Wagnalls, 1926), 423.

72. Alma Mahler, *Gustav Mahler: Memories and Letters*, 162.

73. Lebrecht, *Mahler Remembered*, 237–39.

74. Bertensson, *Sergei Rachmaninoff*, 164.

75. Malloch, "I Remember Mahler."

76. Gustav Mahler, *Selected Letters*, 345–53; Roman, *Gustav Mahler's American Years, 1907–1911*, 307.

77. McClatchie, *The Mahler Family Letters*, 397; de La Grange, *Mahler*, vol. 4, *A New Life Cut Short*, 718.

78. Roman, *Gustav Mahler's American Years, 1907–1911*, 347–48.

79. All quotations unless stated are from interviews with NL, 1987.

80. Anna Mahler, *Anna Mahler: Her Work* (London: Phaidon, 1975), 11.

81. Anna Mahler, letter to NL dated July 5, 1987.

82. Canetti, *The Play of the Eyes*, 158.

83. Anna Mahler, interview with NL, *Sunday Times Magazine*, April 26, 1987, 45–46.

Chapter 12 · *"To Live for You, To Die for You"* (1910–1911)

1. Alma Mahler, *Gustav Mahler: Memories and Letters*, 173.

2. Gustav Mahler, *Letters to His Wife*, 357.

3. Alma Mahler, *Mein Leben*, 51.

4. de La Grange, *Mahler*, vol. 4, *A New Life Cut Short*, 838.

5. Gustav Mahler, *Letters to His Wife*, 360.

6. Gustav Mahler, *Selected Letters*, 363.

7. de La Grange, *Mahler*, vol. 4, *A New Life Cut Short*, 840.

8. Alma Mahler, *Gustav Mahler: Memories and Letters*, 173.

9. Gustav Mahler, *Facsimile Gustav Mahler Zehnte Symphonie*.

10. Alma Mahler, *Gustav Mahler: Memories and Letters*, 173.

11. Ibid., 175.

12. de La Grange, *Mahler*, vol. 4, *A New Life Cut Short*, 871.

13. Ibid., 875.

14. Isaacs, *Gropius*, 35.

15. Alma Mahler, *Gustav Mahler: Memories and Letters*, 176.
16. de La Grange, *Mahler*, vol. 4, *A New Life Cut Short*, 883.
17. Lebrecht, *Mahler Remembered*, 195.
18. Quoted in Jung, *Memories, Dreams, Reflections*, 150 (letter of April 2, 1909).
19. Bauer-Lechner, *Recollections of Gustav Mahler*, 150.
20. Jones, *The Life and Work of Sigmund Freud*, 358.
21. Marie Bonaparte, quoted in de La Grange, *Mahler*, vol. 4, *A New Life Cut Short*, 891.
22. Jones, *The Life and Work of Sigmund Freud*, 358.
23. Garcia, "Gustav Mahler's Choice," 97.
24. de La Grange, *Mahler*, vol. 4, *A New Life Cut Short*, 893.
25. Telegram to his wife, August 27, 1910, Gustav Mahler, *Briefe, 1870–1911*, 338 (the English edition mutates this phrase).
26. Alma Mahler, *Gustav Mahler: Memories and Letters*, 175.
27. Ibid., 335.
28. Reik, *The Haunting Melody*, 343–44.
29. See Appignanesi and Forrester, *Freud's Women*, 329–51.
30. Medvei, *The History of Clinical Endocrinology*, 429, s.v. "Halban."
31. Bonaparte, quoted in de La Grange, *Mahler*, vol. 4, *A New Life Cut Short*, 1656.
32. Jones, *The Life and Work of Sigmund Freud*, 359; see also Lebrecht, *Mahler Remembered*, 281–84.
33. Garcia, "Gustav Mahler's Choice," 96–97.
34. Bonaparte, quoted in de La Grange, *Mahler*, vol. 4, *A New Life Cut Short*, 894.
35. Lebrecht, *Mahler Remembered*, 284.
36. Garcia, "A New Look at Gustav Mahler's Fateful Encounter with Sigmund Freud," 23; see also Poulain-Colombier, "Presto: Les deux patients musiciens de Freud."
37. Appignanesi and Forrester, *Freud's Women*, 343.
38. Garcia, "A New Look at Gustav Mahler's Fateful Encounter with Sigmund Freud"; de La Grange, *Mahler*, vol. 4, *A New Life Cut Short*, 921ff.
39. de La Grange, *Mahler*, vol. 4, *A New Life Cut Short*, 926.
40. Anna Mahler, in conversation with NL, ca. 1988.
41. Maurice Baumfeld quoted in Lebrecht, *Mahler Remembered*, 296.
42. Gustav Mahler, *Mahler's Unknown Letters*, 88.
43. Alma Mahler, *Gustav Mahler: Memories and Letters*, 180.

44. Hans Moldenhauer and Rosaleen Moldenhauer, *Anton von Webern: A Chronicle of His Life* (London: Victor Gollancz, 1978), 135.

45. Stefan, *Gustav Mahler: Eine Studie über Persönlichkeit und Werk*, 115.

46. Cadra, *Diaries*, new translations by Milan Palak and Michael Srba, manuscript in NL's possession.

47. Walter, *Gustav Mahler*, 59.

48. Stefan, *Gustav Mahler: Eine Studie über Persönlichkeit und Werk*, 115.

49. Katia Mann, *Unwritten Memories*, 65.

50. Thomas Mann, *Death in Venice* (London: Martin Secker, 1928), 105–6.

51. Lebrecht, *Mahler Remembered*, 287–88.

52. Reilly, Adler, and Gustav Mahler, *Records of a Friendship*, 112.

53. Roman, *Gustav Mahler's American Years, 1907–1911*, 416–17.

54. Alma Mahler, *Gustav Mahler: Memories and Letters*, 187.

55. Ibid., 189.

56. Busoni, *Letters to His Wife*, 181.

57. Christy and Christy, "Mahler's Final Illness," *Chord and Discord* 3, no. 2 (1988): 7–8, available at www.mahlerarchives.net/archives/mahlerillness.pdf.

58. Baehr, letter to Christy, November 17, 1970, quoted in Christy and Christy, "Mahler's Final Illness."

59. Porter, quoted in ibid.

60. Levy, "Gustav Mahler and Emanuel Libman: Bacterial Endocarditis in 1911," 1631.

61. Feder, *Mahler: A Life in Crisis*, 146.

62. Roman, *Gustav Mahler's American Years, 1907–1911*, 458.

63. Isaacs, *Gropius*, 36.

64. Alma Mahler, *Gustav Mahler: Memories and Letters*, 193–94.

65. Ibid., 194.

66. Ibid., 197.

67. Ibid., 198.

68. *Neue Freie Presse*, May 2, 1911.

69. Alma Mahler, *Gustav Mahler: Memories and Letters*, 200.

70. *Neue Freie Presse*, April 22, 1911, quoted in Blaukopf, *Mahler: A Documentary Study*, 272.

71. *Musical America*, May 13, 1911, quoted in Roman, *Gustav Mahler's American Years, 1907–1911*, 475–76.

72. Quoted by Karpath in de La Grange, *Mahler*, vol. 4, *A New Life Cut Short*, 631–32n84.

73. *Mahler in New York*, booklet accompanying the New York Philharmonic series The Mahler Broadcasts, 1998, 105–6.
74. Roman, *Gustav Mahler's American Years, 1907–1911*, 481–82.
75. de La Grange, *Mahler*, vol. 4, *A New Life Cut Short*.
76. www.bloomberg.com/apps/news?pid=20601088&sid=aNPHGekzv2SU.
77. Alma Mahler, *Gustav Mahler: Memories and Letters*, 199.
78. *Neue Freie Presse*, May 12, 1911.
79. Alma Mahler, *Gustav Mahler: Memories and Letters*, 199.
80. Ibid., 200.
81. de La Grange, *Mahler*, vol. 4, *A New Life Cut Short*, 1271.

Chapter 13 • After Mahler (1911–2010)

1. Yates, *Schnitzler, Hofmannsthal and the Austrian Theatre*, 42.
2. Stefan, *Gustav Mahler: Eine Studie über Persönlichkeit und Werk*, 119.
3. Foerster, *Der Pilger*, 706.
4. Walter, *Gustav Mahler*, 65.
5. Auner, *A Schoenberg Reader*, 96; different translation in de La Grange, *Mahler*, vol. 4, *A New Life Cut Short*, 1260.
6. Lebrecht, *Mahler Remembered*, 315.
7. Alma Mahler, *Mein Leben*, 66.
8. Grun, *Alban Berg: Letters to His Wife*, 147.
9. Mitchell, *Discovering Mahler*, 503.
10. Specht, *Gustav Mahler*, 300; quoted in Floros, *Gustav Mahler: The Symphonies*, 297.
11. Walter, *Briefe: 1894–1962*, 204.
12. de La Grange, *Mahler*, vol. 4, *A New Life Cut Short*, 1459.
13. Obituary, *Chicago Tribune*, December 26, 2005.
14. Walter, *Briefe: 1894–1962*, 371–72.
15. Letter postmarked May 8, 1963, quoted in Deryck Cooke's Introduction to the second edition of the Tenth Symphony, London: Faber Music/AMP, 1989.
16. Photocopy in NL's archive.
17. Cooke letter, May 8, 1963.
18. *Peterborough Daily Telegraph*, August 15, 1964.
19. Ibid., August 14, 1964.
20. *Peterborough Daily Telegraph*, August 17, 1964.
21. de La Grange, *Mahler*, vol. 4, *A New Life Cut Short*, 1453.

22. President Bill Clinton, testimony to grand jury, August 17, 1998, at www.youtube.com/watch?v=j4XT-1-_3y0.; and George W. Bush, June 18, 2002, at www.hud.gov/news/speeches/presremarks.cfm.

23. *Songs of Vienna*, Columbia Records, 1941.

24. *Guardian Saturday Review*, April 19, 2008, 11.

Chapter 14 · A Question of Interpretation

1. Bauer-Lechner, *Erinnerungen an Gustav Mahler*, 29.

2. Blaukopf, *Mahler: A Documentary Study*, 225.

3. Walter, *Theme and Variations*, 188–89.

4. 1997 interview with John Walters, www.earbox.com/inter002.html.

5. Heyworth, *Conversations with Klemperer*, 34.

6. David Matthews, note to Riccardo Chailly's Decca recording of Mahler's version of the Schumann symphonies.

7. Dr. Ernst J. M. Lert, "The Conductor Mahler: A Psychological Study," *Chord and Discord* 1, no. 9 (1938): 10–28; www.mahlerarchives.net/archives/mahlerconductor.pdf.

8. Anna Mahler, comment to NL.

9. Fülop, *Mahler Discography*, 446–47.

10. Jacket note by Andreas Kluge to 1994 Sony Classical release.

11. Daniel Barenboim, "Love, The Hard Way," *The Guardian*, August 31, 2001; www.guardian.co.uk/education/2001/aug/31/arts.higher education.

12. See *Mahler-Feestboek*, 127.

13. Kaplan Foundation, "The Correct Movement Order of Mahler's Sixth Symphony."

14. Gilbert Kaplan, "Restoring Order in a Cataclysmic Symphony," *New York Times*, December 14, 2003.

15. See Mitchell, *The Mahler Companion*, 372–75.

16. *The Lebrecht Interview*, BBC Radio 3, July 16, 2007.

17. All Tennstedt quotes, unless specified, are from my talks with him, 1983–97.

18. *Time*, March 7, 1977, article by William Bender.

19. Quoted in *New York Times* obituary, January 13, 1998.

20. Judy Grahame, e-mail to NL, March 2, 2008.

21. Norman Lebrecht, "Taking on the World," *Independent Magazine*, April 11, 1992, 45.

22. Snowman, *Hallelujah*, 59.

23. *The Lebrecht Interview,* BBC Radio 3, July 16, 2007.
24. E-mail from Peter Alward, February 29, 2008.
25. Jacket note by Eva Reisinger to Westminster release, 2002.
26. http://lsoontour.wordpress.com/2009/11/17/its-not-about-the-music/.
27. Gareth Davies, e-mail to NL, December 3, 2009.
28. *The Guardian,* August 8, 2009, R10.
29. Ken Russell, interview with NL, 1985.
30. See www.imdb.com/title/tt0212827/news#ni0099901.
31. Stefan, *Gustav Mahler: Eine Studie über Persönlichkeit und Werk,* 1.
32. Blaukopf, *Mahler: A Documentary Study,* 1, 256.

BIBLIOGRAPHY

Principal Works Cited

Adler, Guido. *Gustav Mahler.* Vienna: Universal Edition, 1911. 2nd ed., 1916.

Auner, Joseph, ed. *A Schoenberg Reader.* New Haven and London: Yale University Press, 2003.

Bahr-Mildenburg, Anna. *Erinnerungen.* Vienna: Wiener Literarische Anhalt, 1921.

Bauer-Lechner, Natalie. *Erinnerungen an Gustav Mahler.* Leipzig and Vienna: E. P. Tal, 1923.

———. *Gustav Mahler in den Erinnerungen.* Edited by Herbert Killian and Knud Martner. Hamburg: K. D. Wagner, 1984.

———. *Recollections of Gustav Mahler.* Translated by Dika Newlin. Edited and annotated by Peter Franklin. Cambridge: Cambridge University Press, 1980.

Blaukopf, Herta, and Kurt Blaukopf. *Die Wiener Philharmoniker.* Vienna and Hamburg: Paul Zsolnay, 1986.

Blaukopf, Kurt. *Mahler.* Translated by Inge Goodwin. London: Allen Lane, 1973.

———, ed. *Mahler: A Documentary Study.* New York: Oxford University Press, 1976.

Borchardt, Georg, ed. *Mahler: Meine Zeit wird kommen: Aspekte der Mahler-Rezeption.* Hamburg: Dölling und Gallitz Verlag, 1996.

Brand, Juliane, Christopher Hailey, and Donald Harris, eds. *The Berg-Schoenberg Correspondence.* Basingstoke: Macmillan Press, 1987.

Brod, Max. *Gustav Mahler: Beispiel einer deutsch-jüdischen Symbiose.* Frankfurt-am-Main: Ner-Tamid Verlag, 1961.

———. *Israel's Music.* Tel Aviv: Sefer Press, 1951.

Castagné, André, Michel Chalon, and Patrick Florençon, eds. *Gustav Mahler et l'ironie dans la culture viennoise au tournant du siècle, actes du colloque de Montpellier, 16–18 juillet 1996.* Montpellier: Editions Climats, 2001.

Cooke, Deryck. *Gustav Mahler: An Introduction to His Music.* London: Faber Music, 1980.

————. *Mahler 1860–1911*. London: BBC, 1960.

————. *Vindications: Essays on Romantic Music*. London: Faber & Faber, 1982.

de La Grange, Henry-Louis. *Mahler*. Vol. 1. London: Victor Gollancz, 1974.

————. *Gustav Mahler*. Vol. 2. *Vienna: The Years of Challenge (1897–1904)*. Oxford: Oxford University Press, 1995.

————. *Gustav Mahler*. Vol. 3. *Vienna: Triumph and Disillusion (1904–1907)*. Oxford: Oxford University Press, 1999.

————. *Gustav Mahler*. Vol. 4. *A New Life Cut Short (1907–1911)*. Oxford: Oxford University Press, 2008.

Feder, Stuart. *Mahler: A Life in Crisis*. New Haven and London: Yale University Press, 2004.

Floros, Constantin. *Gustav Mahler: The Symphonies*. Translated by Vernon Wicker. Portland, Ore.: Amadeus Press, 1993. Originally published as *Gustav Mahler III: Die Symphonien* (Wiesbaden: Breitkopf und Härtel, 1985).

Foerster, J. B. *Der Pilger*. Prague: Artia, 1955.

Franklin, Peter. *Mahler Symphony No. 3*. Cambridge: Cambridge University Press, 1991.

Fülop, Peter. *Mahler Discography*. New York: The Kaplan Foundation, 1995.

Graf, Max. *Composer and Critic*. New York: W. W. Norton, 1946.

————. *Legends of a Musical City*. New York: Philosophical Library, 1945.

Grun, Bernard, ed. and trans. *Alban Berg: Letters to His Wife*. London: Faber & Faber, 1971.

Hamann, Brigitte. *Hitler's Vienna: A Dictator's Apprenticeship*. New York and Oxford: Oxford University Press, 1999.

Hefling, Stephen. *Mahler: Das Lied von der Erde*. Cambridge: Cambridge University Press, 2000.

————. *Mahler Studies*. Cambridge: Cambridge University Press, 1997.

Heyworth, Peter, ed. *Conversations with Klemperer*. London: Victor Gollancz, 1973.

Isaacs, Reginald. *Gropius: An Illustrated Biography of the Creator of the Bauhaus*. Boston: Little, Brown and Company, 1991. Abridged from original *Walter Gropius, Der Mensch und sein Werk*. Berlin: Gebr. Mann Verlag, 1983–84.

Kaplan, Gilbert E. *Introduction to Facsimile of Gustav Mahler Second Symphony in C Minor, "Resurrection."* New York: Kaplan Foundation, 1986.

————, ed. *The Mahler Album*. New York: Kaplan Foundation, 1995.

Klemperer, Otto. *Klemperer on Music: Shavings from a Musician's Workbench*. Edited by Martin Anderson. London: Toccata Press, 1986.

Kolodin, Irving. *The Metropolitan Opera, 1883–1966: A Candid History*. New York: Alfred A. Knopf, 1966.

Lea, Henry A. *Gustav Mahler: Man on the Margin*. Bonn: Bouvier, 1985.

Lebrecht, Norman. *Mahler Remembered*. London: Faber & Faber, 1987.

————. *The Maestro Myth: Great Conductors in Pursuit of Power*. New York: Carol Publishing Corporation, 1992.

Mahler, Alma. *Gustav Mahler: Memories and Letters*. Translated by Basil Creighton. London: W. Clowes and Son, 1946. 3rd rev. ed., edited by Donald Mitchell and Knud Martner. London: J. Murray, 1973.

————. *Mein Leben*. Frankfurt: Fischer, 1960. Translated by E. B. Ashton as *And the Bridge Is Love*. New York: Harcourt Brace, 1958.

————. *Diaries 1898–1902*. Translated and abridged by Antony Beaumont. London: Faber & Faber, 1999.

Mahler, Gustav. *Adagietto. Facsimile, Documentation, Recording*. Edited by Gilbert E. Kaplan. New York: Kaplan Foundation, 1992.

————. *Briefe, 1870–1911*. Vienna: Paul Zsolnay, 1924.

————. *Letters to His Wife*. Edited by Henry-Louis de La Grange and Günther Weiss, in collaboration with Knud Martner. Translated by Antony Beaumont. London: Faber & Faber, 2004.

————. *Mahler's Unknown Letters*. Edited by Herta Blaukopf. Translated by Richard Stokes. London: Victor Gollancz, 1986.

————. *Mein lieber Trotzkopf, meine süsse Mohnblume: Briefe an Anna von Mildenburg*. Edited and with a commentary by Franz Willnauer. Vienna: Paul Zsolnay Verlag, 2006.

————. *Selected Letters*. Edited by Knud Martner, Eithne Wilkins, and Ernst Kaiser. Translated by Bill Hopkins. London: Faber & Faber, 1979.

Mahler, Gustav, and Richard Strauss. *Gustav Mahler—Richard Strauss: Correspondence, 1888–1911*. Edited by Herta Blaukopf. Translated by Edmund Jephcott. London: Faber & Faber, 1984.

McClatchie, Stephen, ed. and trans. *The Mahler Family Letters*. Oxford: Oxford University Press, 2006.

Meysels, Lucian O. *In meinem Salon ist Österreich: Berta Zuckerkandl und ihre Zeit*. Vienna: INW, 1994.

Mitchell, Donald. *Discovering Mahler: Writings on Mahler, 1955–2005*. Suffolk: Boydell Press, 2007.

————. *Gustav Mahler: The Early Years*. London: Rockliff, 1958. 2nd ed., revised by Paul Banks and David Matthews. London: Faber & Faber, 1980.

———. *Gustav Mahler: Songs and Symphonies of Life and Death.* London: Faber & Faber, 1985.

———. *Gustav Mahler: The Wunderhorn Years.* London: Faber & Faber, 1975.

———, ed. *Gustav Mahler: The World Listens.* Haarlem: TEMA Uitgevers, 1995.

———, and Andrew Nicholson, eds. *The Mahler Companion.* Oxford: Oxford University Press, 1999.

Museen der Stadt Wien. *Traum und Wirklichkeit in Wien, 1870–1930.* Special exhibition catalog of Historiches Museum der Stadt Wien. Vienna: Museen der Stadt Wien, 1985.

Pfohl, Ferdinand. *Gustav Mahler: Eindrücke und Erinnerungen aus den Hamburger Jahren.* Edited by Knud Martner. Hamburg: Karl Dieter Wagner, 1973.

Reilly, Edward R., Guido Adler, and Gustav Mahler. *Records of a Friendship.* Cambridge: Cambridge University Press, 1982.

Reeser, Eduard. *Gustav Mahler und Holland.* Vienna: IGMG, 1980.

Reik, Theodor. *The Haunting Melody.* New York: Farrar, Straus & Young, 1953.

Ritter, William. *William Ritter chevalier de Gustav Mahler: Écrits, correspondance, documents.* Edited by Claude Meylan. Bern: Peter Lang, 2000.

Roller, Alfred. *Die Bildnisse von Gustav Mahler.* Leipzig and Vienna: E. P. Tal, 1922.

Roman, Zoltan. *Gustav Mahler and Hungary.* Budapest: Akademiai Kiado, 1991.

———. *Gustav Mahler's American Years, 1907–1911.* New York: Pendragon Press, 1989.

Schoenberg, Arnold. *Schoenberg Letters.* Edited by Erwin Stein. London: Faber & Faber, 1964.

Specht, Richard. *Gustav Mahler.* Stuttgart and Berlin: DVA, 1913; 18th printing, 1925.

Stefan, Paul. *Gustav Mahler: Eine Studie über Persönlichkeit und Werk.* Munich: Piper & Co., 1910. U.S. edition, Schirmer, 1912.

———, ed. *Gustav Mahler: Ein Bild seiner Persönlichkeit in Widmungen.* Munich: Piper & Co., 1910. See also by same author: *Gustav Mahlers Erbe.* Munich: Weber, 1908; *Das Grab in Wien.* Berlin: Eric Reiss, 1913.

Sverak, Vlastimil, Renata Pisková, Helena Nebdalova, and Petr Dvořák. *Počátek cesty: Gustav Mahler a Jihlava.* Jihlava: Statni okresni archiv, 2000.

Szeps-Zuckerkandl, Bertha. *My Life and History.* London: Cassell, 1938.

Wagner, May H. *Gustav Mahler and the New York Philharmonic Orchestra Tour America.* Lanham, MD: Scarecrow Press, 2006.

Walter, Bruno. *Briefe: 1894–1962.* Frankfurt: Fischer, 1969.

———. *Gustav Mahler.* Translated by James A. Galston. London: Kegan, Paul, Trench, Trubner & Co.,1937.

———. *Theme and Variations.* Translated by James A. Galston. London: Hamish Hamilton, 1947.

———. *Von der Musik und vom Musizieren.* Frankfurt: Fischer, 1957.

Willnauer, Franz. *Gustav Mahler und die Wiener Oper.* Munich and Vienna: Jugend und Volk, 1979. Reprint, 1993.

Zuckerkandl, Bertha. *Österreich intim. Erinnerungen 1892–1942.* Frankfurt: Ullstein, 1970.

Zweig, Stefan. *The World of Yesterday.* London: Cassell, 1943.

Zychowicz, James L., ed. *The Seventh Symphony of Gustav Mahler: A Symposium.* Cincinnati: University of Cincinnati College of Music, 1990.

Other Books Cited

Adler, Tom, with Anika Scott. *Lost to the World.* Philadelphia: Xlibris, 2002.

Adorno, Theodor Wiesengrund. *Mahler, eine musikalische Physiognomik.* Frankfurt: Suhrkamp, 1960.

———. *Mahler: A Musical-Physiognomy.* Translated by Edmund Jephcott. Chicago: Chicago University Press, 1992.

———. *Quasi una Fantasia: Essays on Modern Music.* London: Verso, 1992.

Appignanesi, Lisa, and John Forrester. *Freud's Women.* Rev. ed. London: Phoenix, 2005.

Aspertsberger, Friedbert, and Erich Wolfgang Partsch, eds. *Mahler-Gespräche.* Innsbruck: Studien Verlag, 2002.

Bailey, Colin B., ed. *Gustav Klimt: Modernism in the Making.* New York: Harry N. Abrams, 2001.

Barham, Jeremy, ed. *Perspectives on Gustav Mahler.* Burlington: Ashgate, 2005.

Beaumont, Antony. *Zemlinsky.* London: Faber & Faber, 2000.

Bertensson, Sergei, and Jay Leyda. *Sergei Rachmaninoff: A Life in Music.* New York: New York University Press, 1956.

Bertin, Celia. *Marie Bonaparte: A Life.* London: Quartet Books, 1983.

Bethge, Hans. *Die Chinesische Flöte.* Leipzig: Insel-Bücherei, 1907.

Brown, Malcolm Hammick, ed. *A Shostakovich Casebook.* Bloomington: Indiana University Press, 2004.

Busoni, Ferruccio. *Letters to His Wife.* London: Edward Arnold, 1938.

Canetti, Elias. *The Play of the Eyes.* Translated by Ralph Mannheim. New York: Farrar, Straus & Giroux, 1986.

Cardus, Neville. *Gustav Mahler: His Mind and His Music.* Vol. 1. London: Victor Gollancz, 1965.

Carnegy, Patrick. *Wagner and the Art of the Theatre.* New Haven and London: Yale University Press, 2006.

Carr, Jonathan. *The Real Mahler.* London: Constable, 1997.

Cherlin, Michael, Halina Filipowicz, and Richard L. Rudolph. *The Great Tradition and Its Legacy: The Evolution of Dramatic and Musical Theatre in Austria and Central Europe.* London: Berghahn Books, 2004.

Cooke, Mervyn. *A History of Film Music.* Cambridge: Cambridge University Press, 2008.

Damrosch, Walter. *My Musical Life.* New York: Scribner, 1923.

Davenport, Marcia. *Too Strong for Fantasy.* London: William Collins, 1968.

Dukas, Helen, and Banesh Hoffmann, eds. *Albert Einstein: The Human Side: New Glimpses from His Archives.* Princeton: Princeton University Press, 1989.

Evans, Richard J. *Death in Hamburg: Society and Politics in the Cholera Years, 1830–1910.* London: Penguin Books, 1987.

Farrar, Geraldine. *Such Sweet Compulsion.* New York: Greystone, 1938.

Fiedler, Johanna. *Molto Agitato: The Mayhem Behind the Music at the Metropolitan Opera.* New York: Doubleday, 2001.

Gay, Peter. *Freud: A Life for Our Time.* London: J. M. Dent, 1988.

———. *A Godless Jew.* New Haven and London: Yale University Press, 1987.

Giroud, Françoise. *Alma Mahler, or the Art of Being Loved.* Translated by R. M. Stock. Oxford: Oxford University Press, 1991.

Grass, Günter. *Peeling the Onion.* Translated by Michael Henry Heim. London: Harvill Secker, 2007.

Gresser, Moshe. *Dual Allegiance: Freud as a Modern Jew.* Albany: State University of New York Press, 1994.

Grunfeld, Frederic V. *Rodin.* London: Hutchinson, 1987.

Grünfeld, Heinrich. *In Dur und Moll.* Leipzig: Grethlein, 1923.

Hanak, Peter. *The Garden and the Workshop: Essays on the Cultural History of Vienna and Budapest.* Princeton: Princeton University Press, 1998.

Harwood, Ronald. *Mahler's Conversion.* London: Faber & Faber, 2001.

Heller, Sharon. *Freud A–Z*. London: John Wiley, 2005.

Hellsberg, Clemens. *Demokratie der Könige: Die Geschichte der Wiener Philharmoniker*. Zurich: Schweizer Verlagshaus, 1992.

Heymann-Wenzel, Cordula, and Johannes Laas, eds. *Musik und Biographie*. Würzburg: Königshausen & Neumann, 2004.

Heyworth, Peter. *Otto Klemperer, His Life and Times*. Vol. 1. Cambridge: Cambridge University Press, 1983.

———. *Otto Klemperer, His Life and Times*. Vol. 2. Cambridge: Cambridge University Press, 1996.

Hilmes, Oliver. *Witwe im Wahn: Das Leben der Alma Mahler-Werfel*. Munich: Siedler, 2004.

Janik, Allan, and Stephen Toulmin. *Wittgenstein's Vienna*. New York: Simon & Schuster, 1973.

Jones, Ernest. *The Life and Work of Sigmund Freud*. Edited and abridged by Lionel Trilling and Steven Marcus. London: Penguin Books, 1964.

Jung, Carl Gustav. *Memories, Dreams, Reflections*. Translated by Richard and Clara Winston. New York: Pantheon Books, 1963.

Jungk, Peter Stephan. *A Life Torn by History: Franz Werfel, 1890–1945*. London: Weidenfeld & Nicolson, 1990.

Karbusicky, Vladimir. *Mahler in Hamburg: Chronik einer Freundschaft*. Hamburg: Von Bockel Verlag, 1996.

Karpath, Ludwig. *Begegnung mit dem Genius*. Vienna: Fiba, 1934.

Keegan, Suzanne. *Bride of Love: The Life and Times of Alma Maria-Werfel*. London: Secker & Warburg, 1991.

Kenyon, Nicholas. *Simon Rattle: From Birmingham to Berlin*. London: Faber & Faber, 2001.

Köhler, Joachim. *Richard Wagner: The Last of the Titans*. Translated by Stewart Spencer. New Haven and London: Yale University Press, 2004.

Kokoschka, Oskar. *My Life*. Translated by David Britt. London: Thames & Hudson, 1974.

Lukacs, John. *Budapest 1900*. London: Weidenfeld & Nicolson, 1998.

Mahler-Feestboek. Amsterdam: Concertgebouw, 1920.

Mann, Katia. *Unwritten Memories*. London: Andre Deutsch, 1975.

Martin, George. *The Damrosch Dynasty*. Boston: Houghton Mifflin, 1983.

McColl, Sandra. *Music Criticism in Vienna, 1896–97*. Oxford: Clarendon Press, 1996.

Medvei, Victor Cornelius. *The History of Clinical Endocrinology*. London: Taylor and Francis, 1993.

Monson, Karen. *Alma Mahler: Muse to Genius.* London: William Collins, 1984.

Morton, Frederic. *A Nervous Splendour, Vienna 1888–1889.* London: Weidenfeld & Nicolson, 1980.

Nejedlý, Zdeněk. *Gustav Mahler.* Prague: Statní Nakladatelství, 1958.

Newman, Richard, and Karen Kirtley. *Alma Rosé: Vienna to Auschwitz.* New York: Amadeus Press, 2003.

Painter, Karen, ed. *Mahler and His World.* Princeton: Princeton University Press, 2002.

Pople, Anthony, ed. *Theory, Analysis and Meaning in Music.* Cambridge: Cambridge University Press, 2006.

Porter, Roy. *The Greatest Benefit to Mankind.* London: HarperCollins, 1997.

Prokofiev, Sergei. *Diaries 1915–1923: Behind the Mask.* Edited and translated by Anthony Phillips. London: Faber & Faber, 2008.

Reed, Philip, ed. *Britten and Mahler: Essays in Honour of Donald Mitchell on His 70th Birthday.* Woodbridge: Boydell Press, 1995.

Roazen, Paul. *Freud and His Followers.* London: Allen Lane, 1974.

Ross, Alex. *The Rest Is Noise.* New York: Farrar, Straus & Giroux, 2007.

Ryding, Erik, and Rebecca Pechefsky. *Bruno Walter: A World Elsewhere.* New Haven and London: Yale University Press, 2001.

Schnitzler, Arthur. *My Youth in Vienna.* Translated by Catherine Hutter. London: Weidenfeld & Nicolson, 1971.

Snowman, Daniel. *Hallelujah: An Informal History of the London Philharmonic Choir.* London: LPC, 2007.

Spiel, Hilde. *Vienna's Golden Autumn, 1866–1938.* London: Weidenfeld & Nicolson, 1987.

Susskind, Charles. *Janacek and Brod.* New Haven and London: Yale University Press, 1985.

Walker, Alan. *Hans von Bülow: A Life and Times.* New York: Oxford University Press, 2010.

Walker, Frank. *Hugo Wolf.* 2nd rev. ed. London: J. M. Dent, 1968.

Wechsberg, Joseph. *The Opera.* London: Weidenfeld & Nicolson, 1972.

Weidinger, Alfred. *Kokoschka and Alma Mahler.* Translated by Fiona Elliott. Munich and New York: Prestel, 1996.

Werfel, Franz. *Embezzled Heaven.* New York: Viking, 1940.

Whitford, Frank. *Oskar Kokoschka.* London: Weidenfeld & Nicolson, 1986.

Whyte, George R. *The Accused: The Dreyfus Trilogy.* Bonn: Inter Nationes, 1996.

Wilhelm, Kurt. *Richard Strauss, An Intimate Portrait.* Translated by Mary Whittall. London: Thames & Hudson, 1989.

Wolf, Hugo. *Eine Persönlichkeit in Briefe, Familienbriefe.* Edited by Edmund von Hellmer. Leipzig: Breitkopf & Härtel, 1912.

Wullschlager, Jackie. *Chagall: Life and Exile.* London: Allen Lane, 2008.

Yates, W. E. *Schnitzler, Hofmannsthal and the Austrian Theatre.* New Haven and London: Yale University Press, 1992.

Yoffe, Elkhonon. *Tchaikovsky in America.* New York: Oxford University Press, 1986.

Manuscripts, Theses, Pamphlets, Periodicals, Exhibition Catalogs, Dissertations

Anizan, Anne-Laure. "Paul Painlévé (1863–1933): un scientifique en politique." Thesis, Institut d'Études Politiques de Paris, 2006.

Die Ära Gustav Mahler, Wiener Hofoperndirektion 1897–1907. Vienna: Theater Museum, 1997.

Bailey, Colin, ed. *Gustav Klimt: Modernism in the Making.* Exhibition catalog for National Gallery of Canada. Ottawa, June–September, 2001.

Bosworth, M. "The Ellis Island U.S. Arrival Records for Gustav Mahler, 1907–10." *Naturlaut* 6, no. 2: 2–3.

Cadra, Janko. *Diaries of Janko Cadra* (1882–1927), in the Archives of Fine Arts and Literature of the Slovak Foundation, Martin, Slovakia. Translations by Milan Palak (booklet, 2005) and Michael Srba (private communication, 2009).

Christy, Nicholas P., and Beverly M. Christy. "Mahler's Final Illness." From the Department of Medicine, Roosevelt Hospital, and the College of Physicians and Surgeons, Columbia University. New York: 1998. www.mahlerarchives.net/archives/mahlerillness.pdf.

Collins, T. M. "A Life of Otto H. Kahn: Finance, Art, and Questions of Modernity." PhD diss., New York University, 1998.

Draper, K. "A Voice for Modernism in Elsa von Bienenfeld's Music Reviews." Graduation thesis, Brigham Young University, 2005.

Garcia, Emanuel E., M.D. "A New Look at Gustav Mahler's Fateful Encounter with Sigmund Freud." *Journal of the Conductors' Guild* 12, nos. 1 and 2 (Winter/Spring 1991): 10–30.

———. "Gustav Mahler's Choice: A Note on Adolescence, Genius and Psychosomatics." In *The Psychoanalytic Study of the Child*, ed. Albert J. Solnit et al., vol. 55, 87–110. New Haven and London: Yale University Press, 2000.

Hefling, S. "Mahler's Totenfeier and the Problem of Program Music." *19th-Century Music* 13 (Summer 1988): 27–53.

Jaroš, Zdeněk. *Guide to Mahler's Jihlava.* Municipality of Jihlava, 2000.

Korngold, Julius. *Memoirs.* Manuscript copy in NL archives.

Die Korngolds: Klischee, Kritik und Komposition. Catalog for an exhibition at the Jewish Museum, Vienna, November 2007–May 2008.

Kristan, M. "Josef Hoffmann und die Villenkolonie auf der Hohe Warte." Notes to a special exhibition for the Vienna International Arts and Antiques Fair, Vienna, Leopold Museum, November 2007.

Levy, D. "Gustav Mahler and Emanuel Libman: Bacterial Endocarditis in 1911." *British Medical Journal* 293 (December 20–27, 1986).

Loschnigg, F. "The Cultural Education of Gustav Mahler." PhD diss., University of Wisconsin-Madison, 1976.

"Mahler et la France." *Musical: Revue du Théâtre Musical du Châtelet* (Paris) 9 (1989).

Mahler, Gustav. *Gustav Mahler IX. Symphonie, Facsimile nach der Handschrift.* Edited by Erwin Ratz. Vienna: Universal Edition, 1971.

———. *Facsimile, Gustav Mahler Zehnte Symphonie; Skizzenblätter.* Vienna: Paul Zsolnay, 1924.

Mahler Tentoonstelling, Muziekcentrum Vredenburg Utrecht, November 13–30, 1986.

Martner, Knud. *Gustav Mahler im Konzertsaal* (manuscript, to be published by Ashgate in 2010–11).

———. "Verwelkte Blütenträume: Ein Werkverzeichnis der österreichischen Komponistin Alma Maria Schindler (verehelicht Mahler, Gropius, Werfel) nebst Streiflichter auf die Jahren bis 1902." Copenhagen: Privately printed, 2007.

Natter, T., and C. Grunenberg, eds. *Gustav Klimt: Painting Design and Modern Life.* Exhibition catalog for Tate Liverpool, May-August, 2008.

Plutalov, D. PhD diss. on the life and works of Maria Yudina, University of Nebraska-Lincoln (in progress).

Poulain-Colombier, Jacquelyne. "Presto: Les deux patients musiciens de Freud: Le Patient de la Psychanalyse." Paris: L'Harmattan, 2007.

Rose, Louis. "The Psychoanalytic Movement in Vienna: Toward a Science of Culture." PhD diss., Princeton University, 1986.

Rothstein, Edward. "Mahler Goes on Trial: Genius or Fraud or Both?" *New York Times,* November 22, 1994, C18.

Rychetský, Jiří. "Mahler's Favourite Song." *Musical Times* 130, no. 1762 (1989): 729.

Sander, Jaroslav. "The Family History of Gustav Mahler." *Jewish Quarterly* 33/3, no. 123 (1986): 53–54.

Zakrewska, Dorota. "Alienation and Powerlessness: Adam Mickiewicz's 'Ballady' and Chopin's Ballades." *Polish Music Journal* 2, nos. 1–2 (1999), at www.usc.edu/dept/polish_music/PMJ/issue/2.1.99/zakrzewska.html.

Online Resources

www.gustav-mahler.org/mahler/chrono-f.cfm—timeline of his life (in German).

www.bgm.org—La Grange's Mahler "mediathèque."

www.gustavmahler2010.eu/Mahler-a-Cechy.aspx—Czech anniversary plans.

http://gustavmahler.net.free.fr—useful discography.

www.gustav-mahler.org/english—the International GM Society (IGMG).

www.jihlava.com—hometown guide.

www.mahlerarchives.net—varied collection of articles and links.

www.mahler-steinbach.at/englisch/index_en.htm.

www.deathreference.com/Ke-Ma/Mahler-Gustav.html—Mahler's morbidity.

www.universaledition.com/mahler—publisher's site.

www.leonardbernstein.com—one conductor's contribution.

www.dasliedchinese.net—guide to original texts.

www.lehrer.uni-karlsruhe.de/~za1326/meyer/mahler.pdf—helpful analysis of Tenth Symphony (in German, with music examples).

INDEX

Printed in the United States
by Baker & Taylor Publisher Services